Ted Hughes

Twayne's English Authors Series

Kinley E. Roby, Editor

Northeastern University

TEAS 486

Ted Hughes. Photograph © Jane Bown, *Observer,* 1989.

Ted Hughes

Leonard M. Scigaj

Virginia Polytechnic Institute and State University

Twayne Publishers
A Division of G. K. Hall & Co. • *Boston*

Ted Hughes
Leonard M. Scigaj

Copyright 1991 by G. K. Hall & Co.
All rights reserved.
Published by Twayne Publishers
A division of G. K. Hall & Co.
70 Lincoln Street
Boston, Massachusetts 02111

Copyediting supervised by Barbara Sutton.
Book production by Gabrielle B. McDonald.
Typeset in Garamond by Graphic Sciences Corporation of Cedar Rapids, Iowa.

First published 1991.
10 9 8 7 6 5 4 3 2 1

Library of Congress Cataloging-in-Publication Data

Scigaj, Leonard M.
    Ted Hughes / Leonard M. Scigaj.
        p.   cm. — (Twayne's English authors series ; TEAS 486)
    Includes bibliographical references and index.
    ISBN 0-8057-7006-2
    1. Hughes, Ted, 1930-   —Criticism and interpretation.
I. Title.   II. Series.
PR6058.U37Z89   1991
821'.914—dc20   90-25744
                                                CIP

For Walter and Pearl

Contents

Preface

What do we desire in a major poet? That he or she should charm us out of our humdrum lives? Refresh our contact with the natural world? Fuse thought and feeling like Eliot's odor of a rose? Make us feel lucky to experience our humanity? Fascinate us with the reach of a mind that instantly absorbs our attention? Challenge us with new ideas that shock our perceptions out of cozy habit? Articulate the living culture of the present? Help us to comprehend our culture, in the way Dos Passos once quipped a good mechanic understands an internal combustion engine? Astonish us with the presence of the spiritual within the material? Grapple with the themes of love, aggression, death, redemption, and powers within and beyond us?

Auden once responded to the question of what constitutes a major poet in his "Introduction" to *Nineteenth-Century Minor Poets*. He believed that to achieve major status a poet must publish a great deal of quality poetry that incorporates a wide range of subject matter, demonstrates a masterful verse technique, and reveals an originality of vision and style that matures in recognizable stages throughout a career.

The poetry of Ted Hughes amply satisfies Auden's criteria. From structuralist, formalist beginnings, Hughes's poetry has grown enormously. He has enriched his craft and vision by incorporating the surreal inner life, world myth and folklore, and mystical landscape poetry. More recently he has achieved an openness to the external world where language and environment crystallize to form an ecology of values that captures a spiritual dimension. Neither his prodigious output nor his gift for vibrant, arresting metaphors has slackened throughout his long career. His style, which has regularly alternated from the kinetic to the meditative even in his first volumes, has achieved a lean line that is so intense yet so calm that it nearly eliminates the boundary between print and actual experience. Though some may call his vision bleak, it is honest, very sympathetic to humanity, strong in the unvarnished, unsentimental, and unblinkered grasp of experience, and passionately alive, wise from a full engagement in the joy and pain of actual living.

Hughes has been a fixture of the British literary scene for three decades and has been poet laureate of England since December 1984, but he remains little read in the United States. When his name is mentioned even in

American academic circles, discussion centers on *Crow,* a volume Hughes published 20 years ago. Our feminists focus on his first wife, Sylvia Plath, and her decision to take her own life in 1963, and in our Gilbert and Gubar no-man's-land Hughes has become a menacing patriarch lurking in shadows. But these shadows derive from viewing his poetry through lenses that distort the actual events of that first marriage.

Plath was a first-rate, highly accomplished poet, well on her way to becoming a major spokesperson for the plight of women in a society of male privilege; this truth is undeniable and incredibly important. But in her openly expressed desire to manipulate events in her life to expose the real nerves of the cultural present, she succeeded in convincing thousands of her readers that the poetic events of *Ariel* were accurate reflections of her domestic life rather than revealing reflections of her psychic life.

This text attempts to present with clarity and economy a discussion of the major works of Hughes's adult poetry. Hughes is one of the most important writers of children's literature in the United Kingdom today, and he has also written 18 plays and many minor volumes of poetry, but only a few of these works are discussed here, and only insofar as they illuminate the major adult poetry. These areas—children's works, drama, minor poetry volumes—invite the kind of separate, tightly focused studies that an introductory overview cannot provide. Excellent introductory essays to Hughes's children's work and drama are available in *The Achievement of Ted Hughes,* a critical anthology edited by Keith Sagar. Scholars interested in a more exhaustive study of Hughes's literary and stylistic influences, absorption of Oriental texts, and developmental stages should consult my earlier study, *The Poetry of Ted Hughes: Form and Imagination.* The Selected Bibliography lists these and other important introductory or scholarly studies of Hughes.

This study was enriched by my access to unpublished BBC radio scripts written by Hughes that contain important guides to his poetry, and by letters from Ted and Olwyn Hughes responding to my questions about biographical material. Keith Sagar has helped to identify younger British poets influenced by Hughes. I have researched Plath and Hughes at the Smith College Neilson Library Rare Book Room and the Lilly Research Library of the University of Indiana, have absorbed the available scholarly books and essays on both Hughes and Plath, and have read carefully the recently published biographies of Plath by Linda Wagner-Martin and Anne Stevenson.

My objective was not simply to summarize the views of others on Hughes's poetry or to repeat insights from my first study of Hughes, but to extend my research into new and useful areas of interpretation. Each chapter takes a fresh approach to individual Hughes poetry volumes while emphasizing a core of ideas and a continuity of values that has only deepened with time. This text is the first to consider Hughes's early poetry in terms of his absorption of midcentury structuralism. My focus on language and ecology throughout the text takes Hughes research in entirely new directions. Other highlights include a new interpretation of the eye imagery in *The Hawk in the Rain*, the first consideration of the relevance for *Crow* of Hughes's published letter "A Reply to My Critics," and the first discussion of *River* to consider ecology and the Animal Master myths of tribal societies.

I emphasize central groups of poems within each of Hughes's major volumes, viewed from a middle distance. Until we comprehend how Hughes's major themes operate in a sufficient body of poems in major volumes, we cannot judge the strengths and weaknesses of individual poems. Part of the problem is the alarming refusal of contemporary reviewers of Hughes's poetry to assimilate scholarship that has been available for years. Even such a fine critic as Helen Vendler preferred to bludgeon Hughes in a *New Yorker* review (31 December 1984) with a special pleading ax that severed poems of violence from their organizational context within volumes while refusing to consider the fine Hughes studies by Sagar, Gifford and Roberts, and Hirschberg—all of which were in print at least three years prior to the review and offer mythic, psychological, and cultural rationales for the violence. This Twayne volume should facilitate a more just and comprehensive assessment of Hughes's poetry.

Now that this Twayne introductory volume is completed for the benefit of the general reader and undergraduate student, the next project in Hughes scholarship should be a more sophisticated assessment of his poetry that incorporates the social, semiotic, and phenomenological approaches of postmodern and feminist criticism. Since 1960 Hughes's attitude toward language has changed abruptly. He no longer seeks to master the world through words, and he becomes hyperaware of how cultural assumptions embedded in linguistic systems seek to exploit nature and women. Since 1970 he has endeavored to produce a clear and simple poetic line that invites the reader to experience his grasp of the fresh wonders of nature. When he does write as a critic of culture in his more recent poetry, his satire incorporates the precision of a surgeon instead of the earlier surreal violence.

I would like to thank Virginia Tech for a half-year Research Assignment Sabbatical that gave me the time to write a draft of half of this text, and the National Endowment for the Humanities for a travel grant that

allowed me to research Hughes and Plath texts at Smith College and the
University of Indiana. Thanks also to Ruth Mortimer and her staff at the
Neilson Rare Book Room of Smith College, and to Saundra Taylor and
her staff at the Lilly Research Library, Indiana University; both staffs were
extremely helpful and courteous. Thanks also to the staffs of Harvard
University's Widener and Houghton libraries for permission to use their
resources, and to the British Broadcasting Corporation for permission to
quote from unpublished radio scripts written by Hughes.

I would like to thank Ted and Olwyn Hughes for their responses to chapter 1 of this text, and for their generous help with copyright permissions. To
Chris and Bette Noble of Cambridge, and Bill Timberlake and Holly
Stocking of Bloomington—friends who allowed me to share the warmth of
their homes while I pursued my research—an equally warm thank-you.
Special thanks to my wife and colleague Nancy Simmons for her advice and
support, for her expert editorial and proofreading skills, and especially for
her timely reminder that rocks have rights.

Acknowledgments

I am grateful to Ted Hughes, and to the British Broadcasting Corporation, for permission to quote unpublished BBC radio scripts written and broadcast by him. I am also grateful to Ted Hughes, and to the Lilly Research Library of Indiana University, for permission to quote from unpublished Hughes correspondence.

For permission to quote from the copyrighted poetry of Ted Hughes, I am especially grateful to the following:

Faber & Faber, Ltd., for quotation from Hughes volumes published by them: *The Hawk in the Rain,* © Ted Hughes 1957; *Lupercal,* © Ted Hughes 1960; *Wodwo,* © Ted Hughes 1967; *Crow,* © Ted Hughes 1970; 1972, *Season Songs,* © Ted Hughes 1976; *Gaudete,* © Ted Hughes 1977; *Cave Birds,* © Ted Hughes 1978; *Remains of Elmet,* © Ted Hughes 1979; *Moortown,* © Ted Hughes 1979; *River,* © Ted Hughes 1983; *Flowers and Insects,* © Ted Hughes 1986; and *Wolfwatching,* © Ted Hughes 1989.

Farrar, Straus & Giroux, Inc., for quotation from their published Hughes volume, *Wolfwatching,* © Ted Hughes 1991.

Harper & Row, Publishers, Inc., for quotation from Hughes volumes published by them: *The Hawk in the Rain,* © Ted Hughes 1957; *Lupercal,* © Ted Hughes 1960; *Wodwo,* © Ted Hughes 1967; *Crow,* © Ted Hughes 1971; *Gaudete,* © Ted Hughes 1977; *Remains of Elmet,* © Ted Hughes 1979; *Moortown,* © Ted Hughes 1980; and *River,* © Ted Hughes 1983.

Olwyn Hughes, for reprinting of "Crow the Just" from the Rainbow Press volume, *Poems: Ruth Fainlight, Ted Hughes, Alan Sillitoe,* © Ted Hughes 1971, and for poems not yet collected in book form.

Alfred A. Knopf, Inc., for quotation from their published Hughes volume, *Flowers and Insects,* © Ted Hughes 1986.

Viking Penguin, Inc., for quotation from Hughes volumes published by them: *Season Songs,* © Ted Hughes 1975, and *Cave Birds,* © Ted Hughes 1978.

Abbreviations in the Text

Quotations from the poems of Ted Hughes used throughout this text derive from the American Harper & Row, Viking, Knopf, or Farrar, Straus & Giroux editions listed in the Selected Bibliography. Page numbers in parentheses are added whenever poem titles are omitted.

To simplify notation, secondary works frequently cited in the text appear in parentheses according to the following abbreviations:

Blake	Blake, William. *The Poetry and Prose of William Blake.* Rev. ed. Edited by David V. Erdman. Garden City, N.Y.: Doubleday, 1968.
Book of the Dead	Evans-Wentz, W. Y., ed. *The Tibetan Book of the Dead.* 3d ed. Translated by Lama Kazi Dawa-Samdup. 1957. Reprint. London: Oxford University Press, 1974.
Campbell 1960	Campbell, Joseph. *The Masks of God: Primitive Mythology.* New York: Viking, 1960.
Campbell 1962	_____. *The Masks of God: Oriental Mythology.* New York: Viking, 1962.
Campbell 1968	_____. *The Masks of God: Creative Mythology.* New York: Viking, 1968.
Eliade	Eliade, Mircea. *Shamanism: Archaic Techniques of Ecstasy.* 2d ed. Translated by Willard R. Trask. Princeton: Princeton University Press, 1969.
"Elmet"	Hughes, Ted. "Elmet." *BBC Radio 3.* Produced by Fraser Steel. Recorded 3 May 1980.
Faas 1	Faas, Ekbert. "Ted Hughes and *Crow.*" 1970. Reprinted in Faas, *Ted Hughes: The Unaccommodated Universe,* 197–208. Santa Barbara, Calif.: Black Sparrow, 1980.
Faas 2	_____. "Ted Hughes and Gaudete," *Ted Hughes: The Unaccommodated Universe,* 208–215.

Graves
    Graves, Robert. *The White Goddess: A Historical Grammar of Poetic Myth.* 2d ed. New York: Farrar, Straus, & Giroux, 1966.

Jung 5
    Jung, Carl Gustav. *Symbols of Transformation: An Analysis of the Prelude to a Case of Schizophrenia.* 2d ed. Translated by R. F. C. Hull. Bollingen Series 20, vol. 5. Edited by Sir Herbert Read et al. Princeton: Princeton University Press, 1967.

Jung 8
    _____. *The Structure and Dynamics of the Psyche.* Translated by R. F. C. Hull. Bollingen Series 20, vol. 8. Edited by Sir Herbert Read et al. New York: Pantheon, 1960.

Jung 9a
    _____. *Archetypes and the Collective Unconscious.* Translated by R. F. C. Hull. Bollingen Series 20, vol. 9, part 1. Edited by Sir Herbert Read et al. New York: Pantheon, 1964.

Jung 9b
    _____. *Aion: Researches into the Phenomenology of the Self.* Translated by R. F. C. Hull. Bollingen Series 20, vol. 9, part 2. Edited by Sir Herbert Read et al. New York: Pantheon, 1959.

Jung 11
    _____. *Psychology and Religion: West and East.* Translated by R. F. C. Hull. Bollingen Series 20, vol. 11. Edited by Sir Herbert Read et al. New York: Pantheon, 1963.

Jung 12
    _____. *Psychology and Alchemy.* Translated by R. F. C. Hull. Bollingen Series 20, vol. 12. Edited by Sir Herbert Read et al. Princeton: Princeton University Press, 1968.

Jung 13
    _____. *Alchemical Studies.* Translated by R. F. C. Hull. Bollingen Series 20, vol. 13. Edited by Sir Herbert Read et al. Princeton: Princeton University Press, 1967.

Jung 14
    _____. *Mysterium Coniunctionis: An Inquiry into the Separation and Synthesis of Psychic Opposites in Alchemy.* Translated by R. F. C. Hull. Bollingen Series 20, vol. 14. Edited by Sir Herbert Read et al. New York: Pantheon, 1963.

Jung 16
    _____. *The Practice of Psychotherapy: Essays on the*

Psychology of the Transference and Other Subjects. 2d ed. Translated by R. F. C. Hull. Bollingen Series 20, vol. 16. Edited by Sir Herbert Read et al. New York: Pantheon, 1954.

Jung PC ————. "Psychological Commentary." Translated by R. F. C. Hull. In *The Tibetan Book of the Dead,* 3d ed., edited by W. Y. Evans-Wentz, xxxv–li. London: Oxford University Press, 1974.

Journals Plath, Sylvia. *The Journals of Sylvia Plath.* Edited by Ted Hughes and Frances McCullough. New York: Dial, 1982.

Letters Home ————. *Letters Home: Correspondence 1950–1963.* Edited by Aurelia Schober Plath. New York: Harper & Row, 1975.

"Myth 1" Hughes, Ted. "Myth and Education." *Children's Literature in Education* 1 (1970):55–70.

"Myth 2" ————. "Myth and Education." In *Writers, Critics, and Children,* edited by Geoff Fox et al., 77–94. New York: Agathon, 1976. [A completely different essay from "Myth 1."]

Poetry ————. *Poetry in the Making.* London: Faber & Faber, 1967.

"The Rock" ————. "The Rock." In *Writers on Themselves,* edited by Herbert Read, 86–92. London: Cox and Wyman, 1964.

"Reply" ————. "A Reply to My Critics." *Books and Issues* 3–4 (1981):4–6.

Sagar Sagar, Keith. *The Art of Ted Hughes.* 2d ed. London: Cambridge University Press, 1978.

Scigaj Scigaj, Leonard M. *The Poetry of Ted Hughes: Form and Imagination.* Iowa City: University of Iowa Press, 1986.

Smith Smith, A. C. H. *Orghast at Persepolis.* London: Eyre Methuen, 1972.

Zimmer Zimmer, Heinrich. *Myths and Symbols in Indian Art and Civilization.* Edited by Joseph Campbell. New York: Pantheon, 1946.

Chronology

1930   Edward James Hughes born in Mytholmroyd, a town in the Calder Valley of West Yorkshire on the textile route near the Brontë country, on 17 August, the third and last child of William Henry Hughes, a carpenter of Irish, Spanish, and English ancestry, and Edith Farrar Hughes, a descendant of Nicholas Farrar, founder of Little Gidding. Their home stood near Scout Rock, a 600-foot scoop face in the Pennines.

1938   Hughes family moves to Mexborough, South Yorkshire, where parents open a newsagent's and tobacconist's shop. From 1943 through 1949 a number of fine English teachers in the Mexborough Grammar School, especially John Fisher, develop his interest in poetry. Publishes poems in the school magazine *Don and Dearne,* 1946–50.

1948   Wins Open Exhibition to Cambridge University.

1949   Enters RAF for two years, serving as a radio mechanic in an isolated East Yorkshire station, before entering Cambridge.

1951   Enters Pembroke College, Cambridge; studies English under ballads expert M. J. C. Hodgart. Changes in third year to archaeology and anthropology. Parents return to West Yorkshire, living at Todmorden.

1954   Graduates from Cambridge in June. First undergraduate poem, "The Little Boys and the Seasons," published in *Granta* under pseudonym Daniel Hearing. From 1954 through 1956 continues to publish poems in Cambridge poetry magazines while working in London or Cambridge at various minor jobs. Parents move in 1954 to the Beacon, a ridgetop home near Heptonstall.

1956   Publishes four poems in the first and only issue of *St. Botolph's Review,* a poetry magazine edited by David Ross. Meets Sylvia Plath, a Fulbright student at Newnham College, Cambridge, at the first issue party, 25 February. Marries Plath on Bloomsday, 16 June, with a honeymoon at Benidorm, Spain. *Poetry* publishes "Bawdry Embraced" in August—his first nonacademic publication—and

Nation publishes poems in August, November, and December issues.

1957   Teaches English at a secondary school near Cambridge while Plath completes her M.A. in English. Hughes publishes poems in many major magazines, including *Poetry, Spectator, Nation, Harper's, TLS, New Yorker, London Magazine, New Statesman.* First BBC radio reading, "The Martyrdom of Bishop Farrar," 14 April. Sails in June to America with Plath. On 18 September Hughes's first poetry volume, *The Hawk in the Rain,* is published as first prize over 286 other entries in a contest sponsored by the Poetry Center of the Young Men's and Young Women's Hebrew Association. Judges are W. H. Auden, Marianne Moore, and Stephen Spender.

1958   Teaches spring-term English and creative writing classes at Amherst campus of the University of Massachusetts. Poetry reading at Harvard in April. Meets Smith faculty sculptor and graphic artist Leonard Baskin. Moves with Plath to Boston in the fall for a year of writing. Guinness Poetry award.

1959   Resides in Boston until a summer cross-country camping tour. At Yaddo in the fall, Hughes begins a year's work on an (unpublished) oratorio on the *Bardo Thödol,* the Tibetan Book of the Dead. Sails with Plath to England in mid-December. Guggenheim Fellow 1959–60.

1960   *Lupercal* published. Resides in London, where Frieda Rebecca Hughes is born 1 April. Publishes first major adult short stories in *Harper's* ("The Rain Horse") and the Faber *Introduction* ("The Rain Horse," "Sunday," and "Snow"). Begins BBC radio talks and book reviewing. Somerset Maugham Award for *The Hawk in the Rain.*

1961   *Meet My Folks!* published. Hawthornden Prize for *Lupercal.* Moves to Devon home 31 August.

1962   Nicholas Farrar Hughes born 17 January. *Selected Poems with Thom Gunn* published. First recordings of poetry, for Jupiter Records and British Council. Moves to London after separation from Plath at end of September.

1963   Suicide of Sylvia Plath 11 February. With family help Hughes cares for Frieda and Nicholas in London and Yorkshire. *How the Whale Became* and *The Earth-Owl and Other Moon-People* published.

1964   *Nessie the Mannerless Monster* published. Works on unpublished film version of *Gaudete.*

1965 Begins coediting and writing editorials for *Modern Poetry in Translation* with Daniel Weissbort. Continues work for first 10 issues. Begins yearly work as judge for the *Daily Mirror* National Children's Poetry Competition, which has since become the W. H. Smith National Literary Competition.

1966 Moves to Ireland with children (January–May); returns to Devon. Writes most of the *Wodwo* poems and other essays.

1967 *Wodwo* and *Poetry in the Making*, a selection of BBC radio talks for schools, published. First Crow poem, "A Disaster," appears in the 22 July *Scotsman*. Principal organizer of the first Arts Council International Poetry Festival at Queen Elizabeth Hall. In late fall begins work with Peter Brook on script for *Seneca's Oedipus*.

1968 *Seneca's Oedipus* first performed by National Theatre Company at the Old Vic, 19 March, starring John Gielgud and Irene Worth. *The Iron Man* published. Edits *A Choice of Emily Dickinson's Verse*.

1969 *Seneca's Oedipus* published. Assia Gutman Wevill and her daughter Shura die in March. Mother, Edith Farrar Hughes, dies 13 May. City of Florence International Poetry Prize for *Wodwo*. Buys Lumb Bank; later refurbishes it and leases it to the Arvon Foundation to employ writers to tutor creative writing courses. Purchased by Arvon Foundation 31 July 1989. Moves several times back and forth to Ireland in 1969–70; finally decides to remain in Devon.

1970 Marries Carol Orchard in August. *The Coming of the Kings and Other Plays* and *Crow* published.

1971 Completes the script (unpublished) of *Orghast* in Teheran, produced by Peter Brook and his International Center for Theatre Research Company in late August at the Fifth Festival of the Arts of Shiraz, Persepolis, Iran (see A. C. H. Smith, *Orghast at Persepolis* [London: Eyre Metheun, 1972].) Edits *With Fairest Flowers While Summer Lasts*.

1972 *Selected Poems: 1957–1967* published. Buys Devon farm Moortown. Publishes last book review 5 March in *Observer*. Second, augmented, edition of *Crow* published.

1973 Premio Internazionale Taormina Prize.

1974 Queen's Medal for Poetry.

1975 *Season Songs* published. Reads *Crow* and *Cave Birds* poems at Ilkley Literature Festival in May.

1976 *Moon-Whales and Other Moon Poems* published.

1977 *Gaudete* published. Edits Plath's *Johnny Panic and the Bible of Dreams*. Named to the Order of the British Empire.

1978 *Moon-Bells and Other Poems* published. Signal Award. *Cave Birds* published.

1979 *Remains of Elmet* and *Moortown* published.

1980 Heinemann Bequest of the Royal Society.

1981 *Under the North Star* published. Signal Award. Edits Sylvia Plath's *Collected Poems*. Father dies in February.

1982 *Selected Poems: 1957–1981* published. With Frances McCullough edits *The Journals of Sylvia Plath*. With Seamus Heaney edits *The Rattle Bag*.

1983 *River* published.

1984 *What Is the Truth?* published. Named poet laureate of England 19 December.

1985 Guardian Children's Fiction Award for *What Is the Truth?*

1986 *Ffangs the Vampire Bat and the Kiss of Truth* and *Flowers and Insects* published.

1988 *Tales of the Early World* published.

1989 *Wolfwatching* published.

Chapter One
Introduction

Mana from an Ecological Heaven

During one of his British Museum expeditions through the ruins of ancient Ninevah and Babylon in the 1840s, the British archaeologist Austin Layard encountered Saoud, a Bedouin poet whose "wild, though plaintive, strain" so delighted guests, warriors, and chief alike that bodies swayed to the measure. Shouts, sobbing, and laughter arose spontaneously according to the heroic, tragic, or satiric subject matter, and amatory verses brought to all assembled an excitement "almost beyond control." Layard concluded that the excitement these Bedouin poets produce "exceeds that of the grape."[1]

Ted Hughes believes that poetry ideally produces an almost hypnotic, trancelike excitement that has practical, psychological, social, and spiritual benefits. This conception of poetry derives from the development of human communication in tribal cultures. Although contemporary listeners do not make animated gestures and shout unselfconsciously when poets recite their verses, Hughes maintains that poetry does potentially have the power to draw us out of ourselves, activate psychic energies, motivate decisions, and empower actions that lead to achieving practical goals. It can mimic the rhythms of nature to bring peace to the psyche, and in general promote psychological health and social harmony. If properly crafted it can communicate exalted mystical states. Like the tribal shaman, the poet journeys to heal both his or her own psyche and that of society. If the poet has sufficient power to express the excitement and energy experienced on the journey, the participating reader can enhance his or her potential for achieving wholeness, personality growth, spiritual fulfillment, and develop a more cohesive bond with society.

Hughes briefly recounts the meeting of Layard with the Bedouin poet in "The Hanged Man and the Dragonfly," his 1984 introduction to *The Complete Prints of Leonard Baskin*. Hughes considers the excitement generated by Saoud's poetry to be a residue of the ancient "sacred shout" of pain simultaneously mixed with the exaltation that in tribal societies promotes an influx of mana energy, redeeming the afflicted spirit. "Mana" for humans in tribal cultures is a vitalistic spiritual force; humans possessed by mana de-

1

velop a holy, magical, charismatic psychic state that can heal the psyche and promote self-possession in themselves and in those around them. Mana energy derives from nature's spiritual power circuit and is potentially a property of any being or thing: animals, warriors, tribal healers, chiefs, weapons, or ritual objects. Hughes believes that literature can generate feeling states equivalent to being possessed by mana energy and especially activate the healing properties of mana. The fact that creative writing often does produce a feeling of liberation and peace, of expanded consciousness and enlarged vision, demonstrates for Hughes "the biological inevitability of art, as the psychological component of the body's own system of immunity and self-repair."[2]

Hughes has always believed that poetry is a form of intensified communication that has healing qualities. In an unpublished 1963 BBC broadcast Hughes distinguished "genuine" poetry from mere verse by the psychic excitement that the poet captures and communicates. Though it is impossible to pinpoint the origins of this power, until the poet "feels this thing stir in him," and until "he can get that obscure excitement out into his work, he is merely writing verse." For Hughes this "special kind of excitement . . . is what some primitive peoples call 'mana,' [a] magical power, an intense mysterious fury which speaks directly into the depths of our imaginations and has a sway over us which we can't easily explain. 'Mana' is what makes one drummer or singer infinitely more gripping and meaningful than his rivals."[3]

Mana power, the driving force of Hughes's poetic language, is not just an application of a fanciful anthropological term. Hughes has read many of the works of the Swiss psychoanalyst Carl Jung, who found in his research many surprising connections between the concept of mana in the animistic beliefs of tribal cultures and the modern concept of libido or psychic energy. A magical intensity, power, or force, mana is for humans in tribal societies inseparable from the object within which it resides, and flows outward and inward as moods of excitement or elation ebb and flow (Jung 8:61–65, 233–34).[4] A shaman possessed of ecstatic mana converts the neurotic libidinal blockages of his or her "patients" into healing energies. So too can the modern shaman—the poet—according to Hughes ("Myth 1," 58 ff.).[5]

Hughes completed a degree in anthropology at Cambridge University in 1954, and throughout his career has concerned himself with the psychological and social functions of literature. The fact that tribal groups and civilized societies since the third millenium B.C. have resorted to song and its later written equivalent in poetry for therapeutic reasons attests to the continued presence of human powers and needs that poetry activates and satisfies—powers and needs that for Hughes are critical for psychic health and the welfare of the human community. Early in his career, in the first of his many reviews for the *Listener* (1962), Hughes affirmed the therapeutic psychological dimension of oral poetry in tribal societies. Of C. M. Bowra's *Primitive Song*, Hughes wrote that "the bulk of the songs are power-charms, tools and practical agents in the business of gaining desired ends, or deflecting the spirits of misfortune from planting their larvae in the psyche."[6]

At first glance it seems that parallels between tribal and contemporary societies are very limited. In our technologically advanced age we are not naive and unsophisticated. We do not fear lightning, nor do we believe in the miraculous. We do not listen to poetry as part of a group that shares a common body of beliefs; we read poetry in isolation, too often as an escape from daily tedium. Though we are dimly aware of global ecological issues such as water and soil pollution, the eroding ozone layer, and the greenhouse effect, we are not alert to minute changes in our natural environment because we have few worries about daily survival. So much the worse for us, believes Hughes, for we have purchased our sophistication at great cost. The progress of Western civilization, especially during the last 300 years since the emergence of the New Science and the onset of the Industrial Revolution, has exiled us from our rightful place in nature into the pseudosecurity of machines and rational analysis. At the same time we have alienated ourselves from our own nature and its healing powers.

Science and technology glorified the analytical powers of the human cerebral cortex and largely ignored human emotional and instinctual needs. The humane impulses of sharing and sympathy that bind preindustrial communities together have atrophied as science and technology championed utilitarian ego logic. Rational humanism led to two world wars and massive urban discontent, and allowed technology to become the tool of materialists who have succeeded in placing our global ecology in peril. We may not fear lightning, but the technological barricades we have developed to insulate us from the environment and to manipulate natural resources indicate a fearful withdrawal from any experiential knowledge of the natural world that created us.

In the late 1960s, while Hughes was writing his Crow poems to show us the consequences of a feverish flight from nature into rational analysis, the ecologist Paul Shepard wrote that nature cannot be translated into abstractions like "usable energy and commodities." He advocated an ecologically responsible literature, like that of the classical Greeks and the Navajo Indians, where nature was our second skin and the self was "a center of organiza-

4 TED HUGHES

tion, constantly drawing on and influencing the surroundings, whose skin and behavior are soft zones contacting the world instead of excluding it." Shepard asserted that what the Greeks and Navajos displayed in their worship was "a deep sense of engagement with the landscape, with profound connections to surroundings and to natural processes central to all life."[7] The poetry of Ted Hughes is the ecological and psychological Velcro that reattaches us to vital natural rhythms and expresses the necessary balance between the needs of the self and the limits of nature.

Ecology is the study of nature understood as a dynamically interrelated system held in a delicate balance (*dikê*, the master principle beneath Sophoclean tragedy).[8] The *eikos,* or "house," signified for the Greeks not only the physical dwelling, but the warm hearth's *eiko*-logical bond of individual to community—in its economic, moral, and spiritual dimensions.[9] Not to reverence nature, and not to recognize one's limits and the limits of nature, is to make oneself a tragic figure in a tragic cycle (as in the *eikos,* or House, of Atreus). Creon, the dictatorial rationalist of Sophocles' *Antigone,* tried to make his punishment of Polyneices an abstract lesson or example, but his sacreligious refusal to allow burial of the warrior's body amounted to a multileveled ecological disaster, offending humane community customs, the good will of the gods, and nature.

Similar disasters occurred in *Crow* (1970), Hughes's most famous work. Crow's habit of utilitarian, rational analysis ultimately created social, ecological, and cosmic havoc. In "Crow and Stone," near the end of the volume, Crow's passion for rational analysis led him to such obsessive interference in the myths and environment of humans that he warred against matter itself, creating cosmic dust like nuclear fallout and "holding the very globe in terror."[10] Crow's disastrous escapades, though they depict the consequences of Western science and technology's secret will to power, thankfully occurred only in a cartoonish landscape. *Crow* was a jeremiad and a moral fable in which Hughes the prophet decried a schizoid wilderness where the affluent West lay dazed upon the psychoanalyst's couch or anesthetized by mass media, while most of the globe suffered ecological damage and economic deprivation. We have met the enemy and Crow is us.

The need for poetry to advocate a therapeutic return to the natural world has never been greater. The most important theme in Hughes's poetry throughout his career is exactly this therapeutic return to the wonders, limits, mysteries, and healing powers of the natural world, after a satiric analysis of the misdirected Western rational/technological bias that alienates humans from the cycles of nature. This theme is very deeply embedded in Hughes's life.

The Menace below the Moors

Hughes's English roots allowed him to experience nature's beauty and healing powers, as well as the environmental devastation caused by the Industrial Revolution. Ted Hughes was born Edward James Hughes, the youngest of three children, on 17 August 1930 in Mytholmroyd, a town located in the Calder Valley—a deep gorge cut through the Yorkshire Pennines. Hughes's lifelong love of fishing, that attached him very directly to the rhythms of nature and produced many fine poems, including the exquisite *River* (1983), began at age three in a canal a few yards behind the row house of his birth. A few hundred yards further south loomed Scout Rock, a 600-foot high scoop face in the surrounding hills that cast a shadowy gloom on his young life. In his childhood Hughes enjoyed hiking and hunting with his older brother Gerald in the area surrounding Scout Rock.

In 1963 Hughes broadcast a BBC radio program about Scout Rock, where he wrote that "all that I imagined happened elsewhere, out in the world, the rock sealed from me, since in England the world seems to lie to the south." Liberation soon became equated with the "gentle female watery line" of the high moors above Scout Rock, where after arduous climbing one is bathed in a light "at once both gloomily purplish and incredibly clear." The rock, however, stubbornly imposed itself as "a darkening presence," like a "watchfully threatening" patriarch ("The Rock"). Fay Godwin's photographs of the Mytholmroyd area, preserved in Hughes's *Remains of Elmet* (1978), included many views of the moors, the canal, local landmarks, and dwellings, and one of Scout Rock itself (on page 71 of both the Faber and the Harper and Row editions).

Hughes equated the stoniness of Scout Rock with the oppression of the Industrial Revolution, the remains of which he experienced firsthand in his childhood. Mytholmroyd rests on an east-west truck route between the textile centers of Halifax, Bradford, Huddersfield, and Leeds to the east, and what Hughes in *Elmet* called the "rotten lung" of smoggy Manchester to the west. Manchester, an hour's drive away, drenched him weekly in "acid rain fall-out." "The Long Tunnel Ceiling" in *Elmet* expresses Hughes's memories of trying to fish under a canal bridge, in the shadow of the Moderna blanket factory, while the "lorries" (trucks) clattering above scared the fish and wrecked the youthful angler's concentration: "Lorries from Rochdale, baled plump and towering / With worsteds and cottons, over my head met / Lorries from Bradford, and fought past each other." Much of the forceful energy that occurs in Hughes's poetry articulates an aggressively utilitarian ethos, as here with the lorries fighting past each other. The Industrial Revolution's ecological devastation has been woven into his head like a Bradford worsted since childhood.

When Hughes was eight his father, William, a carpenter who made portable buildings of all shapes and sizes, moved the family about 40 miles southeast when he and Hughes's mother, Edith, opened a newsagent's and tobacconist's shop in Mexborough. As he mastered his high school subjects, benefiting especially from excellent English teachers such as John Fisher, Hughes began to write stories and verse to amuse his friends and classmates. He won an Open Exhibition scholarship to Cambridge University in 1948, but before he entered in 1951 he served two years in the RAF as a ground radio mechanic in a remote East Yorkshire station where he read avidly in his leisure time.

During his first two years at Cambridge Hughes studied English under the supervision of the ballads expert M. J. C. Hodgart. Finding the English program unabsorbing, he changed his program of studies to anthropology in his third year, graduating in June 1954. While he studied for his anthropology tripos (honors exam), he steeped himself in folklore and Yeats. The pivotal switch to anthropology occurred when Hughes experienced a revelatory dream after laboring at a paper on Samuel Johnson. Someone like himself, but with a fox's head and a body flayed with fire, entered his room, placed a burning human hand on the essay, and said "You are destroying us."[11] Dreams for Hughes have always conveyed important bulletins from the subconscious. The therapeutic function of dreams and the self-repairing powers of the psyche constitute two of his central points of agreement with the psychotherapy of Carl Jung.

The Beacon

While Hughes studied at the university, his parents in 1951 returned to the Mytholmroyd area, and since 1954 lived atop the high moors in a ridgetop house called the Beacon at nearby Heptonstall. This is the source of the memorable early poem "Wind" from his first volume, *The Hawk in the Rain* (1957). Hughes's language in his early poetry is distinctively muscular and kinetic, and in this poem he matches it with the power of nature to convey how the psyche strains to adjust to extraordinary experiences. But what might result in bombast in another poet is tempered by an acute comprehension of how the psyche absorbs the moment-to-moment rush of sensation. Metaphors harness and direct the energy like a halter and reins on a horse. The house, like a foundering ship in a storm, has been battered by the wind, with woods "crashing," hills "booming," and the windows "blinding wet." Afterward "The hills had new places," while the wind, stubborn in its passing, kept "Flexing like the lens of a mad eye." Strained to its maximum, the house "Rang like some fine green goblet" just before shattering, while outside the force was so strong that "a black- / Back gull bent like an iron bar slowly." No one can gainsay the power of language and observation that rivets the reader to his chair like the poem's occupants to that windtaxed house.

In his introductory remarks to "Wind" in *Poetry in the Making* (1967), his excellent collection of BBC radio talks for children about how to write, Hughes described the wind of the poem as a vividly experienced natural event that forces one to see things anew ("The hills had new places") and also as "simply inspiration," an excitement akin to the Old Testament prophets' experience of being "carried off to their visions in a great wind." His accompanying description of the view from the Beacon, another of the thousands of instances of mana power in his writing, fastens us to nature with the grip of his language. At the Beacon "the wind blows without obstruction across the tops of the moors . . . . The grass of the fields there is of a particularly brilliant watered green, and the stone walls of the enclosures that cover the hillsides like a great net thrown over whales, look coal black" (*Poetry*, 33).

Later in his life, during visits home, the Beacon brought the serenity of nature to Hughes's fingertips, healing the psyche. On one 1960 trip to the Beacon, Hughes wrote in a letter that upon arrival he had immediately lapsed into a 24-hour "bottomless torpor, sinking in this enormous blissful silence. I think this must be the most beautiful spot in England . . . . The silence here is overpowering—because the hills seem to embody it—you can see it—everything is spellbound by it. . . . When you leave the door open here it seems to come right into the house."[12] But Hughes did not need to revisit Yorkshire to keep his roots in nature strong; they have remained whole and intact throughout his life. They tap springs of creativity that produce his best poetry. Hughes's rootedness in the ecology of nature transforms endlessly according to the dictates of an extremely healthy, agile, feather-touch imagination to become the spirit beacon of his verse.

It is not an accident that, of the large body of Oriental literature and philosophy that has influenced Hughes's writing as the result of his readings in folklore, Taoism is a major source for the serenity and mystical silence of many *Elmet* poems. The natural harmony that produces the spirit breath of the imagination in Taoism and the accommodation to the rhythms of ecological change and renewal in nature that end in moments of visionary silence—in apprehensions of the ultimate Tao, the empty Nameless beyond the phenomenal world—recall moods and spiritual states that Hughes had already experienced on his native West Yorkshire moors. In the *Elmet* poem "Open to Huge Light," for instance, the high moor grass under the "huge light" and the seige of wind is borne "through visions / From emptiness to brighter emptiness / With music and with silence." One important way to view the development of Hughes's poetry is to observe gains in the mana power of meditative energy: a greater intensity of concentration that strips away wordy baggage to arrive at a direct grasp of the essence. Instead of the muscular verbosity of the early "Wind," a spare austerity suffices in *Remains of Elmet*.

At sundown the moors glimpsed from atop Heptonstall can heal and offer spiritual reconciliation even in their starkness. The undulating moor-lines that form a backdrop to the town cemetery seem to Hughes like the extended wings of "a family of dark swans" that carry the spirits of departed relatives heavenward in the *Elmet* poem "Heptonstall Cemetery." In this poem Hughes accepted the death of his mother Edith and his uncle Walter. He could even envision the departed spirit of Sylvia Plath as one of the dark swans' "Living feathers" undergoing spiritual rebirth as they beat "low through storm-silver / Toward the Atlantic."

Dark Swan

After Hughes completed his Cambridge degree in anthropology in June 1954, he began publishing in Cambridge poetry magazines such as *Granta* during the next two years while he worked in London or Cambridge at various jobs, including factory night watchman, zoo attendant, rose gardener, schoolteacher, and reader for J. Arthur Rank, the film producer. Hughes maintained his literary friendships at Cambridge, and early in 1956 when David Ross and others decided to launch their own poetry magazine, *St. Botolph's Review*, it contained four Hughes poems in its only issue. At the review's 25 February celebration party, Hughes met Sylvia Plath, an American poet who was studying English on a Fulbright grant at Cambridge.[13] Each was impressed with the other's work, and the personal attraction was immediate. The relationship promised to be intensely fulfilling for both. They married on Bloomsday, 16 June 1956, after a courtship of less than four months.

An intellectual cross-fertilization of interests and cultures developed that reinforced their roles as artists. They shared their love for Blake and Lawrence and traded insights about many of the masters. Plath, a Bostonian and summa cum laude graduate of Smith, already had many prize-winning publications in poetry and fiction, and used her American efficiency to type Hughes's poems and ensure that batches of them were always under consideration at various magazines. Hughes opened up Plath's grasp of nature with his firsthand knowledge of the English countryside, and helped her through her periodic bouts of writer's block. Plath exchanged her knowledge of American poetry and the New Criticism for Hughes's knowledge of Shakespeare and Graves's *The White Goddess.* Together they explored common interests in poetry, other fine arts, and psychology.

During the next year, while Plath completed her degree at Cambridge and Hughes taught in the secondary school system, both had poems accepted by such major magazines as *Poetry* and *Atlantic.* Hughes won a Guggenheim fellowship in 1959 to continue his creative writing and in 1960 won both the Somerset Maugham Award for literary promise and the Hawthornden Prize for his second poetry volume, *Lupercal.* But his most important prize had been his first.

In October 1956 Plath typed 40 of Hughes's poems and sent them to a contest sponsored by the Poetry Center of the Young Men's and Young Women's Hebrew Association of New York. She used for the first time the nickname "Ted" on his book manuscript. The judges of the contest—W. H. Auden, Stephen Spender, and Marianne Moore—chose the manuscript, over 286 other entries, for first prize: publication by Harper and Brothers. Hughes learned of the prize in February 1957, and has been understandably superstitious since then about using any other name than "Ted Hughes." Plath accepted an instructorship at Smith a month later and in May Faber and Faber, with congratulations from T. S. Eliot, agreed to publish the British edition. By the time both editions of *The Hawk in the Rain* appeared in September, the couple had been living in Massachusetts for three months.

The Hawk in the Rain revealed Hughes's immense talent, expressed in a powerful, muscular line that absorbed the best of the moderns without neutralizing the strength of his own grasp of nature. Critics praised his vitality and accuracy of observation, his vividly sensuous and very physical imagery, the blunt honesty and dramatic immediacy of his presentation, and his deep exploration of universal themes. A few noted occasional echoes of Hopkins, Graves, and other moderns, but most were struck by Hughes's dramatic originality. Negative criticism was directed at occasionally gruff rhetoric, clotted metaphors, or strong verbs that wrenched the syntax.

Hughes taught at the nearby Amherst campus of the University of Massachusetts in the spring of 1958 while Plath labored at grading themes at Smith, agonized over whether she really wanted a Ph.D. and an academic career, and experienced the deflation of observing at close hand the pettiness of professors she had idolized just two years earlier. Hughes enjoyed his teaching immensely, but preferred a career where he could be his own master. When Plath finally decided that teaching drained her creative energies, they moved to Boston in the summer to write for a year, supported by their savings from teaching.

Hughes labored steadily and patiently over his craft in the tiny Beacon Hill apartment, generating many of the poems that would fill his even more successful second poetry volume, *Lupercal* (1960). As he alternated between reading and writing, he extended his thematic range and his grasp of English history, used the Roman Lupercalia ritual to tap his myth and anthropology background, and continued to write literature for children. Plath, exhausted in body and spirit from a full year of teaching, found creative writing more difficult than ever and succumbed to periods of depression and writer's block. She took a part-time job as a medical secretary, audited Robert Lowell's workshop in confessional poetry at Boston University in the spring of 1959, and struggled with desires to begin a family.

Plath had attempted suicide in August 1953, two and a half years before she met Hughes. Typing medical case summaries at Massachusetts General Hospital five years later gave her material for stories, but periods of depression and her inability to write continued. By December 1958 she was again seeing Dr. Ruth Beuscher, the therapist who had helped her through the emotional trauma of the outpatient electric shock therapy that had preceded her attempted suicide. With the help of Dr. Beuscher, Plath explored the probable reasons for the suicide attempt and uncovered a tangle of emotions and blocked personality development relating to her father's death when she was eight, her subsequent resentment toward her mother, and her fear of abandonment by father figures—including Ted, identified as a substitute father (*Journals*, 276–87; *Letters Home*, 289).

But prospects gradually brightened in 1959. Hughes and Plath enjoyed a successful camping trip to the West Coast in the summer. Then they accepted an invitation from the Yaddo writers' colony at Saratoga Springs, New York, to spend a relaxed three months working at their creative writing before leaving for England in December. At Yaddo both writers began to explore their inner worlds more directly, but in divergent ways. Hughes met the Chinese composer Chou Wen-Chung, who interested him in writing an oratorio for a multimedia composition he was creating on the *Bardo Thödol*, the Tibetan Book of the Dead (hereafter cited in the text as *Book of the Dead*). Hughes worked at the oratorio off and on through November 1960 (*Letters Home*, 354, 399). Though lack of funding killed the project and the oratorio remains unpublished, he mined it for many of the surrealistic poems of *Wodwo* (1967), his third volume of poetry. At Yaddo Plath became influenced by Roethke's death-and-rebirth pattern in his *Praise to the End* sequence; combining Roethke's mythic round with her therapy revelations and her workshop training in confessional poetry, she was able to face her suicide attempt for the first time in "Poem for a Birthday." Yet the more she searched her own experience, the less optimistic her poetry became.

The *Bardo Thödol* abounds in imagery expressing psychic dissociation, withdrawal, and nightmarish violence. Long familiar with the Bon/Buddhist background of the *Bardo,* Hughes tried to render its surrealism faithfully and also found it a powerful addition to his style, an effective way to bring home to the reader the dire consequences of the mythification of science and technology in the West. The standard Evans-Wentz translation of the *Bardo* is prefaced (since the 1957 third edition) by Carl Jung's lengthy introductory essay. Hughes, who had been reading Jung's blend of psychoanalysis, myth, the occult, dream interpretation, and cultural criticism since the late 1940s, now found a surrealistic method to combine Jung with his own folklore and anthropology readings in a spellbinding way.

Like the American poets Gary Snyder and Allen Ginsberg, Hughes learned that Oriental philosophy and psychology offered an alternative to Western rationalism and utilitarian egocentricity. During the sixties Hughes read Zen and Sufi literature, and Hindu Upanishads, and in the seventies Indian Tamil poetry and Taoist writers. From the time of contact with the *Bardo* until the late seventies, Hughes's combination of surrealism, the myths and folklore of ancient and tribal societies, and various Oriental influences helped to make his poetry strikingly original, but also baffling to most reviewers.

Many British literary reviewers who experienced World War II as adults found poems like "Hawk Roosting" (*Lupercal*) and "Second Glance at a Jaguar" (*Wodwo*) to be unbearable emulations of violence for its own sake. After *Crow,* a few accused Hughes of an adolescent indulgence in nihilistic violence.[14] These critics, untrained in psychology and anthropology, were unaware of the social and moral dimensions of Hughes's belief in mana power. As in Jung and shamanism, one cannot be healed when psychic energy is repressed; one must wrestle with it ("Myth 1," Faas 1). Believing very strongly in the capacity of humans to grow, Hughes in his sixties poetry expressed intermediary stages of psychological wrestling with personal and cultural demons in graphic imagery.

Plath became pregnant while on the camping trip out west, and on 1 April 1960 gave birth to Frieda Rebecca Hughes in London. After she recovered from childbirth, Plath worked on *The Bell Jar* in the mornings while Ted cared for Frieda, and the parents switched writing and childcare roles in the afternoons. Though from this time on they divided childcare responsibilities equally and kept their own writing time sacrosanct, Plath remained subject to extreme mood swings and occasional jealousies.[15] Hughes was becoming an increasingly well-known poet, with even better reviews for *Lupercal,* which created many social opportunities and obligations. Tall and handsome, Hughes had a virile presence and an appealing, well-tuned cello of a voice. The BBC soon "took him up" and Hughes became extremely effective at composing radio scripts about writing for children and adolescents, earning $3 per minute of airtime in the early sixties.

In April Plath again became pregnant, and in the summer she and Hughes found an old rectory with a thatched roof in rural Devon that would distance them from urban pressures and the London social round to afford more time to write and also provide needed space for their growing family. They purchased Court Green and moved there at the end of August 1961. Nicholas Farrar Hughes arrived on 17 January 1962.

Although world events and the death of a neighbor in 1961–62 occasionally depressed her, on a much higher plane Plath was becoming extremely self-absorbed. She was beginning to incubate *Ariel*'s vision of numbed withdrawal where the land's end is "Cramped on nothing" ("Finisterre") or "looks out on nothing" ("Blackberrying"), where the clouds spread their "vacuous sheets" ("Little Fugue") and where the mind "cannot see where there is to get to" ("The Moon and the Yew Tree"). From "Tulips," a poem about her appendectomy in March 1961, through the spring of 1962, Plath's poems record her actual mental states without her earlier distanced craftsmanship. With the exception of *Three Women* and "New Year on Dartmoor," poems about the birth of Nicholas, the artistic record during this period reveals an increasingly bleak vision. She was gradually descending the stairs of her psyche to confront the "Black asininity" she describes in "Wintering," the last of the five beekeeping poems in *Ariel.*

The domestic climate became more tenuous and strained. Despite enjoying his time with the children, carpentry, and gardening at Court Green, Hughes became increasingly alienated by Plath's moodiness and self-absorption. On Friday, 18 May, the Canadian poet David Wevill and his wife, Assia Gutman Wevill, arrived for a weekend. The four had first met when the Wevills took over the small Primrose Hill flat Hughes and Plath had vacated when they moved to Devon. Assia became attracted to Hughes during the visit and about a month later they began an affair in London.

When Plath learned of the affair, she insisted that Hughes leave the home; by early September the couple agreed to a six-month separation, with Hughes to live in Spain and Plath in Ireland. By the time the two settled on an adequate support payment for the children and Hughes moved his belongings in early October, Plath had already begun the great flurry of poems that completed *Ariel*.

Plath moved herself and the children to a London flat in the late fall of 1962 only to encounter the hardships of the worst English winter of the century. Though many of the fine *Ariel* poems written after Hughes's departure convert her anger into the desire for an autonomous self through death and rebirth motifs, the separation and the weather wore on her. She became depressed; her doctor prescribed an antidepressant and also arranged for a live-in nurse until a hospital bed could be arranged. Hours before the nurse arrived, depression caused a total collapse: in the early morning of 11 February 1963 Plath committed suicide by gassing herself in the kitchen oven. With family help from his mother, aunt, sister Olwyn, and later his second wife Carol Orchard, Hughes raised Frieda and Nicholas, who are now both adults pursuing very worthwhile careers.

Reconciliation and Renewal

Three weeks after Plath's death the sculptor Leonard Baskin, a member of the Smith College art faculty and a family friend, arrived to try to lift Hughes's spirits by asking him to write a poem about Baskin's crow engravings, to be printed at his Gehenna Press. "The Anatomy of Crow" never materialized, and Baskin heard no more of his suggestion until Hughes's Crow poems began appearing in the summer of 1967. Meanwhile Hughes continued his reviewing, his BBC talks for adolescents, and his children's verse, until in 1966 he began the last group of poems that appeared in *Wodwo*. A review that Hughes published in December 1965 on two books of folklore rekindled a long-standing interest in the Trickster narratives of tribal societies, one of the major sources for Crow's escapades.[16] It would be untrue, however, to suggest that Hughes needs commissions, or myth or folklore texts to generate creative ideas, or to claim that any direct correspondence exists between his reading and creative projects: the reading is an alluvium, a deposit that is moved and mixed many times by the strong river of his creativity.

Hughes originally conceived *Crow* to have a medieval epic plot where the protagonist, after many trials and ordeals, learns how to end his alienation from Nature and win Nature as his bride. But the deaths of Assia and her daughter Shura in March 1969 brought the sequence to an abrupt halt, with most of the early poems written, but few from the concluding transformation and betrothal sections. The creative collaboration with Baskin, however, has flowered over the years. Baskin has since produced excellent illustrations for many of Hughes's volumes, including the children's work. Baskin's very remarkable graphic work has also been the source of Hughes's inspiration for *Cave Birds* (1978) and *Flowers and Insects* (1986).

Since 1971 many of Hughes's volumes and poem sequences have first appeared in limited editions by various printers for the Rainbow Press, a publishing imprint owned by Hughes and his sister Olwyn. Originally they intended each volume to have a slightly different shade of leather binding, forming a rainbow spectrum across a shelf. Olwyn, who holds an arts degree from the University of London and has often worked in Paris as a secretary for theater agencies and other organizations, sometimes did the rough planning and chose the design and materials for these elegant limited editions until the press ceased publishing new volumes in 1981.

In 1967 the British theater director Peter Brook decided to produce a version of Seneca's *Oedipus* with the National Theatre Company at the Old Vic in March 1968, with John Gielgud and Irene Worth in the lead roles. His assistant, Geoffrey Reeves, suggested that Ted Hughes be commissioned to adapt an existing translation by David Turner. Hughes's spare rendition, a series of unpunctuated psychodrama tropes, emphasized the suffering and spiritual anguish of the protagonists, and rendered the gory violence of Seneca in a staccato of sharply visualized concrete images that strain painfully toward illumination. When Brook decided to take his International Center for Theatre Research to Iran to perform a composite drama based upon Western myths of suffering and illumination, he asked Hughes to join him in Teheran in 1971 and write the text.

The result, the *Orghast* drama (1971: unpublished), brought Hughes toward a middle position: his animus against Western rationalism was expressed through the Krogon tyrant of the drama, but he placed a new emphasis on the fruits of suffering. In the success of Sogis in part 2 of the drama, Hughes rewrote Ripley's ordeal from *The Wound,* with greater emphasis upon the results: spiritual illumination. As Hughes conflated elements of Aeschylus's *Prometheus Bound* with elements of Calderón's *La vida es sueño* (Life is a dream) and bits from Seneca, Manichaean myths, and dozens of other texts, he began to feel more optimistic about the worth of suffering.

Hughes now appeared to be tapping the power center of world mythology where, as Joseph Campbell observed, suffering can produce an enlargement of consciousness and illumination in the realm of spirit (Campbell 1968, 647–78). After searching these Western myths, Hughes and Brook developed one of the main themes of *Orghast,* which is also one of Brook's main beliefs about a necessary theater—that the gifts of language and fire are analogous, inner/outer components of the development of Western culture (Smith, 39). Themes of transformation and illumination also occur in the 1973 minor works *Prometheus on His Crag* and *Orpheus.*

Two events in his private life in the early seventies furthered Hughes's reconciliation with nature's pattern of death and rebirth. In 1970 he married Carol Orchard, the daughter of a Devon farmer. Then in 1972 he bought a cattle farm in Devon, called Moortown, which Carol's father Jack Orchard managed until his death in 1976. The 1975 volume *Season Songs* contains many poems enriched by the vivid imagery of farm life. As a regular farmhand at Moortown in the seventies, Hughes carried a pocket journal and made occasional notes in rough verse. His purpose was to catch the actual event and his response to it with a minimum of distortion from memory or artistic craftsmanship. The result was *Moortown Elegies* (1978), which a year later became the opening section of *Moortown.*

In the seventies Hughes's deepening involvement with Western mythology, a second marriage, and a strong Taoist influence later in the decade led to a renewed interest in the feminine. In the poetic colloquies of the *Gaudete* "Epilogue," which Hughes began in 1975, the Reverend Nicholas Lumb, an Anglican country parson who has been fornicating clandestinely with the village wives under the pretext of engendering a savior, learns to expand his understanding of the feminine beyond his erotic compulsions. His suffering brings him a deeper knowledge of life and a new reverence for the feminine.

As with Baskin's crow engravings, most of Hughes's projects since the midseventies have been at least in part inspired by the visual arts. The hermetic psychodrama *Cave Birds* (1978) began when Hughes in 1974 saw a group of Baskin's weirdly anthropoid drawings of cave birds. The two collaborated upon a second group of drawings and poems, and Hughes then added a dramatic organization when the Ilkley Festival commissioned him to do a stage reading in May 1975. The final reconciliation with the feminine in this volume produced one of the finest love poems Hughes has written, "Bride and groom lie hidden for three days," where man and woman refashion each other in intense, moment-by-moment astonishment. The combination of Taoism and Fay Godwin's photographs in *Remains of Elmet* (1979) brought a Proustian recollection of childhood and a consent to its worth under the benign influence of the undulating feminine moorlines.

An almost translucent spiritual glow surrounds the imagery of *River* (1983) and *Flowers and Insects* (1986). Here one finds what Blake called the "organized innocence of wisdom" (a marginal note to Night 7b of *The Four Zoas*) as Hughes uses the natural object as a signature that instantly reveals spiritual truths. The river is itself both the stream of moment-to-moment consciousness and a conduit for the spiritually healing energy of nature, a "down-roping / Of the living honey" from the sky above in "River Barrow." As Blake could see a world in a grain of sand, so Hughes in *Flowers and Insects* finds the apogee of lived life in a violet's fragile delicacy: "Only a purple flower—this amulet / (Once Prospero's)—holds it all, a moment, / In a rinsed globe of light." In his most recent work Hughes is able to capture directly the moment of consciousness as events unfold before it.

In *Wolfwatching,* his latest poetry volume (1989), Hughes achieves a remarkable flexibility of style. The poems alternate between poignant portraits of aging relatives whose absorption of modern machine culture has disconnected them from the landscape, and poems about whales and sparrow hawks that are so united with their environment that they suggest ecological and spiritual dimensions.

Intellectual Influences

Hughes is one of the most widely and deeply read of poets. Even to enumerate his major reading interests would be an exhausting task. He has read omnivorously in Occidental and Oriental folklore, myth, and religion. Major Western literary influences include the Bible, the ancient Greeks, Chaucer, the ballads, Shakespeare, Donne, Milton, Blake, Shelley, Hopkins, Yeats, Owen, Eliot, Lawrence, Dylan Thomas, Beckett, Vasco Popa, and the Americans Whitman, Dickinson, and Ransom. A more worthwhile task would be to place Hughes's poetry and thinking in an intellectual tradition.

To consider Hughes's poetry as simply advocating a return to nature would be to reduce it to triteness. Certainly Hughes has much in common with the American self-reliance theme of Emerson and the "simplify, simplify" ideas of Thoreau. But his poetic style mainly continues the inspirational tradition whose sources include early lyric poets such as Sappho, the Dionysian dithyramb, the Old Testament prophets, the shamanistic and epic bards of tribal societies and ancient cultures, and which continues to flow through the work of Blake, Shelley, and Yeats. In terms of shamanic descents to an underworld and flights to a spiritual source, Hughes belongs to a wide European tradition that includes Goethe, Novalis, Lorca, Rilke, Rimbaud, Baudelaire, Nerval, and Valéry, among others. Intellectually and thematically Hughes has most in common with Blake, Yeats, and Lawrence, especially in their critique of the empirical tradition of Locke and Newton that led to the Industrial Revolution, their critique of Protestant Christianity, and their advocacy of unitive states of being and visionary perception to repair the divorce of the perceiving subject from its object.

Only the creative forge of Los in Blake's *Jerusalem* can heal the lapse in imaginative vision that put the giant Albion into a sleep of reason and divided his senses into four disputatious, isolated zoas. Albion's sleep is the result of the empiricism of the New Science and its technological consequence, the Industrial Revolution. Since that time religion, according to Blake, has ceased to relate body to soul and to transform human energies into spiritually satisfying communal bonds. Therefore, art must show the way. In "The Hanged Man and the Dragonfly," Hughes alludes four times to Blake's "human form divine," a postulate of innocent yet unified Edenic perception in the early *Songs* and *The Everlasting Gospel*. Albion's lapsed vision, his satanic empiricism, destroyed this perception (*Milton*: plate 32; *Jerusalem*: plate 27). To see the divine within the human form we must learn not to perceive God, but to exercise our own divinity—to "perceive *as* God" by transcending dualism through imaginative vision.[17]

By focusing only upon the empirically verifiable and ignoring what is otherwise experiential for humans, Locke offered a model of behavior in which the perceiving subject was a passive tabula rasa that abstracted primary qualities such as mass and weight to fit into general categories. In Blake's poetry this is the dungeon vision of Ulro, where Urizen, or "your reason," abstracts and separates space and time from the self with geometrical precision. Newton reduced the universe to mechanics and the sleepy monocular vision of universally applied mathematical laws. As Blake once said in a famous letter, "May God us keep / From Single vision & Newtons sleep" (Blake, 722).

Yeats, who collaborated on an edition of Blake in 1893, advocated a unity of being where opposites such as body and spirit, self and soul, subject and object unify in the excitement of visionary perception, as in the concluding chestnut tree and dancer images of "Among School Children." In such a state of exalted vision "The body is not bruised to pleasure soul, / Nor beauty born out of its own despair, / Nor blear-eyed wisdom out of midnight oil." When one perceives holistically and participates in the excitement of the moment of perception, one does not lapse into a mode of analysis that would divide the tree into its parts or abstract dance from dancer. Hughes admired Yeats's use of folklore and the occult in the quest for this integrated perception. Yeats continued Blake's critique of the empirical tradition with poems such as "Fragments," where Eve as spinning jenny is wrenched from the side of Locke, a degraded Adam, as "The Garden died."

One sees Lawrence's critique of the Industrial Revolution in the mechanical "go" of Gerald Crich and the impotence of Clifford Chatterley, whose machine—a wheelchair—crushes the creeping-jenny and the forget-me-nots in the woods. In his *Studies in Classic American Literature,* his psychoanalytic essays, and his pornography essay Lawrence criticized the mentalized consciousness divorced from the senses by the Puritans and Protestant Christianity, and proposed a dark passional wholeness, a proud singleness that can give freely and create a star-equilibrium of two autonomous individuals, as with Birkin and Ursula or Mellors and Connie. In his poems Lawrence celebrated the otherness of animals with wonder, directness, and honest fidelity to feeling.

Hughes absorbed the rich heritage of Blake, Yeats, and Lawrence long before his career as a poet began. But in Hughes's view more than an Edenic unity of being died as a result of the New Science and the Industrial Revolution. Hughes's father was one of only 17 survivors of an entire battalion of the Lancashire Fusiliers whose total strength was replaced *three* times at Gallipoli. Conversations after the Sunday family dinner frequently focused upon memories of the Great War, when Hughes was a child, and the cenotaphs of the Lancashire Fusiliers who fought bravely and died at Gallipoli still dot the West Yorkshire hillsides.

Any discussion of violence and death in Hughes should begin with these cenotaphs. Hughes agrees with Jung that a cause-effect relationship exists between the analytic and mechanical culture of the Industrial Revolution and the world wars of the twentieth century. For Jung the psyche ideally functions as a paradoxically united tension of opposites. The conscious ego ideally exists as an integrated whole where thinking, feeling, sensation, and intuition work in harmony. The ego should periodically dip back into the Self, a larger totality that includes conscious and unconscious contents, for instinctual and goal-directed energies whenever it needs to reorient itself or find a new self-image to replace one it has outgrown.[18] But our post-Industrial Revolution culture develops only the rational portion of the ego, and herein lies our problem.

Crow's Malaise

The rational portion of the ego thrives on processing information. It feels secure only when it receives logical explanations for events. All that is alogical it fearfully withdraws from and represses. Jung maintained that the nonrational psychic centers contain powerful libidinal energies: when an individual or a culture represses them, the bottled-up energies may explode into violence after projecting the inner chaos and fears upon a scapegoat. In one essay Jung intimated that Hitler functioned as a symbol of collective violence in a totalitarian state where introspection lapsed into passive acceptance and all repressed, chaotic energy and fears were projected onto an ethnic scapegoat, creating the Holocaust.[19] Hughes in "Scapegoats and Rabies" (*Wodwo*) concluded that all humans in the West are scapegoats, having become acculturated to an empiricism and a machine technology that makes us passive tabulae rasae, ready to channel our mechanical "go" unthinkingly into lockstep formations on demand. Our neurotic, reckless energy is a function of our refusal to develop sufficient introspection to foster real individuality. In "Scapegoats and Rabies" humans become windup machines ready to explode into cenotaphs.

Crow is our Western cultural paragon of atrophied introspection and fearfully egocentric withdrawal from nature. In 1970, the year of the first British edition of *Crow,* Hughes also published a very enthusiastic review of Max Nicholson's *The Environmental Revolution* in which he lamented public ignorance of basic conservation issues. The reasons for this ignorance are indigenous to Western culture. One passage functions as an especially succinct introduction to the *Crow* poems—a clear blend of Jungian psychology and Hughes's thoughts on ecology:

The fundamental guiding ideas of our Western Civilization are against Conservation. They derive from Reformed Christianity and from Old Testament Puritanism. This is generally accepted. They are based on the assumption that the earth is a heap of raw materials given to man by God for his exclusive profit and use. The creepy crawlies which infest it are devils of dirt and without a soul, also put there for his exclusive profit and use. By the skin of her teeth, woman escaped the same role. The subtly apotheosized misogyny of Reformed Christianity is proportionate to the fanatic rejection of Nature, and the result has been to exile man from Mother Nature—from both inner and outer nature. The story of the mind exiled from Nature is the story of Western Man. It is the story of his progressively more desperate search for mechanical and rational and symbolic securities, which will substitute for the spirit-confidence of the Nature he has lost.[20]

Completely lacking in introspection and utterly dependent upon the defense mechanisms of a fragile ego, Crow is never at home in nature because he has exiled himself from both inner and outer nature. He expresses his anxiety through an obsessive analytic energy that consistently appropriates nature to his utilitarian designs. In "A Horrible Religious Error," for instance, the serpent appears, the preeminent pre-Christian symbol of transformation and renewal in nature (Campbell 1968, 154). Adam and Eve, recognizing its power to help them grow, kneel in worship. But Crow "only peered" at the snake. After analysis, a violent appropriation follows: he "Grabbed this creature by the slackskin nape, / Beat the hell out of it, and ate it."

Lacking a developed inner life, Crow's responses are predictably egocentric while he projects his inner chaos outward. Crow sits in the Black Beast's chair and hides in its bed, but he will never recognize that "The Black Beast" is himself. By the end of the poem he projects his inner vacuum outward and exhausts his neurotic energy by flailing at black holes in the divorced scientific space created from his own fears, like Blake's Urizen. He has exiled himself from inner and outer nature; he becomes obsessed with the vacuum of outer space rather than face the vacuum of his inner space.

A Float in Yoga and the Tao

How can one avoid Crow's fate? How can one develop significant depth in one's inner life and reconnect oneself with nature? Hughes suggests that one ought to go fishing in the unconscious for sustenance. In an early BBC radio talk about fishing (1961), Hughes characterized the inner life of humans as "the world of final reality, the world of memory, emotion, imagination, intelligence, and natural common sense," and real thinking became a process of breaking into that inner life to "capture answers and evidence to support the answers, out of it." Hughes was describing a process of reconnecting the conscious ego with one's unconscious resources—the Jungian Self. After nervous energy abated and he forgot the distractions of duties and schedules, Hughes would stare at the red dot of his fishing float in a slightly mesmerized way and after a while feel connected with his subconscious and with nature in a much more fundamental way than that achieved by using his analytic reasoning to compile data and facts. According to Hughes, once the distractions dissolve, "you enter one of the orders of bliss," where you are suspended in a "concentrated patient excitement."[21] The process of meditation Hughes described is an ancient one. In his *Yoga Sutras,* Patanjali spoke of ceasing the flow of conventional decision making as a prelude to connecting with the living present. One relieved oneself of inner tensions through concentrating on a single point.[22] Actually Hughes was a decade ahead of his time. Although in America the Zen-influenced Beat poets of the late fifties used Oriental thinking as an antidote to the goal-oriented success myths of Western society, only in the seventies did it become common for therapists to suggest classes in transcendental meditation for executives and office workers to relieve their stress and frazzled nerves. As the above story suggests, Hughes does not advocate extinguishing the ego or transcending the phenomenal world in *nirvāṇa*, as does Yoga. He uses Oriental influences as various as Zen, Yoga, Taoism, Indian Upanishads, and Vacanas to heighten his contact with a more essential self and to reconnect himself with the vital rhythms of nature.

This is especially true of Hughes's interest in Taoism since the midseventies. The predynastic Chinese developed their grasp of the *Tao,* or "Way" — the Nameless eternal order or the absolute, undifferentiated substance, often likened to a womblike emptiness, from which all phenomena emanate—through becoming absorbed in nature. Gradually one senses a natural harmony in the rhythms of change from the dark, intuitive, feminine yin to the bright and assertive masculine yang.[23] This not only reconnects the individual to nature in a fundamental way and sensitizes him or her to deeper psychic energies within the self, but also occasionally leads to glimpses of a spiritual energy at the heart of existence during rare moments of visionary trance. Hughes's poem "Go Fishing," from the incomparable *River,* is his most successful rendering of the process by which we avoid Crow's malaise.

"Go Fishing" suggests that nature offers a soothing, healing bath in preconceptual, wordless states of feeling and contact with natural rhythms essential to psychic health. The reader wades into the river water of Hughes's language as the persona wades into the river. Here one's brain mists away as one also bathes in the "underbeing" of the subconscious. The purely rational dissolves in the poem's invitation to drink in or "gulp" the sensuality of nature through images and connotations that revitalize the sensations of touch, taste, and sight. The hushed sibilation of "s," "h," and "w" sounds rock the reader endlessly in soothing cradles of auditory sensations. The lack of periods almost hypnotizes the reader into accepting the poem's challenge to meditate upon inner psychic states and forget discursive thought.

The mana energy of Hughes's language manifests itself as a controlled inner excitement, a delighted yet healing plasm available just beneath the "drift / Of water-mesh" and the "weight of earth-taste light." The language is effective enough to refresh the senses and revitalize our capacity to experi-

ence the touch of nature, our ecological second skin. If the reader becomes
absorbed in the poem's quiet intensity, it is possible to experience a glimpse
of the Tao while undergoing a cleansing rebirth into the "new and nameless." After completing this therapeutic healing process, the reader is less apt
to labor under repressed energies, and is ready for the community of humans, the social contact implied in the poem's last line. Psychological
wholeness leads to communal bonding—the main moral message of
Hughes's art.

Language as Mediating Mandala

Hughes is especially concerned with the affective function of language,
with using the mana power of his poetry to help the reader activate and integrate psychic energies. Whether one considers these energies to be the
Freudian id, ego, and superego, or a more generalized Jungian psychic energy activated by archetypal situations occurring in the personal unconscious, is really for reader and interpreter to decide as each makes free
metaphorical applications to his/her own life ("Myth 1," 66). These psychic
energies are shared by all humans, and the writer must be responsible when
activating and organizing them in the structure of the text.

Hughes's insistence upon the therapeutic function of language is broadly
structuralist in its underlying assumption that the forms of communication
of tribal and more advanced cultures express and activate psychic energies
shared by all humans. Freud and Jung believed that the events in a dream
are structured by the dreamer in meaningfully distorted ways that express
the actual state of the psyche—the relative state of repression, derangement,
or integration of instincts or psychic energies shared by all humans.[24] Lévi–
Strauss believes that myths are linguistic structures that reveal the habit of
the human mind to perceive life's problems in terms of binary oppositions
that the myths themselves mediate or palliate.[25] When structured by the responsible creative artist, language for Hughes is the mediator that can activate, release, and integrate psychic energies common to all humans. For
Hughes the poet is the consummate therapist.

Hughes called for responsible creative writing in the first of his two
"Myth and Education" essays. By "seasoning [the reader's] inner personality
by fantasies," the reader develops a rich and confident inner world worthy of
introspection as well as "an imagination which can deal with both the outer
world and our inner life" ("Myth 1," 59, 61). This language in creative writing is not so much the source of meaning as it is a therapeutic tool, a mediator between the reader's inner life and the world of nature outside the self.

In the same essay Hughes extended his affective emphasis on language by stating that creative fantasies can release the reader's repressed energies and effect at least a momentary cure for the neurotic. Hughes cited Freud's therapeutic technique as working toward the release and recognition of demonic, repressed energy, for the personality will grow into wholeness only when the energy has been welcomed into conscious life ("Myth 1," 66). Thus what might appear to be gratuitous violence enacted by an obsessively analytic, would-be hero in *Crow,* or outrageous sexual behavior embodied by the Reverend Lumb in *Gaudete,* is really an invitation to explore one's repressed demonic energies within an organized structure that ultimately integrates these energies into a coherent whole.

Hughes's analysis of his children's story *The Iron Man,* his only extended interpretation of one of his own creative works, concerns exactly such an activation and release of repressed energy to promote psychic health in the reader. When a huge iron giant appears in a rural town, the boy Hogarth agrees to help the farmers trap it in a pit and bury it because it has been eating their tractors. But the giant will not stay buried. When the giant resurrects himself in the spring, Hogarth convinces the farmers to let the giant eat junkyard scrap. Later the giant saves the town from a demonic "space-bat-angel-dragon"; after winning an ordeal by fire, the giant forces the dragon to change its threats into the music of the spheres. Through his initiative, Hogarth, the child-ego, repossesses his subjective world with its emotional and spiritual resources (the space-bat-angel-dragon) and redeems his outer world, which had shrunk to a threatening machine technology. All components of Hogarth's world embrace in mutually supportive ways that will facilitate development ("Myth 1," 63–67).

As the reader follows *The Iron Man,* he or she identifies with the boy as potential hero and subliminally experiences a similar release of repressed demonic energies. If the repressed energies are not released, one may become as potentially dangerous as the jaguar in the *Wodwo* poem "Second Glance at a Jaguar," which Hughes has characterized as a "symbol of man's baser nature shoved down into the id and growing cannibal murderous with deprivation" (Faas 1, 199). Though few single poems effect as complete an integration of psychic energies as a five-part story like *The Iron Man,* the remaining chapters of this study will reveal that Hughes structures each volume of poetry to lead to a final psychic integration.

Hughes feels he can legitimately make such large claims for the therapeutic function of poetic language because language itself, according to some anthropologists, originated from primeval grunts that expressed basic physiological needs, and because the spoken word is heard by the auditory nerves that connect to the cerebellum, which controls the muscular and sympathetic nervous systems in humans. When Hughes developed his *Orghast* drama in the summer of 1971, a substantial portion of the dialogue came from a language he improvised to speak more directly to the mental states of the audience through sound patterns and musical structure. Hughes cited two beliefs of Lévi–Strauss as rationales for the invented language. Sound patterns in music make us conscious of our physiological roots. Meanwhile the musical structure of mythic motifs encloses the audience in timeless patterns for the duration of the drama to explore and integrate their psychic energies by appealing subliminally to common mental structures. Hence the audience did not need a dictionary for Hughes's invented language, for the sound conveyed the sense directly: the *Orghast* root *ull* conveyed "swallow" and *gr* conveyed the tearing action of eating meat (Smith, 43–47). Once again Hughes conceived language to be an all-purpose tool for communicating desires and for establishing an agreement with reality outside the self. (*Poetry*, 119).

If Hughes's goal is psychic coherence, integration, and harmony, he presents in his poems at least as much turbulence, dissociation, incoherence, and violence—a wealth of Derridean *différence* in each volume, if not in each word. One of the most striking postmodern qualities about this very structuralist poet is his working axiom that any achieved integration and harmony is a very fragile and temporary state, always subject to being undermined by change and further experience. As in the "Finale" of *Cave Birds,* a goblin pops up at the end of every ritual.

Structuralism and mana power in Hughes are opposed, however, to the poststructuralism of Jacques Derrida and the deconstructionists, who do not recognize universals of human experience or any assumed connection between language and psychic energies. For Derrideans no necessary relation exists between the words on the page (the signifers) and the concepts to which the words refer (the signified). Each act of reading is a totally unique interaction between a reader and a work; no "text" exists without this interaction. Words and print reveal the absence of the objects to which they refer. The reader is free to relate his or her past experience to the signifiers no matter what may have been the author's intent.[26] Hughes has 25 centuries of oral and written literary evidence to support his positions about constants within the psyche, the purpose of literature, and the author's controlling intentions; deconstructionists, on the other hand, reduce textual activity to the free and ever-changing encounter between a reader and a work.

Actually, as chapter 5 reveals, Hughes's more recent meditations on the relation of language to human experience resemble Martin Heidegger's observation that language is a uniquely human activity that expresses the potential coherence of self and the natural elements to constitute "world." For Hughes language is a therapeutic tool, not a suspect entity that has no essence or thinghood.

Although Hughes has never compared his poems to mandalas, these intricate visual structures have a therapeutic function that is similar to Hughes's conviction that literature creates an "imaginative blueprint" within the mind of the reader that heals by integrating psychic forces ("Myth 1"). Mandalas are intricately drawn circular paintings depicting the self occupying the center of patterns usually involving a harmonious balance of the four natural elements. In Tibetan Buddhism mandalas are visual aids used to heal psychic dissociation; both the viewer and the artist who creates them can organize and heal the inner life by contemplating mandalas with absorbed intensity. According to Jung, they invite the viewer to become the whole, integrated self depicted in the complex organization of paired opposites of inner and outer, rational and instinctive, conscious and subconscious life. In general they function as therapeutic devices, suggesting that the disoriented psyche has a self-regulating capacity. They activate one's inner life and invite introspection and self-exploration (Jung 9a: 355–90). Many of Hughes's poems and all of his volumes of poetry are mandalas intricately organized to promote wholeness and harmony in the reader.

As models for integrating inner and outer forces, Hughes's poems have had a very direct influence upon other contemporary poets, especially Seamus Heaney. Hughes greeted the earliest of Heaney's bog poems with enthusiasm and encouraged his fellow poet to continue employing this anthropological perspective. Hughes's deftly organized poetic amalgams of myth and anthropology have also influenced the poetry of George MacBeth, Peter Redgrove, Ted Walker, Richard Murphy, Ken Smith, and Heathcote Williams. The volumes R. S. Thomas published in the 1970s contained poems that show an unmistakable *Crow* influence. But Thomas West is correct in concluding that Hughes is a very original talent who will not readily spawn imitators and does not need them to prop his work with the pseudolegitimacy of a "movement." His importance for younger British poets lies in providing and example of confident talent pursuing and successfully achieving a unique personal idiom.[27]

Though a few critics misunderstand the function of violence in his work, most applaud the poetry of Ted Hughes as serious, important, and powerfully gripping. Hughes has been a mainstay of the British literary scene since the early sixties, broadcasting more than two dozen self-scripted BBC talks and more than a dozen plays, judging poetry contests, reviewing books, and recording and giving public readings of samples from his many volumes of adult and children's poetry. He is arguably the most important writer of adult and children's poetry in England at present. Through all of this, and through his numerous introductions and translations of East European poets (see the Selected Bibliography), he has immeasurably extended our understanding of poetry and has provided a sure guide to living with intensity and fulfillment. In recognition of the importance and substance of the most fully achieved body of work of any living British poet, Ted Hughes was named poet laureate of England on 19 December 1984.

Chapter Two

Erecting a Here: *The Hawk in the Rain* and *Lupercal*

The Organizing Eye: *The Hawk in the Rain*

"Things fall apart; the centre cannot hold," Yeats wrote in "The Second Coming." The nostalgia for a lost center, arguably one of the most salient features of modernist thought, derives to a great extent from the loss of the communally shared values and beliefs that religion and ritual once provided. In his undergraduate anthropology studies, Ted Hughes read such works as Edward Evans-Pritchard's accounts of Azande witchcraft in North Africa, R. F. Fortune's discussion of sorcery among the Dobu in the Pacific Islands, and Arnold van Gennep's summary of rites of passage among distant and isolated tribal societies.[1] From these and many other studies he learned that religion had always been the one center for organizing the inner energies of humans and reducing the otherness of nature by enfolding mind and environment into one coherent whole. But as he read Yeats and Eliot, Hughes also learned that religion had ceased to play a vital role in twentieth-century Western culture.

From Yeats and Eliot, and especially from their precursor Blake, Hughes also inherited a central tenet of modernism: that the world of art must replace religion and provide an organizing center for the things that fall apart. Hughes invested this tenet with psychological force, believing that the organizing center must incorporate rational, instinctual, and spiritual components. Otherwise, repressed energies will explode into violence. Hence his comments in a 1971 interview: "When the wise men know how to create rituals and dogma, [nature's] energy can be contained. When the old rituals and dogma have lost credit and disintegrated, and no new ones have been formed, the energy cannot be contained, and so its effect is destructive. . . . We have settled for . . . the rigidly rationalist outlook." Hughes called this outlook a deathly refusal of nature's energy. He advocated that we "accept the energy, and find methods of turning it to good, of keeping it under control—rituals, the machinery of religion. The old method is the only one" (Faas 1, 200–201).

Hughes's early poetry offers a controlling center by reuniting humans
with the supporting energies of their environment through structuralist
organization. Hughes writes in "Things Present," the opening poem of
Lupercal, that his poems "Embody a now, erect a here." On the blank page
they erect a mandala or blueprint for integrating psychic life, and for integrating the self with nature. The eye of the hawk in the title poem of his
first volume, *The Hawk in the Rain* (1957), is a multipurpose formalist
lens. The hawk organizes its world by bringing it to a controlling focus.
Analogically, the hawk's eye is the aesthetic control exerted by the poet as
craftsman, organizing the world of the poem. That eye is also part of a motif
of eye imagery that appears in three of every four poems in the volume,
knitting the 40 poems into one organized whole even though each poem is
sharply individualized and the volume does not contain a common persona
or theme. But most importantly the eye imagery invites the reader to enter
into each poem's world, so that Hughes may organize the reader's energies
into a coherent whole with a stable center that does hold. Each poem in
Hawk becomes a mandala for psychic organization, a polestar of reliable orientation for future self-development.

The persona of "The Hawk in the Rain" is caught in the mutable world
of change and decay, presented in the poem in terms of noise and unceasing
movement. He sees himself as a morsel to be swallowed by the earth after
having lived a life of unreflecting, dogged habit, never rising above the
physical cycle of birth and death. He sloughs through a "banging wind" and
the ubiquitous English rain that "hacks [his] head to the bone." The hawk is
an ideal to strive toward, for its skill and strength organize the noisy turbulence of nature into a "weightless quiet" as long as its energy holds and its
"still eye" can concentrate all to a focused purpose, a "diamond point of will
that polestars / The sea drowner's endurance." The hawk is the free artificer
of the world he composes for himself.

Many of Hughes's poems are about animals, which early in his career
won him the unflattering label "zoo laureate" from readers and critics who
wanted to dismiss his work without making an honest effort at comprehension. But the early animal poems that initially appear to be simple rendi-
tions of Hughes's zookeeper experiences are really serious attempts to
awaken the reader's eye. The early poems are not simple descriptions of external events recorded with camera-eye realism; the world of nature has
been assimilated by the poet into the poem and organized into a prear-
ranged, meaning-bearing system, in the manner of humans in tribal societies, who, according to Lévi-Strauss, use the binary logic of their minds to
humanize an alien nature, mediating or reconciling in their myths human

needs with nature's restrictions. As Hughes himself said in a 1960 BBC radio talk, "Usually, in a poem that seems to be about a bird, animal or fish, it is evident that the poet is in fact writing about some element of human nature in the guise of a creature."[2] The hawk becomes a symbol of the human ability to attain an integrated life that sustains the isolated soul, directs one's energies, and provides a self-regulating guide to future action. Nature seems to attain an ecological balance effortlessly, without reflection. Humans must attain this same balance through conscious reflection and goal-directed action. The hawk's purpose is no doubt predatory, but the persona of the poem is captivated only by the hawk's self-control and the strong, steady control it exercises over its environment. Ultimately the hawk embodies a supernormal intuition of the persona's highest goal-directed energies—what Jung would call the God image within the self.[3] Only when the hawk's strenuous effort flags and his concentration relaxes does he die. That future death is foretold in the poem *not* as the hawk crashing onto a representational earth, but as his self-organized world falling apart, minus the hold of its Yeatsian center. When the hawk cannot sustain his organized vision, his world turns upside down and crashes *upon him* at the conclusion of the poem. Things fall apart when the center of organization cannot hold.

Hughes conveys the hawk's moment-by-moment control of his own self-created order through lines 6 and 7: "His wings hold all creation in a weightless quiet, / Steady as a hallucination in the streaming air." A hallucination is a self-created, temporary projection that suffices until the "weather" comes "the wrong way." Though the changeable weather of the poem may echo the mutability theme in Dylan Thomas's "Poem in October," the hawk is definitely not the hangman agent of a mutable nature borrowed from Thomas's "Over Sir John's Hill." In "The Hawk in the Rain" the hawk embodies the resilient human spirit's potential for wresting a satisfying, fulfilling life from nature through effort and through creating personal values. One must organize a world to live a worthwhile life, the poem seems to say, and an unorganized life is not worth living.

The majority of the poems in *The Hawk in the Rain* display a highly organized craftsmanship that itself is meaning bearing—a continual attempt to achieve a holistic balance of inner and outer worlds. The hawk appears again in "The Dove-Breeder," but with a different symbolic value, the result of mediating different opposites. "The Dove-Breeder" of the poem's title is a man whose prissy concern for pedigree and show in his dovecote reveals a lack of personal experience in love. He grooms fantails and pouters with fastidious care, carefully working his way through an award system that indi-

cates his need for public approval. The hawk embodies the fierce charge of
sensuosity that sweeps through the dove breeder when an extraordinary experience of love crashes into his carefully constructed public image like a
hawk raiding a dovecote.

The body of the poem elaborates through an extended metaphor what
happens when an overpowering rush of the erotic "struck" into the life of a
"mild-mannered" male. Though the hawk enters the poem as the excess of
eros to balance the defective eros of the prissy dove breeder, the dove breeder
assimilates this entry of eros into his life, and the poem ends with the hawk
tamed, in a mediatory balance: "Now he rides the morning mist / With a
big-eyed hawk on his fist." "The Dove-Breeder" functions as a model for the
release and final control of deep psychic energies.

"People are energetic animals," according to Hughes.[4] Yet in the late fifties Hughes saw the English approaching experience too tamely. The English national ethos of rational and pragmatic common sense produced a
whole generation of poets who turned their backs upon the Holocaust,
numbed by the carnage they had lived through as adults. In 1956, just one
year before the publication of Hawk, Robert Conquest had introduced the
poetry of "the Movement"—Philip Larkin, Kingsley Amis, John Wain,
Donald Davie, Elizabeth Jennings, and others—in his New Lines anthology. Conquest in his introduction proclaimed that these poets took a stance
of cagey skepticism toward life, and demanded that poetry consist of everyday language and realism. The elaborate metaphors, high style, psychoanalytic scrutiny of the id, and large themes of forties poets like Dylan Thomas
and Robert Graves were anathema, their force and probity reduced in
Movement poems to a thin, witty urbanity that often lacked substance.

"The Thought-Fox" can be considered a response to the reductive stance
of Movement poets. For Hughes, thinking is not a process of cool rational
analysis, but an invasion of the "sudden sharp hot stink" of nature into the
poet's quiet cerebrations. A foxy eye brings with its concentrated purpose
the "widening deepening greenness" of the natural world that we apprehend
through our five senses. The fox mediates the opposites of the rich vitality of
the natural world and the poet's cool meditation. As the footprints of its
bold body enter the poet's head, "the page is printed." Where the camera-
eye realism of Movement poets would record nothing but a ticking clock
and starless window, nature has invaded the poet's aesthetic world, filling
the blank page with its redolence.

Through mediating this invasion of the "sudden sharp hot stink,"
Hughes from his earliest poetry emphasized the importance of recognizing
nature as an ecological second skin. As he designed his poems according to

formalist principles to reconcile nature and the human mind through language, Hughes also raised his readers' awareness of that delicate balance point, that intuitional zone where at each moment humans subconsciously readjust the demands of the natural world and the human mind. This indicates a deep awareness of interdependence, of the dynamics of ecological balance that Movement poets missed with their emphasis upon wit and rational judgment.

Anthropology and the New Criticism   The mediation of opposites in the structure and eye imagery of Hughes's early poetry derived primarily from two sources: his undergraduate reading in the social systems of African and other early cultures and his early immersion in the New Criticism of John Crowe Ransom. A good deal of the anthropology Hughes read as an undergraduate took issue with Lucien Lévy-Bruhl's contention that the thinking of humans in such cultures was prelogical, an immersion in sorcery, magic, and illogical contradictions such as complete totemic identification with animals. On the Cambridge reading list for the anthropology tripos in 1954 were Edward Evans-Pritchard's *The Nuer* and *Witchcraft, Oracles, and Magic among the Azande,* works that specified how the social consciousness of humans in young cultures is controlled by hidden, value-laden assumptions that they become acculturated to unreflectively from birth onward. Institutional practices dictated rewards and penalties that reinforced these assumptions, with magic and other nonlogical elements occupying very minor roles, often as social lubricants. Evans-Pritchard demonstrated that both the Nuer and the Azande had developed institutional structures indicative of logical complexity.[5]

The work of Margaret Mead and Ruth Benedict, also on the Cambridge anthropology reading list, emphasized the importance of social structures to mold individuals whose perceptions are initially malleable, elastic—not genetically determined. From her studies of three very different cultures in New Guinea not 100 miles apart (the Arapesh, Mundugumor, and Tchambuli), Mead concluded in *Sex and Temperament in Three Primitive Societies* that aggressive, competitive behavior is not sexually determined but encoded in a culture's social practices and revalidated through habit and tradition.[6]

Claude Lévi-Strauss inherited this tendency to champion the structural abilities of humans in nonadvanced, third world cultures. In his studies of the language and myths of such cultures, especially the Tsimshian "Story of Asdiwal" and Bororo fire and cooking myths, Lévi-Strauss affirmed a capacity in the inhabitants of these cultures for structuring thought into complex linguistic and mythic systems that mediated between the discontinuous worlds of external nature and human consciousness. For Lévi-Strauss, these myths did not simply legitimate a culture by affixing a point of origin and inculcating a reassuring massage of repetitious practices. They revealed a structural tendency of the human mind to work by means of binary analysis: to achieve some measure of order and predictability in the alogical and often mysterious world beyond the senses, humans create myths to reconcile opposites and mediate contradictions. These myths are psycho- and *eiko*-logical blueprints that always work in the direction of reducing harmful excess and achieving moderation and social balance. One creates a personal cosmos and an ordered society by reconciling the contradictory claims of earth and sky, life and death, nature and culture, and raw meat and hungry stomachs through the structural organization of myths.[7]

Lévi-Strauss's analysis of totemism also revealed the acute logical powers of binary analysis and structural reconciliation in the human mind. According to Lévi-Strauss, humans in nonadvanced societies ensured incest prohibitions by creating totemic systems that applied the homologous world of separate animal species to underscore tribal clan divisions. In this respect the totem served as a mediatory structural device: a member of the bear clan could marry with anyone *except* another member of the bear clan, for whom the bear was a sacred talisman of mana power.[8] As humans have displayed their capacity to organize natural phenomena to suit social needs from early cultures forward, so Hughes converted the hawk's acute strength of vision and energy or the fox's quiet stealth from the world beyond the self into mediatory designs called poems. In the postwar torpor of England Hughes thought it important to write poems about vitality.

The work of Lévi-Strauss describes fairly exactly the structuralist bent of Hughes's early poetry. The intellectual capacities of humans in tribal cultures for developing complex, coherent social structures are similar to those of the poetic craftsman and his personae. From the times of early cultures to the present humans have regularly expressed in language the desire to order reality and moderate excess in socially beneficial ways. If the individual is malleable and if cultural structures can train perceptions, then so too can poetic structures when read at pivotal points in one's development. Yet though Hughes was aware of the intellectual complexity of tribal social structures from his undergraduate readings, he could not in his earliest poetry have been directly influenced by Lévi-Strauss, for Lévi-Strauss's major works did not begin to appear until the early sixties, and his early papers collected in *Structural Anthropology* did not appear in English until 1958.

Hughes was riding a modernist zeitgeist, synthesizing in his early poetry new findings in psychology and anthropology. Poet and anthropologist were working along parallel lines.

The structuralist tendency toward reconciling opposites in the mediatory realm of symbol and artistic design that Hughes acquired from his undergraduate anthropology readings blossomed into a central feature of his early poetry after he read the poetry of John Crowe Ransom and the New Criticism of Ransom and Cleanth Brooks during the three years prior to the publication of *Hawk* (Scigaj, 33–35). The American New Criticism, in part a second stage of the Imagist movement, emphasized the power of the poet to fuse his intended meaning with sensuous images that suggested the concrete "thinginess" of objects through the synthesizing power of Coleridge's secondary imagination. This would eliminate the poetry of abstractions and the use of imagery from nature merely to illustrate stale moral precepts.[9] As in Lévi-Strauss's theory of how myths reveal the logic of the human mind, New Critical theory revealed how in the mediatory ground of the poem the poet incorporated and arranged concrete elements of the outer world of nature to flesh out the intended meaning germinating in his mind.

Self-realization or Satire   It would not be reductive to realize that Hughes structured most of the poems in *The Hawk in the Rain* in ways that reinforce his express notion of the poem as a "blueprint," a mandala for organizing our inner world and promoting an ecologically sound balance between inner and outer worlds ("Myth 1," 66–67). The frequent eye imagery assists the reader in evaluating the persona's success at achieving an integrated self and a balanced relation to nature. If the persona is willing to wrestle with the disorganized psyche or tumultuous invasions of concrete experience from the world outside the self, the psyche heals itself. Here Hughes affirms a faith in human powers of self-development akin to Jung's belief in the self-regulating psyche. But if the persona represses what it refuses to recognize either in the self or in nature, and retreats behind a fragile ego or rational defense mechanisms, the persona retains his or her incompleteness, and a satiric tone in the poem reflects the poet's disdain. Blake's maxim "As the Eye—Such the Object" (Blake, 645) applies to the majority of the poems in *Hawk*. Nevertheless, the poem as a structured entity always reconciles through its organization the opposites it treats.

The explosion of enraged energy at the conclusion of "Macaw and Little Miss," for instance, is a function of the girl's repressed eroticism. Hughes places the macaw "In a cage of wire-ribs / The size of a man's head," cueing the reader to a psychological dimension. The macaw's eyes are "stoking devils" from some fiery medieval hell. Meanwhile the girl fondles, caresses, and rocks the caged macaw, calling him "Poor Polly." She lives in a self-constructed fairyland, though at night she has recurring dreams of a warrior who comes "Smashing and burning and rending towards her loin." The opposition becomes violent at the end of the poem. When the macaw refuses to respond to the girl's fondling, she petulantly strikes the cage, and the concluding shrieks of the macaw symbolize an explosion of the girl's repressed erotic desires. Unlike the dove breeder, the girl refuses to wrestle with the birth of erotic desire. The structure of the poem balances opposites that the girl refuses to integrate on the psychological level.

Conversely, the eyes of the jaguar in "The Jaguar" are "satisfied to be blind in fire," like Blake's Tiger. The jaguar's activity is congruent with his power to transform every energetic moment into an inner visionary freedom. "Stone Walls doe not a Prison make," wrote Lovelace in "To Althea, from Prison." The spectators at the zoo are the imprisoned in Hughes's poem, for they lack the vitality and inner freedom of the jaguar. They stand riveted and mesmerized at the cage bars, but their psychological inertia is of a piece with the nursery-wall indolence of the rest of the zoo animals.

Much of the satire in *Hawk* appears directed at the postwar complacency of Englishmen, and is of a piece with the complaints of the angry young men writers of the fifties who decried England's lapse from heroism into a postwar welfare state suffering from chronic unemployment. Like Jimmy Porter in John Osborne's *Look Back in Anger,* Hughes aims satiric barbs at the lack of vitality in contemporary Englishmen. In *Hawk* these are usually the urbanites who lack daily contact with the natural cycles of nature. The girl of "Secretary," for instance, cloisters "her lovely eyes" at night by doing housework for her parents. At daybreak she "scuttles down the gauntlet of lust / Like a clockwork mouse" to the office to spend her days "ducking, peeping" among men "like a starling under the bellies of bulls." The blunt sexuality of the seemingly out-of-place rural imagery is a perfectly apt revelation of what the secretary's eyes hide from herself. She lacks the strength to inspect what she represses; only the poem's structure balances the opposites of starlings and bulls.

Satire dominates "The Hag," "Vampire," and "Egghead," with eye imagery once again highlighting the essential opposites. The speaker of "The Hag" prefers the fairy-tale hag whose tortures directly reveal her envy and spite for the princesses she traps. Today, however, the hag is the well-meaning but inwardly spiteful suburban mother who keeps her daughter at home for the summer when college classes end. She has "locked up" her daughter's "pretty eyes in a brick house"—an action consonant with a shut heart that prefers to thrive on "Nine bolts of spite than on one leash of love." The "Vampire" is the life-of-the-party extrovert whose wit causes everyone to laugh themselves senseless as he saps their vitality to brighten his egocentric limelight. His eyes alternately "brighten" and "grimace" to command attention. He leaves the party grinning, his ego recharged with the group's vitality just as a vampire leaves satiated with his victim's blood. As in "The Hag," metaphors from fairy tales and weird tales reveal psychological deficiencies in contemporary urbanites.

Hughes saves his most acerbic satire in *Hawk* for "Egghead," his critique of the defense mechanisms of the Freudian ego. Though in daily life the egoist may greet everyone he meets with a handshake and a smiling hello, the surface patter is really meant to limit personal contact to superficial levels. So he "shuts out the world's knocking / With a welcome" and with "wide-eyed deafnesses / Of prudence." His cheerily thin veneer is really a barricade, a defense mechanism to keep intact an ego as fragile as an eggshell. This is one of the few poems in *Hawk* where the speaker's satiric barbs get out of hand; his indictment is so heated that imagery and poetic line become numbingly vituperative, with the accuser revealing his own "circumventing sleights / Of stupefaction, juggleries of benumbing." When Hughes chooses not to use a structural plan of mediating opposites and lets speakers soliloquize with the darkly passionate stridency of a Jacobean tragedy, declamatory rhetoric almost overtakes the poem. Similar problems mar "Fair Choice," "Incompatibilities," and "Complaint."

Hughes reinforces his critique of postwar English complacency by contrasting satiric poems about timid contemporary urbanites with poems containing personae from more heroic periods in England's past who swagger across the printed page with blunt directness, speaking their minds, making hard choices, and engaging in actions that often have violent or irrevocable consequences. Diction and subject matter define a parade of characters beginning with the demonic Shakespearean tragic hero in a Hamlet-like rage ("Fair Choice"), the dark revenge and disarming candor of the proud Jacobean ("The Decay of Vanity"), the embittered boldness of the Restoration misanthrope ("Soliloquy of a Misanthrope"), the worldly-wise directness of the eighteenth-century blade ("Billet-Doux"), the radical action of the romantic isolato ("Invitation to the Dance"), the flash of violent action that gives the lie to fin de siècle concepts of universal brotherhood ("Law in the Country of the Cats"), and the blunt realism ("Fallgrief's Girl-Friends") and iconoclasm ("Complaint") of the Lawrentian laborer. The grim, sardonic humor and disarming directness in these poems capture the reader's attention, though at times the syntax becomes contorted or the poetic line too crammed with imagery.

Hughes's early poetry concurs with the intuitions of humans in tribal cultures that confrontations with animals can initiate personality growth, *if* one welcomes the world's knocking. The persona of "Meeting" initially exudes self-confidence as he views himself in a mirror. But his self-examination leads to the recollection of once having been scrutinized by a menacing black goat on an empty mountain slope. The imagery of the poem conveys the chilling effect of having been searched by "A square-pupilled yellow-eyed look" and an eye that dwarfed his bulk with its "living hanging hemisphere." The goat may represent demonic energies buried deeper within the self that the initial self-scrutiny at the mirror uncovers. The meeting with the darker self thus qualifies the initial Faustian swagger.

In *Hawk* the world often knocks with new experience that, if welcomed, can shatter stereotypes and lead to healthier norms of behavior. A comic treatment of this situation occurs in "The Conversion of the Reverend Skinner," where a black whore slaps the minister after he rebukes her proposition with his high moral tone. The slap wakens the minister to his own snobbery and leads to a healthier attitude about sexuality. His puritanical pride vanishes as he begins to feel a kinship with imperfect humans, and the poem ends with the minister blessing God's defiled.

Every new birth is a confrontation with the forces of genetic development and regression. In "Childbirth" the devolutionary genetic forces that Freud considered in his concept of the primal horde try to overtake the foetus at the moment of birth. "The huge-eyed looming horde from / Under the floor of the heart" meet their opposite, the newly born child, symbol of nature's evolutionary forces. Hughes's youthful optimism concerning nature's ability to rectify imbalances appears most prominently at the conclusion of "Childbirth," for here the infant in its utter dependency mediates progressive and regressive forces in the genes. As Hughes said in the Nicholson review, "Nature's obsession, after all, is to survive. As far as she is concerned, every new baby is a completely fresh start."

Love and Violence: The Ambiguities of Desire   Hughes in *Hawk* displays a very mature grasp of the ambiguities of love and the distance between desire and fulfillment that a poststructuralist concerned with the fleeting presence and absence of desire would find very intriguing. "Parlor-Piece" follows Cleanth Brooks's New Critical assertion that tensions of opposites in poems reflect ambiguities and complexities that do in fact exist in real life.[10] The two lovers express their ardor paradoxically by their speechlessness as they strain against the restraint of teatime conventions. They conform not simply because conventions require sedate conduct, but because both maintain an adult recognition of the limits of their self-control, and because they prefer not to trivialize their love with small talk. Yet the tension is not one of stalemate, for the eyes of each are filled with the other in the stillness and silence of mutual regard. Flood imagery does not douse fire imagery; both are temporarily held in check, achieving a taut tension between desire and fulfillment.

When eyes are filled with love, a selfless mutuality of regard occurs that integrates inner energies and outer world into a timeless moment of unity. Four years before Plath met Hughes, she wrote in her journal that her ideal love relationship was the Lawrentian tension of equilibrated stars, as in the "Excurse" chapter of *Women in Love.* Here both lovers retain their autonomy as individuals, but freely give love that holds both in a star-equilibrium—in Plath's words "a balanced tension, adaptable to circumstances, in which there is an elasticity of pull, tension, yet firm unity. Two stars, polarized" (*Journals,* 43). In *The Hawk in the Rain,* dedicated to Plath, Hughes achieves a timeless moment of mutuality and unity in the first two stanzas of "September," where loving eyes are so enraptured with the other that time and space are not divorced from the self, as in Blake's Ulro, but rather transcended in the embrace of love, in a Lawrentian darkness of knowing. Equipoised eyes rest in stillness, in a mirrored self-sufficiency of lambent quietude; time vanishes in a dark embrace where each respects the "star" or autonomy of the other. The strength of this embrace walls out the noise and neurotic rush of daily schedules, as in a yogin's meditation. But moments of transcendent love in *Hawk* are fleeting, impermanent, subject to natural cycles and the vagaries of psychic mood; the last two stanzas of "September" descend to tumult and time.

Poems in *Hawk* also scrutinize the irascibility that appears with much greater regularity in imperfect humans than the moments of bliss that one finds perhaps too regularly in Graves and Thomas. "Incompatibilities" gazes unflinchingly at the possessiveness that usually accompanies love. One allotropic form of love is an anxiety-ridden restlessness: union with the beloved brings a simultaneous and paradoxically gnawing sense of isolation as a selfish desire for possession and control "cold-chisels two selfs single." Here desire dives into the eyes of the other to possess "the star that lights the face," but clutches instead an emptiness like a black hole. As possessiveness steals the autonomy of the other, so also it robs the self of stability. The oscillation between moments of union and isolation recalls the punishment for thieves in Dante's hell—an ad nauseam conversion from reptile to ashes to reptile again.

Just as chilling is the study of love degenerating into competition in "A Modest Proposal." Hughes depicts the "universal wolf" of appetite from Shakespeare's *Troilus and Cressida* (1.3.121) as a struggle for dominance between two wolves that will end only with the complete submission of one to the other. Taunts and leers alternate with feelings of inadequacy in a manic-depressive cycle of vicious skirmishes with "Eyes brighter than is natural." The poem ends with the wolves peering at a scene of concord that they can never attain, symbolized by the lord's ebullient return home from hunting, with his cloak floating and his greyhounds prancing obediently at his side. Poetic structure mediates the oppositions of the lord's stable society and the wolves' dark thickets of irascibility; through extended metaphor and pictorial contrast Hughes offers a revealing glimpse of the competition and publication pressures he and Plath endured as they struggled to advance their careers.

Hughes asserted that his early poems were not about violence but about "the war between vitality and death," and he hoped to achieve a "formal and balanced" peace for the "inner figure of stresses," as in a musical composition.[11] These formalist aesthetics hold true for the entirety of *Hawk,* including the six war poems placed near the end. In contrast to Hughes's sixties social psychology, where war reveals a culture's repressed libido that has exploded into rage and scapegoat projection, these early poems present war as an opportunity for heroism or an invasion of the extraordinary that ironically reveals the inadequacies of sheltered citizens.

The mutilated, incinerated airman's body that drops onto the farmers' fields in "The Casualty" reveals the helplessness of the townsfolk. Their eyes, greedy for sensationalism, are nevertheless stunned and branded by the tactile reality of war. Gruesome details appear between laundry lines to grip their psyches and rivet their eyes. "Bayonet Charge," like many Wilfred Owen poems, presents the stark reality of war with deflating irony. One searing instant of a hare's surrealistically writhing face, roused by smacking bullets, is enough to shock a soldier out of all his conventional beliefs in God and country, propelling him into a terrified retreat.

Less effective is the bomber pilot's emulation of ancient heroes who confronted war directly, as opposed to his removed technological reliance, in "The Ancient Heroes and the Bomber Pilot." A straightforward statement with a flat conclusion, the poem lacks the dramatic interest and structural tension of opposites of the New Critical efforts. "Griefs for Dead Soldiers" is more successful, for here Hughes conveys an effective contrast between pub-

lic and private grief while sustaining a genuinely elegaic mood. The resolution fits human experience: the actual, concrete facticity and finality of
death in the spadework of the burial party outfaces public monument and
widow's grief in the poem's concluding section.

"Two Wise Generals" and "Six Young Men," the best of the war poems
in *Hawk,* are fine examples of rendering the actual complexity of life
through a New Critical structural reliance upon irony and paradox. The
"wise" generals find both of their sleeping armies massacred after pretend-
ing with jaded wisdom to divide lands and other spoils by some abstract
method and gentleman's agreement. Whether each had been duplicitous or
not, the poem asserts that Black Douglas, the fourteenth-century Scottish
nobleman who died fighting the Moors in Spain en route to burying his
dead king's heart in Palestine, is infinitely more honorable than the effete
generals because of his courageously direct action. Throughout *Hawk* one
must grapple with experience in the concrete moment of its happening to
earn the praise of Hughes; timidity or evasion brings censure.

Though the photograph and landmarks endure in "Six Young Men," the
men grouped at the center of the picture did not; each lost his life in World
War 1. Yet details in the photo, itself a deadly factual memento, bring to
the mind of the speaker vivid memories of each man's "smoking blood" and
eccentric behavior. Celluloid survives after a camera's flash, though equally
instantaneous shots rendered all six men lifeless within six months. The
photo depicts a familiar backyard pose that paradoxically shocks one into a
consciousness of death's defamiliarization. Viewing the photo numbs the
psyches of those whose lives the men once touched; "contradictory permanent horrors" remain to chill the survivors' blood.

Paradox and ironic reversal succeed in rendering a complex historical
event with believable fidelity in "The Martyrdom of Bishop Farrar," the
concluding poem of *Hawk.* Unlike the timidity of the contemporary urbanites in many other *Hawk* poems, Bishop Farrar affirms his convictions to the
point of death as Bloody Mary burns him at the stake to set an example.
The townsfolk are more convinced of his faith than after any of Farrar's ser-
mons, though his death is wordless. They warm to his religious persuasion
not because his reasoning has convinced them, but because of the sensationalism and concrete immediacy of his pain. As he dies in silent agony, the
townsfolk pocket his wordless ordeal hot as bakers' buns. Hughes ends the
poem with complex ambiguity, for the fire sends a lifetime of sermonizing
up in smoke, to heedless skies, while poet and reader shrink from Farrar's
almost inhuman "cold-kept miserdom of shrieks." The poem convinces because many events leave us with mixed emotions, unresolved questions of

motivation, and a sadness at the profound discrepancy between intention and result. While we admire the strength of Farrar's convictions, we also shrink from his inhumanly self-destructive resolve.

Though a few poems in *Hawk* suffer from an excess of heated rhetoric or crammed imagery, the vast majority contain very unique and clear distillations of conflicts that are fully realized with a remarkable power and economy. Some of the war poems contain echoes of Owen or of Audenesque disenchantment, and others touches of Thomas or Ransom, but the influences are fully assimilated into dramatic scenes whose texture and substance are unmistakably Hughes's own. The reader feels rewarded for his effort, for at every turn Hughes grapples with the larger issues surrounding the war between vitality and death. The poems are not fluffy pastries, iced with small subjects and thin feelings, but a hearty meal complemented by a bottle of full-bodied wine. Second helpings are even more enjoyable.

Most of the reviews of *Hawk* were very laudatory, with many in agreement that the poems are alive with feeling and vigor, clear and accurate observation, bold drama, and a high tension of imaginative effort. The most perceptive summary comments, however, came from Sylvia Plath in a letter to her mother: "Ted writes with color, splendor and vigorous music about love, birth, war, death, animals. . . . His book can't be typed. It has rugged, violent war poems . . . delicate, exquisite nature poems . . . [and] powerful animal poems. . . . He combines intellect and grace of complex form, with lyrical music, male vigor and vitality, and moral commitment and love and awe of the world" (*Letters Home,* 298).

Touch This Frozen One: *Lupercal*

Kafka once wrote in a letter to a friend that the purpose of art is not to make the reader happy, but to enliven his mind: "a book must be the ax for the frozen sea inside us."[12] In *Lupercal* Hughes continues his war between vitality and apathy, but from a more personal and historical point of view. He relaxes his hold on formalist structure to enable himself to concentrate more deeply upon the real-world object or event, and this frees his pen to touch the reader's frozen emotional life through the power of his language and the strength of his meditative mood. Hughes had spent about six years reading Yeats in the fifties (Faas 1, 202); a Yeatsian concentrated presence of mind is the signature of a *Lupercal* poem. Gone are the dramatic confrontations of opposites and structured resolutions of individual *Hawk* poems—macaws versus little misses, poet versus fox, mirror-gazer versus black goat, wolves versus lord, etc.

Individual *Hawk* poems were organized through eye imagery or the structural mediation of opposites, but from *Lupercal* forward Hughes organizes every volume by means of leitmotifs and myths that knit groups of poems together. Like the racers of the Roman Lupercalia festival in the volume's title poem, poetic language becomes the goat's-hide whip that strikes the readers' passing eyes to reinvigorate the psyche and enliven the perceptions. An unmistakable gain in directness leads to a deeper scrutiny of the real world and more somber meditations upon its love-and-death struggles.

Hughes wrote most of the poems of *Lupercal* in a tiny apartment in the Beacon Hill section of Boston, where he and Plath occupied bay window desks in adjacent rooms. As in "The Thought-Fox" or "Thrushes," Hughes was aware at every moment of the ironies of the city-bound desk poet trying to write about nature. Once again his anthropology background came to his aid. He began to realize that, instead of working out highly stylized dramatic encounters, he must choose and link individual words that would enliven the reader like a wolf's-head mask worn by a shaman. The mana power of his language would evoke and finally control his readers' emotional lives and reconnect them to nature.

Hughes acted this process out in life as well as in his poems. Plath wrote in a 28 December 1958 journal entry that "Ted labored all yesterday afternoon and evening making a wolf-mask out of Agatha's old, falling-apart sealskin. It is remarkably fuzzy and wolfish" (*Journals*, 285). In "February," the month of the Roman Lupercalia festival, the poetic feet of Hughes's words look for vitality. In a listless postwar country where wolves have been extinct for many decades, Hughes searches for the "vanished head" and "the teeth, the quick eyes" of a wolflike energy. Each poem in *Lupercal* becomes a process wherein the poet organizes this energy into "Wolf-masks, mouths clamped well onto the world."

Masks were often used by the shamans of tribal societies to invoke the vitalistic energy of animals and to control that energy to benefit the group through the shaman's ecstatic flight to a source of power. According to Eliade, the Siberian shaman used animal masks to "enter the spirit world by his own inner light," and the Chinese used wolf masks to aid concentration and to participate in what tribal societies believed to be the prodigious spiritual energy of animals (Eliade, 148, 166–68, 179). The control Hughes's psyche exerted in creating the poem would contain the aggressive component of this mana energy, ensuring that the wolves do not "choose his head."

Hughes prescribed the invocation and control of animal energy as therapy for his readers, to revitalize their grip on life in a deadening world of apathy awash in consumer goods. The Lupercalia myth, used to structure the entire volume, also functions to summon and control the vitalistic mana energy that humans in tribal societies thought necessary to ensure the renewal of life for the coming spring. In pre-Christian Rome runners clad in loincloths would gather on 15 February to be marked with dogs' blood and to run up and down the Via Sacra through the Forum Valley, striking bystanders with whips of goat's hide. All barren women so struck were thought to regain their fertility (Scigaj, 63–64).

At this point in Hughes's life the use of this ritual was apt, for he and Plath with trepidation had decided to start a family, but Plath was having trouble conceiving because she was not ovulating regularly (*Journals*, 311; *Letters Home*, 352). At one level *Lupercal*, once again dedicated to Plath, was a prayer for family fertility. At another level the ritual embodied Hughes's hopes to succeed in revivifying his readers with linguistic invocations of mana energy, while controlling the predatory portion of this energy through his structure and a very moral acumen that directs his observations. The Roman ritual was itself a remnant of a pastoral ritual used in preempire times to protect against wolf packs interfering with the spring birthing of lambs, for shepherds thought that the wolves' howling embodied ancestral evil in a month dedicated to Februus, god of the dead.[13] Wolf-mask poems function as mandalas to promote psychic health.

Each section of "Lupercalia" is a meditation upon one of the elements of the Lupercal ritual: dog, woman, goat, and racer. Throughout Hughes concentrates on particular qualities of the participants that are worth emulating. The clear, spare, yet strong language does not call attention to itself or depend upon stylized effects, as in *Hawk*, but meditates intensely upon the object or event. The dog embodies in its scars and plain life-style a tough readiness and a fierce indomitability even at its moment of sacrificial death in section 1. It had "A mouth like an incinerator," and the fire of its mana energy, the "brute's quick" of its blood, becomes in section 2 the "spark" that ends the woman's barrenness, allays the threat of ancestral evil, and restores her to "the wheel of the living."

The very unangelic goats of section 3 live in a rank thriving, but their eyes, that startle women with a "sudden reared stare," are not merely brutish. They contain a "golden element," a filiment of the divine that focuses the mountain light to a searing inquisitorial stare, a stinging slap from the blue that lights the dog's bloody tinder. The final section focuses not only upon the lean muscularity of the racers and the slashing rhythm of their efforts, but also upon the necessary cosmic round of reinvigoration to which all cultures in some form give their assent. The efforts of "Their oiled bodies brass-bright / In a drift of dust" evoke a sense of plenitude and a final prayer from the poet to a decidedly unorthodox god whose elemental power circuit invigorates human history. Simultaneously Hughes hopes that the mana power of his language will "Touch this frozen one"—the frozen sensibilities of his reader.

Lupercal takes a deep and serious look at vitality and violence in English history, and especially at the decline of religion as a force to control love and deathly aggression. According to Max Weber, whose *Protestant Ethic and the Rise of Capitalism* Hughes no doubt read at Cambridge, tangible goods enhanced prestige for the laborers in God's earthly vineyard. Though in theory the inner certitude of the Calvinist Elect was expected to be enough to lead the soul to heaven, in practice intense industrious activity—the Protestant work ethic—could increase that certainty. Religious inspiration devolves into materialism as a result.[14] In "Nicholas Ferrer" Hughes meditates upon an ancestor, the founder of Little Gidding, whose retreat into asceticism was a deliberate rejection of his culture's materialism.

Ferrer in 1626 left a promising career as a member of Parliament to develop his experiment in Christian communal living at a manor home in rural Huntingdonshire. Though Hughes admires Ferrer for his decision, in the poem he sees this choice as only a tidy housekeeping, a far cry from the "fire of the martyrs." The home, a decayed relic now, is of a piece with a religious fire that burned down to "the blue calm / They called God's look" and the "shut heart" of the isolated Protestant living by his or her own inner light. Try as he may to buck the cultural currents of his time, Ferrer's decision was of a piece with the practicality and estrangement from nature that Hughes suggests in the birds and sun of the landscape.

Wandering Elementals   Not far away from the burned-out fire of faith is the "square-shouldered self-respect" of the "plump, cuffed citizen" who leads a profitable life in the satiric poem "The Good Life." Devolution into materialism is also the focus in "Fourth of July," where the American holiday's dull rituals are the end result of Columbus's acquisitive, capitalistic "huckstering." In this atmosphere the mind's spiritual and instinctual energies are left dormant, uninspired by newspaper headlines. Opportunities to develop the self through enlisting one's psychic energies do not exist in this world; these "wandering elementals" are "Ousted," alienated by a surfeit of materialism. Behind both poems is an analysis of the unbridled economic activity that occurred once Protestantism reduced the church's power to inculcate morality. Morality is no longer a public matter of ritual and individual confession, as in Medieval Christianity; it exists only as a struggle within the individual conscience. In 1926 the British economic historian Richard Tawney wrote a fairly popular and persuasive analysis of how Protestant individualism led to post-Renaissance materialism in his *Religion and the Rise of Capitalism.*

The animal poems of *Lupercal* resurrect the "wandering elementals" of readers' spiritual and instinctual energies through the power and immediacy of Hughes's observations as he studies the beneficial and harmful effects of animal energy. It is common in tribal societies to view godly energy in animal rather than human forms—visitations by blessed or demonic animals rather than by our customary angels—for animals have always impressed humans with their remarkable abilities and energies. According to Eliade, in tribal societies animals "can reveal the secrets of the future because they are thought to be receptacles for the souls of the dead or epiphanies of the gods" (Eliade, 98). Yet in *Lupercal* parallel energies in humans that could liberate and lead to personal satisfaction and spiritual growth are often locked in chaotic nightmare visions, for Western culture can only provide outlets for our rational powers and acquisitive impulses. Television violence for Hughes is an exact transcription of our chaotic inner life: television perpetuates the inner chaos because it subliminally encourages viewing in a state of "anesthetized unconcern" (Faas 1, 198). The animal poems in *Lupercal* release, inspect, and organize these locked energies.

Hughes may exhort Odysseus's son Telemachus to take sword and bow and rid the halls of degenerate suitors in "Everyman's Odyssey" at the outset of *Lupercal,* but the majority of the poems portray contemporary Britons as decidedly unheroic, unable to draw the sword, at best daydreaming of a more heroic past. The volume opens with the tramp in "Things Present" dreaming nostalgically of the "stout shoes" of his ancestors, for they "had towers and great names." But their progeny have forgotten how to develop their talents; they have "Honed their bodies away, dreams / The tramp in the sodden ditch." Contemporary Britons are stable grooms dreaming "A Dream of Horses," their "wealth horse-dung and the combings of horses." They dream a surreal nightmare where they cringe in lantern-lit darkness while hearing "a quake of hooves" and a "plunging of horses" that "whinnied and bit and cannoned the world from its place." The horses embody the "wandering elementals" of their spiritual and instinctual energies, now locked in a dream. The poem concludes with a defeatist prayer to be tied and quartered by the horses—by alienated, disorganized energies that rampage through chaotic psyches.

Blent in the Prayer   Conversely, Hughes in most of the animal poems of *Lupercal* prefers to inspect the energies humans share with animals, to revitalize kindred powers in his readers through the concentration and mana power of his language. In the process he carefully scrutinizes the animals, captures the positive aspects of their energies, and then distances himself from their malevolent aspects. "Nothing of our light" of human rational consciousness "Found any reflection" in "The Bull Moses," and yet looking at the bull in the dark byre is like "a sudden shut-eyed look / Backward into the head." The dark byre is a metaphoric of the dark alluvium of the unconscious, and "the locked black of his powers" is akin to powers in humans that reside above and below rational consciousness. As his name indicates, the bull "Moses" fathers his vision of the future as he procreates, and this indicates a visionary, supernormal, or goal-directed spiritual energy. The fact that he is "Shut, while he wombed, to a dark shed" conveys the presence of deep instinctual energies, as does the depth of his meditative stare ("too deep in itself to be called to") and the almost suffocating olfactory imagery: "the warm weight of his breathing, / The ammoniac reek of his litter, the hotly-tongued / Mash of his cud, steamed against me."

Language in "The Bull Moses" is more than descriptively accurate; it captures the reader's attention with a mesmerizing, hypnotic rhythm in stanzas 2 and 4 that portrays the almost mystic strength of the bull's concentration. The persona is willing to inspect the bull's fecund powers and is fascinated by the bull's total unconcern for our daylight world even when the animal is led daily to the pond to drink. As with Moses' commands to the Israelites to follow the Lord's teachings with a singleness of purpose, without deviation to the right or to the left (Deut. 5:32, 17:11, 17:20, 28:14), the bull returns to his byre oblivious of the pigpens on his right or the cow byres on his left. He communes with "some beheld future" that captures all his attention and resides somewhere deeply within him. The poem ends with the persona closing the byre door and pushing in the bolt, as if he found this encounter significant enough to place it safely within his own memory for future consideration.

The ability of cats to survive through a tenacity developed from a rapport between their sensual moods and the phases of the moon is the focus of the four cat poems of *Lupercal*: "Esther's Tomcat," "Of Cats," "Cat and Mouse," and "Wilfred Owen's Photographs." Behind all four is Yeats's use of the cat in "The Cat and the Moon" and his play of the same name to sug-

gest this animal's instinctive ability to survive by adapting to cyclic change
and uniting with its opposite, the phases of the moon. Both "Esther's Tomcat" and "Of Cats" offer examples of cats' unkillable survival abilities. They
are more tenacious and persistent than humans because they operate in
some deep rapport with their sensuality and with moods that change as do
the moon's phases. "Of Cats" begins by suggesting a parallel genetic inheritance between the proverbial nine lives of cats and the stout hearts inherited
by humans from their ancestors. Hughes in "Esther's Tomcat" recognizes an
aggressive stain in both cats and humans as an inevitable component of
these shared survival energies.

In "Cat and Mouse" the cat's quickness and acute eyesight, always ready
to pounce, make it a godly figure of alert, instantaneous power for the
trapped mouse. In "Wilfred Owen's Photographs" the actuality of aggression, once recognized, brings humanitarian change. Once members of Parliament view an actual cat o' nine tails (a nine-corded whip used for
flogging seamen), they are moved to end flogging, just as Wilfred Owen
wanted to scare England out of its refusal to face the slaughter of war by ex-
hibiting photographs in London of trench warfare in all its gory detail. The
survival of cats depends upon their instinctive ability to adapt moment-by-
moment to changing circumstances and psychic moods, whereas rational
powers in humans atrophy in the face of habit and stuffy traditionalism.

Hughes in a 1960 BBC radio interview told Alfred Alvarez that part 1 of
"An Otter" concerned the otter as a representative of the life of prehistoric
animals surviving through hundreds of years of English history while various conquests erupted around them.[15] In the poem Hughes meditates upon
the furtive restlessness of the otter, with its cries and nervous, darting movements in and out of water as if nostalgically seeking some return to a paradisal existence through a three-night rebirth journey like Jonah or Christ.
The otter's energy is an unkillable natural force, as unkillable as the stoat's
in "Strawberry Hill."

Part 2 of "An Otter" concerns the otter's attempt to survive in profane
historical time, where it is hunted as a sportsman's trophy. Hughes communes with its uncanny survival powers, as if to indicate that selfhood in
humans derives from analogous powers of hyperaware concealment as a defense against a hostile environment: "So the self under the eye lies, / Attendant and withdrawn." The mana power of Hughes's language and his
descriptive accuracy combine to create a riveting portrait of the otter's muscular hold on life. His heart is a "big trout muscle" and his grasp is tenacious: "he will lick / The fishbone bare." Most memorable is the capturing
of the otter's nervous energy; he "can take stolen hold / On a bitch otter in a

field full / Of nervous horses, but linger nowhere." Yet like creativity within the human self, the otter can maintain power and potential only in partial concealment—as within the unconscious. When in the poem it is captured and "Yanked above hounds"—hoisted aloft for conscious inspection—its hold on life ends.

"Thrushes" contains the clearest ironic contrast between a poet writing in an urban environment while contemplating the instinctive rightness of animal action. The "bullet and automatic / Purpose" of the thrushes reduces all to "a start, a bounce, a stab." The persona openly envies this reductive action at the same time that he finds it "Terrifying." The "streamlined" efficiency of the thrush is akin to the operations of genius in the creative artist and preferable to our normal situation of squeezing out insights drop by drop, continually distracted by the interfering "Orgy" of our instincts and the "hosannah" of our spiritual energies. The phrase "blent in the prayer" echoes section 2 of "Among School Children." Here Yeats recollected a scene where he and Maud Gonne experienced a moment of union that transcended the usual separation of knowledge and experience—exactly the poet's situation.

Language in "Thrushes" keeps the reader apprised of both the persona's envy of the thrushes' lack of procrastination and the distracting deflections of consciousness, as well as his disapproval of the "Dark deadly eye" attuned to knee-jerk reflex in order to "drag out some writhing thing." Though he envies the thrushes' ability to be at one with their actions, he disapproves of their brutality: what Mozart plucked out of his psyche was certainly *not* "some writhing thing" in a "ravening second." The reader sees the thrushes vividly, but nakedly, unromantically, even as the persona longs to emulate their undistracted behavior—to be so deeply "blent in the prayer" that like the bull Moses he can concentrate on his goal without looking to the right or left. A genius like Mozart embodied in his life and art the concentration and vitality of an optimistic cultural vision in accord with the survival energies of both humans and animals. The greatest indignity in *Lupercal* is to be lifeless, deadly factual, as in "View of a Pig."

In "Historian" Hughes hopes for "a live brain's / Envying to master and last"—to master and survive the energies and facts his contemplation of animals and English history dredges up. Fearsome anticipation of what destructive visions from England's past may visit him seems the focus of "Pike." The pond where the fisherman persona fishes is "as deep as England," and its legendary depths might produce cultural dreams from the past as dark and malevolent as the viselike jaws of a pike. In mood, tone, and historical sweep the poem appears similar to Yeats's somber meditations on disorder at Coole Park. But whereas Yeats found the past orderly and aristocratic and the present chaotic, and found hope in the transfiguring order of art in the swan's flight amid the darkening flood, Hughes finds a malevolent heritage ready to seize his poetic line with visions "immense and old"—an ominous inheritance incapable of change. Neither Yeats nor Lawrence had a sufficient grasp of how inherited aggression casts its shadow before it, but Hughes presses a magnifying glass into his reader's hand with the candor and clarity of lines like "The jaws' hooked clamp and fangs / Not to be changed at this date."

What is it in England's past that is so pikelike, so afflicted with a "malevolent aged grin"? In the 1960 BBC radio interview with Alvarez Hughes stated that he was reading a great deal of pre-Norman Conquest history at this time, and one can readily see in his later work from "The Warriors of the North" in *Wodwo* through *Crow* and *Remains of Elmet* that Roman, Anglo-Saxon, and Norse conquerors left a legacy of "life subdued to its instrument," a utilitarian blight that produced ecological and cultural devastation in favor of the Protestant ethic's "Far, veiled gaze of quietly / Homicidal appraisal" (*Elmet*, 90). The pike in the pond, so vividly realized, are really emblems of a frightening inheritance that Hughes will spend a great deal of his career learning to "master and last."

Hughes's vivid descriptions of his animals troubled some of the Movement-oriented British critics, who thought he was openly advocating violence. "Hawk Roosting" received pride of place in a BBC radio broadcast on violence in poetry, with Philip Hobsbaum equating the "I" of the poem with Hughes himself and arguing that the poem presents an arrogantly superior stance toward his reading public. Keith Sagar and Peter Elfred Lewis have written very substantive replies to counter this naive view (Sagar, 47–50).[16] Lewis points out that Hughes is presenting a dramatic monologue that restricts the hawk's aloofness and confidence to its own point of view, and this arrogant self-sufficiency is most like Edmund in *King Lear,* a position no one would equate with Shakespeare's own.

Sagar concurs, and offers a fine analysis of the larger moral issues Hughes considers in the poem. Sagar develops his remarks from Hughes's own interview comments that he originally intended to portray "Isis, mother of the gods" in the hawk, but since "Christianity kicked the devil out of Job" our culture is left with nature as malevolent energy, "Hitler's familiar spirit" (Faas 1, 199). The god who spoke to Job out of the whirlwind to annihilate his pleas for justice was a god existing beyond our conceptions of morality, a god whose power was so far beyond human understanding that Job was left utterly bewildered. But since Christianity demanded perfect morality, all evil power was relegated to nature—a hopeless dichotomy.

"Hawk Roosting" presents the amoral power of nature with unvarnished frankness. Hawks certainly know nothing of ethics; they live in perfect egotism, without any mediatory realm of consciousness to create moral qualms. The "falsifying dream" and "sophistries" that the hawk lacks in its brutality echo the "distracting devils" of "Thrushes" and by contrast present human consciousness positively, as a buffer zone capable of creating ethical systems. The hawk's utter arrogance is so megalomaniacal that it begs the question in statements like "It took the whole of Creation / To produce my foot, my each feather," and "I kill where I please because it is all mine." Predatory animals will exist as long as the sun's powerhouse fuels nature's creations, and Sagar is correct in affirming that the poem argues that attempts to make nature conform to human morality are doomed.

"Hawk Roosting" contains no persona to envy or emulate the hawk's predatory behavior. But neither does Hughes despair at this unflinching look at nature red in tooth and claw. *Lupercal* contains examples of individuals who function as models of a mature acceptance of life precisely because they accept the daily presence of death without defense mechanisms or childish egotism. Thomas Browne in "Urn Burial" can "abash / The wretch of death that stands in his shoes" because he is "sure / Of its weight." Browne's realistic acceptance of the final oblivion of all human enterprises in *Urn Burial* articulates the melancholy of the late Renaissance as perfectly as Hamlet's soliloquy on Yorick's skull, and Hughes openly praises Browne's realism as "An improvement on the eagle's hook." The manners and music of human culture are heroic especially when they express an undaunted and courageous affirmation of life lived with a quiet acceptance of nature's talons and the finitude shared by all created matter.

Like the hawk's eye of Hughes's first volume, other individuals in *Lupercal* refuse to relax their tenacious hold on the mutable world until the very moment of death. As Nicholas Ferrer outfaced the deathly violence of the Civil War with his piety and individualism, so "The Retired Colonel" embodies the courage of Victorian nationalism. Though to some extent a caricature of the colonial ethos, he displays his convictions with gusto in his very gait as he strolls down the street. He becomes another wolf's-head guardian spirit in a wolfless age. As rough-hewn and unrefined as his name implies, the Crag Jack of "Crag Jack's Apostasy" hopes for "more than the memory / Of a wolf's head, of eagles' feet." He finds conventional religious belief constricting, as if he were buried alive under the weight of tradition, but stanza 2 indicates that in his nonconformism he yet retains an honest need to satisfy a deeply rooted desire for spiritual elevation. His blunt demand for a more compelling presence of the godly in his life than his dream visions allow gains him a Job-like nobility.

Others, admirable for their simplicity, trust only in their vitality and hardihood to survive the struggle against the elements. Less noble but equally tenacious in his grip on the actual world is "Dick Straightup," the octogenarian whose larger-than-life drinking and roistering have gained him a legendary status at the pub. The tramp in "November" sleeps in the outdoors, unafraid of the cold rain and coming winter, as crucified to his mutable world as the dried animal skins on the keeper's gibbet. The persona admires "what strong trust / Slept in him," for his patient acceptance of natural cycles is undeceived by sophistries or defense mechanisms.

Hughes as "Historian" can "master and last" the aggressive forces in animals and English history and outface the mutability of nature because he is strong enough to take risks and somersault like the "Acrobats" onto the nothing of the blank page to free himself of "all sedentary belief." When Hughes ended his April 1958 Harvard reading with "Acrobats," Plath described the poem in her journals as "a perfect metaphor, really, for himself as a poetic acrobat-genius" (*Journals,* 216). Reviewers agreed, with unqualified praise for the entire volume from almost every hand—including Alfred Alvarez, who thought the violence completely contained by Hughes's craft and the implications of that violence skillfully broadened to touch all readers. Stanley Kunitz, Lucas Myers, Alun Jones, and John Holmes echoed one another in admiring the volume for Hughes's ability to become so immersed in the experience described that the final effect is one of complete fusion and an unique immediacy of impact.[17]

Though Hughes was pleased with the triumph of *Lupercal* and flattered to be an increasingly well-known poet when he returned to England in the fall of 1959, dark meditations on the inherited stain of aggression in humans became a major preoccupation in the sixties. "Mayday on Holderness," more than any other *Lupercal* poem, points the way toward the sixties surrealism. Here a May Day landscape meditation elicits nightmare visions of predatory animals: vultures, anacondas, eels, hyenas. Beneath the North Sea in the distance lies the inherited stain of human aggression, the "Cordite oozings of Gallipoli." Though the son of a survivor of Gallipoli, Hughes would take another decade to "master and last" the bombed-out genes he inherited from his father's shattering experience and from the deep English pond that he was so determined to fish.

Chapter Three

Aggression and a New Divinity: *Wodwo* and *Crow*

The Exact Center: *Wodwo*

In the title poem of *Wodwo* (1967), the forest sprite that Sir Gawain battled in the Wirral in *Sir Gawain and the Green Knight* realizes that he is a free spirit, the "exact center" of existence. Hughes characterized the Wodwo as a "half-man half-animal spirit of the forests" engaged in a process of self-discovery (*Poetry,* 62–63). The Wodwo finds his "exact center" by discovering his freedom. The entire volume progresses toward the Wodwo's freedom, a condition that becomes possible when one disencumbers the self of failed cultural beliefs. Living without culturally fixated assumptions, the Wodwo easily integrates himself with nature, his ecological second skin. Self and landscape are not separate, for when he moves about among the trees the Wodwo observes that "that's touching one wall of me." Human, animal, and vegetable worlds cohere without abusing the environment.

The author's note that prefaces *Wodwo* speaks of a "single adventure" in the volume. One way to comprehend this combination of five short stories, the radio play *The Wound,* and 41 very elusive, difficult, haunting poems is to recognize in their progression from opening poem to the concluding "Wodwo" a single persona's adventure toward the goal of achieving the Wodwo's freedom and connectedness. The persona achieves the Wodwo's state by engaging in a process of release, destruction, and revitalization: the release of repressed fears and nightmare visions of aggression, the recognition of these as self-created projections of a defensive ego that must be destroyed or transcended, and finally the attainment of the Wodwo's benign participation in nature. By the end of the volume the reader has learned the process by which one creates one's own mandala of psychic wholeness and ecological balance. In *Wodwo* Hughes analyzes aggression in Western culture by applying the insights of Freud, Jung, and the *Bardo Thödol.* The mana power of his language and his structuralist bent synthesizes all into a "single adventure"—an Oriental pattern of release, destruction, and reintegration with nature.

Genetically Inherited Aggression and a New Divinity

Freud in *Totem and Taboo* (1913) formulated his concept of the "primal horde" by postulating an aggressive taint in humans—a tendency toward violent behavior. According to Freud, this aggressive taint is the inheritance of ancient, balked erotic impulses toward incest, for in the primal horde the castrating authority of the patriarch ensured his exclusive hold on erotic pleasure, which in the dim tribal past supposedly prompted parricide. After World War 1, in *Beyond the Pleasure Principle* (1921), Freud added a second component to his theory of aggressive behavior: a regressive biological urge in all humans, evident especially in the compulsively repetitious behavior of neurotics and children, to overthrow adaptation to the higher functions of reason and regress to more primitive modes of libidinal discharge, including violence. Freud postulated that memory traces of aggressive behavior are inherited and could at any time erupt into violence in the individual or the social group.[1]

Hughes had already considered aggression in such *Hawk* poems as "Childbirth" and "Law in the Country of the Cats," and in the *Lupercal* poem "Mayday on Holderness." Yet in the early sixties his domestic life and intellectual interests often caused deeper meditations on violence. In 1962 Hughes's marriage collapsed, followed by Plath's suicide (11 February 1963), and in the period 1962–65 he wrote two introductory essays to the war poetry of Keith Douglas and two reviews of World War 1 poetry.[2] Given his history and preoccupations at the time, it is not strange to find Hughes in a 1964 review contemplating the "involuntary transmission" of inherited tendencies, for "the possibilities of what a child might absorb from its lineage in this way are awful, which is what alarmed Freud."[3]

Inherited aggression is the thistle of irascibility in the blood in "Thistles," the very powerful opening poem of *Wodwo*. The thistle is a perfect metaphor for aggression in humans. A "revengeful burst" recurs weedlike in each generation, with each spike managing its "plume of blood" in the individual in a way that seems to defeat all attempts at control. The legacy of Viking invaders taints the blood of Englishmen and the consequence is periodic aggressive behavior, a "grasped fistful / Of splintered weapons and Icelandic frost." The referential object in many *Wodwo* poems—thistle, crab, gnat, etc.—serves as a meditative center for a psychic landscape, as in the animal poems of the early poetry. In *Wodwo* the language has a brooding quality, a compelling resonance like the lower register on a church organ, and a self-contained symbolic aura so strong it often deflects interpretation. The surrealistic imagery of psychic dissociation and nightmare distortion is compelling, especially because it parallels moods of alienation and withdrawal from nature. When Hughes fished a pond "as deep as England" in *Lupercal,* he discovered the pikelike aggression in England's cultural heritage. In *Wodwo* he continues his meditations on the problematic Viking inheritance that displaced the comparatively more humane Celtic culture. The Norsemen of "The Warriors of the North" covet the "elaborate, patient gold of the Gaels." Acquisitiveness fuels their icy ruthlessness; booty from abbeys and the rape of burghers' wives thaws their blood. Their aggression becomes culturally fixated in the industriousness of the Protestant ethic and the harsh logic of the Calvinist Elect: a "cash-down, beforehand revenge" flows "Into the iron arteries of Calvin." As in "Thistles," part of the slowly dawning horror generated by the imagery concerns Hughes's recognition that an unchanging cycle of aggression triumphs over any individual's self-control or humanitarian impulses.

"Boom" and "Public Bar TV" present the results of the "cash-down, beforehand revenge": a materialistic culture that feeds the appetites but offers no greater possibilities of self-development or self-fulfillment. A cause-effect logic operates in "Boom." The nuclear blast is the consequence of consumers who cannot control their appetites: they gaze at "glutted shop-windows" and demand ever more insistently to be serviced. "Public Bar TV" offers a clear visual image of the dead end of contemporary Western civilization. Staring at the tube is equivalent to nomads finding foul water and empty horizons; both will lead to extinction.

"Her Husband" and "Second Glance at a Jaguar" continue the study of aggression in contemporary Western culture. Capitalism required cheap resources, energy, and labor, and has forced millions of workers since the latter eighteenth century into lives of unsatisfying servitude. Domestic life deteriorates when the collier returns tense and exhausted from a day of unfulfilling labor. His wife becomes a scapegoat for his irritability. The jaguar of "Second Glance at a Jaguar" possesses an energy that galvanizes his willpower into a frenzy of prolonged concentration like a Buddhist monk chanting a mantra or spinning a prayer wheel. A kindred power in humans, repressed by our culture's fascination with rationality, suffers demonization. Hughes characterized this jaguar as a Dionysian "symbol of man's baser nature shoved down into the id and growing cannibal murderous with deprivation" (Faas 1, 199).

"Ghost Crabs" and "Scapegoats and Rabies" (the latter poem appears in the American edition only) offer the most frightening glimpses of the unending recurrence of aggression in *Wodwo.* Somewhere in Jung's works

Hughes had read that the psyche during sleep regresses to a genetic rein-statement of aboriginal chaos.[4] If this is true, no matter how moral and humane the individual may try to be during the period when conscious-ness controls volition, the ghost crabs of a tainted inheritance will return each night. "Our walls, our bodies, are no problem to them," for "Their hungers are homing elsewhere"—to infect our minds, our psyches. They come from "The sea's cold" like an army landing at a beachhead. Their shell-tops look like "a packed trench of helmets" ready to invade our dreamworld. Grisly images remind one of the jostlings of crabs or lobsters piled high in seafood marts. But, as the crabs "fasten," "mount," and "tear each other to pieces," Hughes visualizes a mindless aggressive power that also exists within the human psyche, "In the roots of blood, in the cycles of concurrence."

In "Scapegoats and Rabies" Hughes meditates on Freud's "compulsion to repeat" component of aggressive behavior. Marching soldiers are "Help-less in the terrible engine of the boots." The surreal nightmare becomes es-pecially horrifying, for the persona is very aware that the soldiers seem to be forever "concentrating / Toward a repeat performance." The soldier of sec-tion 4 is a faceless, anonymous creature whose battle uniform is created by the machine culture, materialism, and escapist entertainment of post-Industrial Revolution England—all of which rob the self of individuality and the capacity for self-development. In section 5 this soldier, badly wounded like Ripley in The Wound, totters back home barely able to sustain his hold on life. The subtitle of section 5, "The Red Carpet," is grimly ironic: instead of signifying a royal welcome, this carpet reddens with an un-remitting flow of blood.

"Out" is a more direct biographical study of aggression. The Gallipoli campaign of World War 1 was much more devastating than that depicted in the romanticized 1981 Peter Weir film, with its limiting Australian ani-mus against the British. During the nine months of the 1915–16 cam-paign, according to Alan Moorehead's Gallipoli (which Plath read in 1960 [Letters Home, 390]), both Allies and Turks lost a quarter of a million men each, with the British accounting for 80 percent of the Allied casualties.[5] Hughes's father, William, who was one of only 17 survivors of an entire battalion of the Lancashire Fusiliers, returned with shrapnel embedded in his breast-pocket paybook.

Hughes considers the consequences of being the "luckless double," the "reassembled infantryman" in "Out." What is his inheritance from a father whose genes absorbed a "four-year mastication by gunfire and mud?" Hughes in section 2 presents his own birth as nature trying to readjust the balance in favor of life, but with enfeebled genes that may contain Freud's "compulsion to repeat." At the moment of birth "The reassembled infantry-man / Tentatively totters out, gazing around with the eyes / Of an ex-hausted clerk." Hughes stated in a 1965 review of an anthology of World War 1 poetry that the continental battlegrounds of the war allowed Englishmen a psychological safety valve for energies repressed by social oppression and military corruption. Britons could siphon off their demonized energies by raging at faraway scapegoats without having to confront the real causes at home. The war front was an unreal nightmare obscuring the "underground of perpetual Somme" that raged within the psyche of each citizen. Meanwhile, the entire scaffolding of Western liberal humanism collapsed, leaving at least the intelligentsia with the acute perception that "suddenly and for the first time Adam's descendants found themselves meaningless."[6]

In section 3 of "Out" Hughes presents this meaningless dimension as a return to a precultural chaos, a regression to an inert state that antedates nature's powers of renewal. All survivors are gripped, anchored in an inertia more powerful than nature's "refreshing of ploughs / In the woe-dark under my mother's eye." Hughes's response is to wash his hands of all worldviews that depend upon an optimistic interpretation of human history. Echoing Robert Graves, in his famous World War 1 memoir *Good-bye to All That*, Hughes bids "goodbye to that bloody-minded" poppy.

In his 1967 essay on the Jugoslav poet Vasco Popa, Hughes wrote that, among artists, belief in Western civilization as an inspiriting ideal has collapsed as the result of two world wars, but survivors like Popa are willing to live in "the unaccommodated Universe" because they have the "simple animal courage of accepting the odds."[7] When Ekbert Faas quizzed Hughes about what he meant by "accepting the odds," Hughes replied that poets like Popa are willing "to invest their hopes in something deeper," a "new divinity" that "won't be under the rubble when the churches collapse" (Faas 1, 207). The poetry of both *Wodwo* and *Crow* reveals that this "new divinity" is a deeper sense of the self as the metaphysical ground of all activity than can be achieved with the Western ego. Hughes's work on the *Bardo Thödol* and his reading of Carl Jung at the very beginning of the sixties gave him an antidote for his obsessions with inherited aggression in Western civilization. Both *Wodwo* and *Crow* record the struggle to find a "new divinity" within the self.

Jung believed that much aggressive behavior occurs after one projects self-created fears onto others. These fears occur habitually because Western culture so overemphasizes rational analysis that reason splits off from its in-

tegrated place in the larger Self and demands logic from its own nonlogical
resources: feeling, intuition, emotion, and instinctual energies. Not finding
comforting logical answers, the dominant rational faculty spurns these resources, and their energy, sealed off in repression, erupts in menacing projections. Aggressive behavior toward objects, persons, and events follows
because they are distorted by the psyche's own alienated, demonized energies (Jung 9a: 38, 229, 346–53; Jung 10: 81–83).[8]

Fear and Surreal Projection   Hughes crafted his *Bardo Thödol*
libretto from the fall of 1959 through November 1960 (*Letters Home,* 354,
399), during the same period he began composing the first poems of
Wodwo. The surrealistic poems and prose of *Wodwo,* as well as Crow's quest
to unite with nature, his self-alienated bride, derive to a great extent from a
fear-and-projection motif at the heart of the *Bardo* that Jung identified in
his "Psychological Commentary," an essay that prefaces the Evans-Wentz
Bardo text in every reprinting since the 1957 third edition. Jung's essay begins by paying tribute to the text for affording him "many fundamental insights" (Jung PC: xxxvi). One of Jung's foremost insights from the *Bardo*
concerned the cause of psychological projections in the "fear of self-sacrifice"
that "lurks deep in every ego" (Jung PC: xlvii). The *Bardo* text and Jung's
commentary reaffirmed Hughes's insights about fear and projection that he
doubtless already knew from his readings in myth and folklore.

According to the *Bardo* philosophy, only the animal nature of humans—
our enchainment to appetites, emotions, habits, and creature comforts—
prevents us from understanding the self as the maker of our own
circumstances (Jung PC: xl). To attain nirvanic liberation from the physical
round of decay and reincarnation in the temporal world, one must, in
Jung's words, "give up the supremacy of egohood" and recognize that "the
'giver' of all 'given' things dwells within us" (Jung PC: xlvi, xl). To achieve
wholeness within the self one must allow repressed material to rise to consciousness, and then recognize the contents as self-created projections of
fears. According to Jung, the ego fears self-sacrifice, but this fear "is often
only the precariously controlled demand of the unconscious forces to burst
out in full strength. No one who strives for selfhood (individuation) is
spared this dangerous passage, for that which is feared also belongs to the
wholeness of the self—the sub-human, or supra-human, world of psychic
'dominants' from which the ego originally emancipated itself with enormous effort, and then only partially, for the sake of a more or less illusory
freedom" (Jung PC: xlvii).

Hughes is not a devotee of any religious orthodoxy and is much too

Western in orientation to advocate striving toward an austere, world-denying nirvanic transcendence of the temporal world. The "new divinity" he advocates is the Wodwo's deeper sense of self directly connected to the environment without the narrowing Western overemphasis upon the rational ego or the sexual taboos and utilitarianism of the Protestant ethic. The *Bardo* pattern of releasing repressed fears, destroying the ego, and developing a more inclusive self as the center of a holistic bond with the environment offered Hughes a way out of his obsessions with inherited aggression and a way back to nature and ecological balance.

Buddhists believe that after the death of the body the spirit wanders for a period of 49 days, during which time it may attain the release of nirvana by recognizing the *Dharma-Kāya* of Clear Light. But if karmic illusions—self-created projections of one's fears and attachments to the phenomenal world—continue to obscure one's vision, the spirit will gradually descend and after 49 days reenter the womb door of the phenomenal world and be reborn amid its transitory decay. An officiating priest recites the *Bardo* over an effigy of the body periodically during the 49-day period; the text exhorts the wandering spirit to recognize the illusoriness of the phenomenal world and to concentrate on the self as the originator of all that it perceives. Actually, the *Bardo* is meant to be used throughout life as a meditative guide to strengthen one's perceptions of the illusory nature of the phenomenal world so that one will be able to attain Buddhahood instantaneously at death.

If one has gained sufficient concentration throughout life, one should immediately recognize the *Dharma-Kāya* of Clear Light and achieve the nirvana of Buddhahood. If one has not achieved sufficient meditative strength, the spirit can strengthen its concentration by heeding the recited *Bardo* exhortations. After four days chances of liberation lessen, for the spirit descends from the clarity of the *Chikkai Bardo* state to the *Chōnyid Bardo,* where one's thoughts—including one's fears—appear in visual images, obscuring the Clear Light of the *Dharma-Kāya* and making nirvanic liberation less likely. After 14 days the soul descends further toward the phenomenal world as it enters the *Sidpa Bardo* and once again experiences physical sensations, emotions, and the cravings of the appetites, symbolized in the text by fierce karmic winds that propel the soul into rebirth at the womb door of phenomenality. As Jung and *Bardo* editor Evans-Wentz observed, the *Bardo* recounts an initiation in reverse, ending with the traditional visit to the House of the Dead that in Greek, Latin, Egyptian, and Indian cultures usually appeared early in the rebirth ordeal (Jung PC: xli–xliii; *Book of the Dead,* 45–53).

The *Bardo* text admonishes the spirit not to fear or desire visions of the earthly world, for these are self-created illusions. One obtains Buddhahood by recognizing that all thought-forms are "the radiance of thine own intellectual faculties come to shine" and by concentrating upon remaining in a state of "non-thought formation" (*Book of the Dead,* 123). Even terrifying apparitions of menacing landscapes—fierce winds, crumbling mountains, angry seas, roaring fires—or of being pursued by terrible beasts (*Book of the Dead,*162) should not cause discomfort, for "in reality, thy body is of the nature of voidness; thou needst not be afraid. The Lords of Death are thine own hallucinations" (*Book of the Dead,* 166–67).

The poems of part 1 of *Wodwo* that are not concerned with fears of genetically inherited aggression present the persona in a state of fear at human finitude. Imagery of rain and darkness, as in the *Sidpa Bardo,* conveys the persona's fear of the world of temporal decay. Hughes frequently adds imagery of silence to convey the persona's neurotic and finally psychotic withdrawal from this unregenerate world. The persona's ego creates the fear, but refuses to release its control because it fears the death of its primacy.

Fear of death dominates many part 1 poems. In "Still Life" the persona envies the stone's invulnerability and is acutely conscious of the harebell's fragile mortality. Worry over the hill's susceptibility to erosion occurs in "Sugar Loaf," where the water's trickle will gradually drop the entire hill into "the small pool's stomach." Imagery of darkness and wind-driven trees occurs in "A Wind Flashes the Grass." Here "Leaves pour blackly across," the shadow of the ploughman's bones "tosses darkly on the air," and branches stir "against the dark, travelling sky" because like the persona "They too are afraid they too are momentary / Streams rivers of shadow."

Some part 1 poems combine mythological allusions with landscapes of surreal estrangement to convey the persona's insecurity or disorientation. In "Fern" the plant is likened to a conductor who orchestrates a paradoxically silent music, as if a Zen adept meant to awaken his audience to the beauties of the natural world. But a consciousness of death intrudes as both earth and fern dance "gravely" in the silence. Compounded with this is the Celtic motif of a dead warrior's return underground as a prelude for rebirth[9] and the Welch use of fern seed to convey invisibility (Graves, 42, 182). "Cadenza" recounts an explosive competition between soloist and orchestra, with the persona imagining himself to be the dead Osiris attended by Isis in her swallow form. Imagery of silence and lightning combines with surreal imagery of a sky diving shut and a sea lifting wings to create a soulscape of severe disorientation. The orchestra explodes when the soloist crashes into it after refusing to end his cadenza.

Military imagery in "Bowled Over" and "Reveille" conveys in each case an awakening to a deathly separation from nature. A consciousness of human aggression, the "bullet on brow" in "Bowled Over," causes the persona such revulsion as to make him desire to desert the ranks of Western culture—its "patched fields, churches." In "Reveille" Adam and Eve once lived in Eden in a mutuality where each was the "everlasting / Holy One of the other." But the serpent awakens each to a consciousness of selfhood, the Blakean specter. Both awake with cries of pain and a sense of separation from nature that devolves to further separation in the Industrial Revolution's abuse of the environment and finally nuclear disaster, the "ashes of the future."

A neurotic fear of involvement in experience occurs in "A Vegetarian." The animals of the poem were each revered at some point in various earlier Western cultures as incarnations of a divine being whose death brought both food and death into the world, propelling humans into participation in the cyclic round of love and death (Campbell 1960: 136–42, 176–202). The persona of "A Vegetarian" wants no contact with carrion but is about to be victimized by the White Goddess in her destructive form, the "hare with the manners of a lady" (Graves, 400–405). This aversion to experience in a world of time and decay—the boar's wound, bull's rending, and relentless sheep's jaw grinding—becomes more psychotic in other part 1 poems, where Hughes follows the advice of Jung and the *Bardo* to let the repressed hallucinations surface with such force as to annihilate the defensive rational ego.

The *Bardo* text exhorts the initiate to "abandon egotism" because it begets fear (*Book of the Dead*, 111–12). The Sanskrit term *nirvāṇa*, literally a cessation of wind (*nir*-to blow out; *vana*-wind), means in one sense to blow out the "flame of selfish longing" (*Book of the Dead*, 97n), to experience the plenitude of existence in its holistic allness, beyond the categorizing and separating of reason. The nirvanic void, as Sir John Woodroffe points out in his foreword to the third edition of Evans-Wentz, is not a negative state, but a kind of "no-thing" or infinite "Is-ness" achieved by negating all limitations, all determinations (*Book of the Dead*, lxxi). To achieve this condition one must also abandon all attractions to and cravings for objects in the phenomenal world and keep the mind in the mood of "endless undistracted *Samādhi*" (*Book of the Dead*, 203), a term in Yoga that signifies a unity or agreement with all of reality.[10]

Poems near the end of part 1 of *Wodwo* present a dissolution of the ego and a search for deeper psychic powers. In sections 1 and 2 of "Root, Stem, Leaf" (American edition only), the persona distances himself from attractions to women and nature, for these attractions bring only unending cyclic change and the agony of loss. In section 3 the persona abandons both his attachment to temporal desires and his ego. He then feels as discarded and forgotten as a lost "heirloom spoon, blackening / Among roots in a thornhedge." Yet the result is a nirvanic sense of the plenitude of all creation, where "Everything is inheriting everything."

"Stations" similarly presents an abandonment of the ego, the "lifeboat coffin" that in "Cadenza" would not be silent. A sense of absence yields to a "surrender to total Emptiness" in the last section of the poem. Here decapitation symbolizes the uselessness of rational thinking. Vocabulary is similarly useless, for it names and thus separates discrete objects. The word "Emptiness," capitalized twice in the poem, signifies in Buddhist thinking the state of *śūnyatā*, a serenity achieved by emptying oneself of all dualistic rational discrimination. D. T. Suzuki finds a perfect description of *śūnyatā* in the *Prajñāparamitā-Hridaya Sutra,* recited by Zen monks upon awakening each morning and before every meal: "Thus, Sariputra, all things have the character of emptiness, they have no beginning, no end, they are faultless and not faultless, they are not perfect and not imperfect. Therefore, O Sariputra, here in this emptiness there is no form, no perception, no name, no concepts, no knowledge. . . . There is no knowledge of Nirvana, no obtaining of it, no not-obtaining of it. . . . When the impediments of consciousness are annihilated, then [one] becomes free of all fear, is beyond the reach of change, enjoying final Nirvana."[11] When one sees reality freshly and preconceptually, without rational categorizing, one revels in the allness of creation.

"The Rescue" and "The Green Wolf" both present states of total personality dissolution and revulsion at the needs of the fleshy body. "The Rescue" is a very enigmatic, self-contained poem that appears to present the body after death waiting for the resurrection of the five senses just as Lazarus waited for the appearance of Christ. The poem presents this waiting surrealistically as an expected rescue by a ship from an island. Instead the persona learns to see "the five" senses for what they are: decayed, mummified apertures of sensual experience, "powdery nerves" handled in silence because abandoned in some shadowy afterworld.

"The Green Wolf" presents an imagined experience of the ego undergoing death by cerebral hemorrhage and fiery immolation. The title alludes to the summer scapegoat victim of the Normandy Beltane fires.[12] Beanflower and hawthorn blossom imagery suggest an unlucky entrapment in the erotic round of birth and death (Graves; 69, 175–76). References to the left side of the body, repeated many times in the poem, suggest the perilous "left-hand-path" of personality dissolution in alchemy, a necessary prelude to rebirth (Campbell 1968, 282ff.). The persona views the impending death of the self as a welcome relief from a state of personality dysfunction so severe that autistic paralysis begins.

"The Bear" is a reworking of the uncollected poem "The Brother's Dream," where a Christian Brother ascends a mountainside in fear and then kills a bear in a cave by ripping it open like Marduk slaying Tiamat to create the world in the Babylonian epic, *Enuma Elish*. After the Christian Brother's experience, the landscape and animals fear him—for an inhuman act of self-destruction.[13] The persona of the *Wodwo* poem, not alienated from his instincts by Christianity, has learned not to make the same mistake. He trusts a destructive power within the self that has a supernormal sense of purpose and growth.

The bear is "the gleam in the pupil," the psyche's capacity for self-directed growth through dissolution; it resides in the "sleeping eye of the mountain," a residence of the deity in many tribal cultures.[14] This power, hibernating within the self most of the time, demands "everything" to effect personality growth, including a dissolution of egocentric self-concepts, now seen in stanza 5 as "dead selves" reflected in the river. The bear is a tenacious power of endurance and continuity within the self, a vital force that offers stability beneath changes in one's self-image.

Surreal Alienation in Part 2   The author's note suggests that the stories and the play *The Wound* in part 2 parallel the progression of the part 1 poems in the "single adventure" of *Wodwo*. Like part 1, the stories of part 2 also lead to an estrangement from nature, eros, and human activity, followed by a complete dissolution of the ego in a visit to the House of the Dead in *The Wound*. In "Sunday" the young Michael feels alienated from a church service so pure that it seems to disinfect the hills. He looks forward to the regular after-service entertainment of Billy Red, who catches rats with his bare teeth to win half-pints of beer. Michael also becomes vaguely interested in a well-to-do girl who arrives with her escort to observe the rat catching at the local pub. The girl is a "thing of scents" with a "powdered profile," the opposite of the "flea-bitten" Billy Red with his "sunken features" and "little withered mouth." These opposites appear to represent the beginning and the end of sexual enticements. Michael, however, sympathizes with the dead rat's bloody end, and leaves the pub disgusted with the entire erotic round of chase and destruction.

The hunter becomes the hunted in "The Harvesting," where the aging Grooby loses consciousness twice while shooting hares from the ends of wheatfields being harvested by a tractor with its attached reaper. Amid the heat and the clang of the reaper Grooby becomes dimly aware that he himself is the victim of life's grim mortality. The story ends with Grooby's second blackout as the tractor, the reaper with its "grinding clatter," and a surrealistic "white, bony greyhound" bear down upon him. Grooby blacks out in the recoil of his rifle as he shoots at a hare flushed out by the reaper, but the reaper and greyhound pursue him, not the hare. He has gone "into a hare"; he is victimized by the cycle of birth and death, as the epigraph chant from the seventeenth-century Allansford witch coven suggests (Graves, 401–402).

Hughes describes the horse in "The Rain Horse" as "a nightmarish leopard," an animal he elsewhere connects with Dionysus (Faas 1, 199). The description is apt, for the horse symbolizes the alienated instinctual energies of the young man in the grey suit, home after twelve years' absence, who "had come too far." Instead of the "meaningful sensation" he expected upon returning home, he feels only dullness and boredom, and "anger against the land that made him feel so outcast." The horse appears just at this moment, and pursues him malevolently only after he represses what the horse signifies. He throws stones at the horse from the safety of a hawthorn hedge, the White Goddess's tree of enforced chastity (Graves, 175–76). The horse's demonic energy "seemed to be actually inside his head," but he represses acknowledging it: he tells the horse to keep his distance and departs feeling confused, frightened, and lobotomized—"as if some important part had been cut out of his brain."

In "The Suitor" the watcher in the trilby (a soft felt hat), who stands next to a darkened smithy, signifies the alienated instinctual portion of the suitor. The suitor has walked five miles in his never-used dancing shoes in the hope of glimpsing a girl who had smiled at him a few times at school. The girl finally appears with an escort, at which time the suitor witnesses the watcher in the trilby receive a beating from the girl's companion. Both the suitor and the man in the trilby are inadequate in love; their alienated eros appears at the end of the story as they crouch back to back under the inaccessible girl's window, with the man in the trilby ironically playing flute notes—an impotent Pan playing "for the sheer idiocy of our situation." As the flute notes climb the girl's second-floor window, the suitor ironically contorts his face into a surreal Dionysian leopard-mask. Many other details in "The Suitor" suggest a surreal portrayal of blocked eros: the girl's house gate, for instance, brandishes the sign "Please shut this," and the backs of dressing table mirrors at the window block the front bedroom from view.

The narrator of "Snow" must endure the cold like an Eskimo shaman in the most surreal of the *Wodwo* stories. If he lets the snow of "paralyzing, yes, lethal thoughts" into his mind, he will sink to lifelessness. He has been walking against the wind in a blizzard for five months without food and needs rational proofs regularly to keep himself from succumbing to total psychosis. He thinks himself to be the survivor of a plane crash, and longs desperately like Kafka's Gregor Samsa to return to his job, parents, and wife—his routine. But reality has become surreal, and his only assurance in the "pouring silent grey" is his chair. To keep "courageous and calm" he considers repeating the Mantra of Chenrazee, a six-syllable chant mentioned in the *Bardo* (*Book of the Dead*, facing 167). The survivor tries hard to still his fear and attachments to the temporal world by walking 14 paces away from his chair, to the point where it is almost obliterated by the snow. The deadpan comedy of the story alternates with a deeply serious revelation of just how difficult it is to starve the ego's needs for rational reassurances. At this point in the "single adventure" the central persona's psyche is in a complete state of personality dissolution, as in "The Green Wolf" in part 1.

All the central characters of the part 1 stories are like the persona of the part 1 poem "A Vegetarian" in their retreat from Western goal-oriented activity, though in the stories the problem is more clearly identified as balked, atrophied, or repressed libido caused by a rational ego demanding to retain control and direct activity. Ripley in *The Wound* is another vegetarian; he would rather eat phallic gherkins like a pregnant woman than respond to the advice of the Girl who wants to help him escape the white chateau. As in "Sunday," the erotic lure splits into negative and positive components: the Girl is Ripley's anima, and the ogresses at the chateau represent the destructive portion of the White Goddess.

In *The Wound,* originally produced as a radio play on the BBC Third Program (1 February 1962), Hughes exploits the possibilities of radio for psychodrama. The entire action of the play actually takes place inside Ripley's head a few seconds after he is shot in battle. He must either summon all his strength and survival energies to live, or capitulate to the world of the dead. Ripley has the same problem as most of the central characters in the part 2 stories: a despondent "what's the use?" of continuing the erotic lure to experience (Jung's anima) in goal-oriented action. Sargent Massey, heartily welcomed by the ogresses at the chateau, is already dead; he is, as Hughes confided in a radio interview, "a projection of the thing that's wrong with Ripley."[15]

What is wrong with Ripley is his unreflective assent to Western culture's mechanical "go," articulated at the outset of the story by Massey's orders to "Keep going!" Like the soldier of "Scapegoats and Rabies," Ripley is "helpless in the terrible engine of the boots." Ripley's lot is evidently not to reason why, but to do and die. Ripley finally does realize that Massey himself is dead and that his logic is deadly when Ripley gazes at Massey's limp body in an armory museum adjacent to the chateau. Without the help of the Girl, his Jungian anima spurring him back to life, he would never get even this far. Ripley's encounters with the Girl contain many double entendres that reveal his ambivalence over returning to the world of the living in this aggressive culture. Just before they meet, the Queen of the ogresses asks Ripley to eat and produces a lengthy list of fish and game to choose from. All were at some point in Western civilization revered as sacred to fertility deities, but Ripley refuses to participate in the erotic lure of love and death, and parries with misogynistic complaints about brothels. Ripley's first encounter with the Girl fares no better: his gherkin jar smashes and he complains she is a 15-year-old "little bitch!" In their second encounter, however, she makes him realize that he has indeed been shot in the head. As Ripley begins to mobilize his psychic energies, he asks with sardonic humor if the outside noise is romantic summer thunder, and the Girl underscores his ambivalence with two replies: "That's your life, working at the hole in your head," followed by "That's the war, working at all the undead." When Ripley stands aghast as the ballroom scene sinks into blackness with the ogresses' arms about the soldiers, the Girl firmly tells him "You can't stay here." Ripley has barely mustered sufficient survival energy to continue.

By the time Ripley returns to his platoon, he is muttering "Marry me" to battle-toughened soldiers in the bleeding mud of war, and one of these soldiers in the last line of the play tells Ripley to "Keep going." Ripley is a survivor, but also clearly a victim of Western aggression. He has no possibility of nurturing his anima in a culture where to reason why is to be the scapegoat victim. The play takes place on midsummer's eve, the time of scapegoat sacrifices in tribal societies.[16] In *The Wound* machine warfare relegates our entire culture to the status of scapegoat victim of its own alienated instincts and repressed, demonized energies.

A New Divinity Realized   Hughes identified two kinds of surrealism in his 1967 Vasco Popa essay: the dadaist "arbitrary imagery of the dream flow," and "the surrealism of folklore," which has not lost its "unifying focus" and commitment to the "outer battle." Folklore surrealism struggles with "practical difficulties so great that they have forced the sufferer temporarily out of the dimension of coherent reality" and into a search for deeper imaginative resources.[17] Hughes definitely agrees with the purpose of folklore surrealism. If parts 1 and 2 of *Wodwo* present the withdrawal and dissolution of the ego, part 3 locates a deeper sense of self, a "new divinity" that returns to nature and with increasing confidence can decide what enriches the self's ability to participate in life with joy and wonder. Part 3 begins with "Theology," a strong expression of the "new divinity" within the self that Hughes struggled to achieve in the sixties. Adam, not Eve, eats the apple of rational knowledge, and with this knowledge dominates Eve. But the serpent eats Eve and all the inheritance of rationalism and alienated instincts that this Christian apple produced. The serpent exits to a paradise unencumbered by corrupting Western dualism—a "new divinity." This paradise may be that of Amitābha of the "All-Discriminating Wisdom," mentioned many times in the *Bardo* text. Amitābha presides over the Western Paradise, where one is reborn miraculously from a lotus blossom (*Book of the Dead*, 189). The Paradise of the serpent in "Theology" does not depend upon an egocentric attachment to things in the temporal realm of corruption.

In one of his discussions of karma, D. T. Suzuki suggests that the only way to live without despair at human suffering is to recognize that suffering underlies all human activities; it is a fact of life that we must learn to accept. Humans are given to rational analysis, to separating good from bad even though *karma* itself originally meant simply "action." The intellect wants to cut up "the seamless piece of cloth called life into several parts" to examine it, says Suzuki, but we must also recognize that karmic "bondage does not really touch our inmost being, which is above all forms of dualism."[18]

Hughes suffers in "Karma" for the millions killed by the Holocaust, Victorian imperialism, the Emperors of Chou, and American slaveholders. He concludes that suffering is the lot of every human born "from the breast / Of the mother" throughout the 150 million years of human history. This position is neither glib nor callous; all of *Wodwo* testifies to the depth and intensity of Hughes's suffering for the legacy of human aggression. By recognizing pain as part of the human condition, Hughes transcends his part 1 obsession with aggression. At the conclusion of "Karma" he asserts that karma is "Not here," not in his inmost being, and that the karmic mirror is composed of "seamless sand" that cannot be divided by the intellect. The karmic mirror in the *Bardo* is the self, which reflects reality. To attain the nirvanic Clear Light of the *Dharma-Kāya* one must wipe all the dust of the phenomenal world from the mirror of the self (*Book of the Dead*, 166–67).

Section 1 of "Song of a Rat" rehearses Michael's sympathy for the dead rat in "Sunday"; the reference in the last line to the blood on its nose-end repeats very directly an image in the short story. Yet the persona merely pities the animal, because it comprehends little. " 'This has no face, it must be God' " and " 'No answer is also an answer' " rehearse Zen *kōans*, philosophical puzzles that transcend the limitations of reason. But the rat cannot even reason: it is bound by animal instinct.

The rat in sections 2 and 3 is not the limited animal of section 1, but another of Hughes's metaphors for energies within humans. Hughes wrote "Song of a Rat" one month after Plath's suicide (Sagar, 61); one can see in the rat's struggles in parts 2 and 3 the struggle of the poet to live in the wake of the suicide. To see the world "wobbling like reflection on water" is to recognize it as the illusory phenomenal world, according to the *Bardo* (*Book of the Dead,* 176, 181). Dandelions, yard cinders, cracked trough, and stars cry out to the rat not to sever its dependency on these phenomenal entities, but the rat transcends its egocentric needs in the last line of section 2 as the rat's head becomes godhead.

In Hindu mythology the rat is frequently associated with the Elephant God Ganesa, he who removes obstacles, because of the rat's persistence in finding a way into the locked granary (Zimmer, 70, 183). In section 3 the Rat, now capitalized, has assumed godhead, has become the source of his own understanding of the world—the "new divinity." When the shadow, the previously unrecognized instinctual energies within the unconscious in Jungian psychology, becomes conscious, it can become integrated with conscious life. Then the individual experiences a renewed sense of purpose and power.[19] This happens at the end of the poem; here the Rat achieves a new self-reliance and leaves its fleshy body of instinctual dependency for the dogs.

Christianity, however, cannot integrate reason and instincts. In "Gog" Hughes writes his own commentary to Revelation. God's assumption of total power—"I am Alpha and Omega" (Rev. 1:11; 21:6; 22:13)— awakens the dragon Gog in section 1. Gog is the instinctual life that God alienated with his proclamation to be champion of the good and the true. The dragon, exiled from heaven, experiences guilt and a fear of the environment. But the persona of section 2 (only the British *Wodwo* contains sections 2 and 3) has achieved a Buddhist perspective. He recognizes, like the persona of "Karma," that nature inevitably creates a world of "Death and death and death." Death is the "dust" on the mirror of nature that she cannot wipe clean, for nature has no capacity for Buddhist enlightenment. Nor does the Christian Knight in section 3.

The Knight in section 3 of "Gog" should be able to pierce the veil of the illusory phenomenal world, like that Rat and the persona of "Karma." This does not happen because the Knight is a Christian knight who cannot transcend his dependency upon the instincts and the phenomenal world. He is a "horseman of iron" doomed to kill the instincts his heritage perpetually alienates. His horse is "shod with vaginas of iron" and his compass is his lance blade and gunsight. The persona of section 3 of "Gog" is not the Knight. He recites the narrative of the Knight's exploits with quiet foreboding and a sense of inevitability. The Knight is the unborn child of Revelation 12: 1–5, a savior who will "rule all nations with a rod of iron." The persona prays that this Knight will transcend his dependency upon the instincts and the "illusion" of a phenomenal world. Transcendence would lead to nonviolence, but aggression will continue, for Christianity will forever fight the human instincts it disowns and represses, a point Hughes developed in the *Lupercal* poem "The Perfect Forms."

All three great men of "Wings" produced work that distanced humans from nature, ancestral wisdom, and any teleology whatsoever. All three depend heavily upon rational analysis, yet all are deficient in distancing themselves from the phenomenal world. The Faber edition of *Wodwo* contains helpful subtitles for the three sections of "Wings": "M. Sartre Considers Current Affairs," "Kafka Writes," and "Einstein Plays Bach." Sartre peers at carrion-eating fish in a "twice-darkened room" where human consciousness produces the second darkness. Consciousness, the "regrow[ing] of the world inside his skull," is necessary for existentialist freedom, for one must consciously choose one's existential projects. This results in an unending series of rational decisions and responsibilities. Guilt and remorse over one's actions in the phenomenal world follow—represented by the flies that pursue Orestes in *Les Mouches*. Sartre is imprisoned in his rational consciousness; no sense of miracle is possible. Angels can only be metaphors for the physical body's exhilarations—a reductive position—so the wings of our most celestial insights are fallen wings, shared with those of the carrion-eating skate.

The owl is sacred to Athena and a favorite folklore symbol for wisdom. But Kafka's wing is broken, stunned by a heavenly glare shining upon a weak-eyed, fallen human intellect. The situation of humans is hopeless, yet we insist upon delusory rational satisfactions such as court adjudications (*The Trial*) and surveyor's maps (*The Castle*). In one of his aphorisms Kafka wrote that since the Fall humans have regularly manifested the capacity to distinguish good and evil, but we become fearful and lack sufficient strength to act upon that knowledge. Hence "the whole visible world is perhaps nothing more than the rationalization of a man who wants to find peace for a moment."[20] Denied any teleological sureties, humans are left to manipulate reason to conceal their weak wills and bodies.

Einstein separated science—the domain of factual relationships and laws—from the sphere of religion—the pursuit of ethical judgments,

human aspirations, and goals. Einstein also separated his love of playing
Bach and Mozart from his scientific research. He believed that music had no
effect on scientific research, but his elder son admitted that Einstein took
refuge in music whenever his research reached a temporary dead end.[21]
Playing Bach may offer Einstein a respite from the scientific problems of
atomic theory but not from the moral problem of contributing to the creation of atomic weapons. Science is never value-free, no matter how much
Einstein wanted to relegate moral questions to the separate province of religion and aesthetic questions to art. If we humans are left only with a world
of scientific fact—"Star peering at star"—in a world without religious
revelation—no manna or pillars of fire—then we are responsible for our tinkering with "the cauldron of the atom" and the nuclear consequences.
Sartrean flies of guilt rise in a nuclear mushroom cloud.

"The Howling of Wolves," "You Drive in a Circle," and "Pibroch" take
steady, clear-eyed, realistic views of nature. Nature is not something to be
feared, as in part 1, but an environment with built-in limitations that humans invest with meaning or scrutinize to capture glimpses of a beyond.
The persona has awakened to an Oriental sense of the human self as generator of values. The wolves have no imaginative life; they have no sense of
"world," and their eyes "never learn" why they respond as they do to certain
cries. The wolf "comprehends little" because its animal behavior is limited
to satisfying appetites. It must "feed its fur." For Blake "the howling of
wolves" manifests an energy that can break through antiquated systems in
The Marriage of Heaven and Hell (plate 8). Yet it is Blake who ascribes this
value to the wolves' energy. The wolves themselves cannot comprehend systems of thought; they lack even the single vision of the eye of human reason.
Eternity is a possibility in the regenerated eye of the human imagination.

Similarly, the sheep in "You Drive in a Circle" are "sodden with the
world, like fossils, / And what is not the world is God." The locus of reality
is mental for Hughes as for Blake: the mind invests the phenomenal world
with meaning. Here Hughes uses a precise Zen term, "no-thinking," or
munen, to convey having achieved a Buddhist sense of identity with the
allness of the universe, beyond attachments, cravings, or dependence upon
the kind of rational discrimination that separates and categorizes.[22] Objective phenomena will not anchor the enlightened spirit; the persona's desti-
nation is the "new divinity" within the self that requires no automobile
journey to reach it. In "Pibroch" Hughes recognizes that the sea's voice is
"meaningless," that the stone is "blind," and that a tree struggles without
mind. Yet this is the environment where humans find their best insights
into a transcendent reality. The "staring angels" of one's best thoughts pierce

through nature's limitations to discover truths beyond the phenomenal world.

In part 3 the central persona of *Wodwo*'s "single adventure" can do more than recognize the limitations of the phenomenal world; it can revel in the beauty of nature by becoming one with the object without fear, without the need to evaluate, systematize, or dominate through egocentric rational analysis. In both "Skylarks" and "Gnat Psalm" Hughes admires the unselfconscious expenditure of energy by the skylark and the gnat. This expenditure represents a free and continuous return of every ounce of strength that nature gave them. To see the world not as possessions owned by individuals, but as a joyous energy transfer where nature transforms itself endlessly, is to see with a deeper sense of self, the "new divinity." In a midsixties review Hughes praised the "wild Heraclitian/Buddhist notion that the entire Universe is basically made of fire" as a more holistic, insightful view of creation than that of systems based on rational first principles.[23] In "Skylarks" and "Gnat Psalm" Hughes revels in the free energy release of all creation fueled by the sun. The persona's empathy becomes so strong as to unite with subject and landscape in one holistic bond.

The skylarks are streamlined fusions of muscle and lungs fashioned with the command to climb and sing. To this command they are obedient with purity and simplicity. Heedless of all else, they fuse with their environment, singing on the in-breath as well as the out-breath. Joy and pain fuse on a plane of experience that logic does not comprehend in section 3, and in section 4 the larks' labor coaxes the persona out of his selfhood to follow their upward flight until his "eye's gossamer snaps." In the last two sections the sacrificial energy of the larks, given to the moment of death, suggests to the persona that the larks must feel as free as humans can be when all the bills are paid, all obligations completed, all work finished—a state of freedom and satisfaction that humans seldom attain. At the end of the poem the enterprises of humans and larks are one because the persona's sympathy embraces all.

The last three poems of *Wodwo* express the "new divinity" most directly. This chapter began with a discussion of the Wodwo's freedom in the last and title poem. "Gnat-Psalm" and "Full Moon and Little Frieda," the remaining two, present the persona's full absorption in the scene described, merging persona, subject, and environment so directly and unselfconsciously as to enlist the reader's imagination in making a three-dimensional experience from two-dimensional print. The self becomes the center of experience in a nonegocentric absorption in the other. Here the self and its ecological second skin are parts of an indivisible whole and the mana power of

Hughes's language conveys exactly a grasp of life as an ecstatic dance. The persona describes the scene without fear of mortality or genetic inheritance. The gnats especially know what it means to achieve a "new divinity":

> Not writing and not fighting but singing
> That the cycles of this Universe are no matter
> That they are not afraid of the sun
> That the one sun is too near
> It blasts their song, which is of all the suns
> That they are their own sun
> Their own brimming over
> At large in the nothing

The gnats' confident knowledge that "they are their own sun" is the clearest expression in *Wodwo* of Jung's interpretation of the *Bardo Thödol's* central message, the realization that the self is the originator of all experience, for "the 'giver' of all 'given' things dwells within us" (Jung PC:xl).

In their frenetic bursts of energy the gnats transcend separateness to achieve a holistic bond that Hughes captures in a perfect image: "Everybody everybody else's yoyo." Dancer and dance are one in a joyous giving where personal commitment and biological imperatives unite: "Ridden to death by your own bodies / Riding your bodies to death." Like the "staring angels" of "Pibroch," the persona at the end of the poem becomes so taken by the furious, dervishlike dancing of the gnats that he experiences an intense moment of union with all creation. He transcends mean selfhood as he grasps "outer space," and this "outer space" simultaneously becomes a fusion with all of creation, for now he sees the world from a cosmic perspective, as Blake did with his grain of sand.

Hughes sees the whole world in the child's purity and innocent identification with nature in "Full Moon and Little Frieda." Self and environment fuse as mirroring artworks. The poem draws on symbols of plenitude and fertility from Indian and Native American cultures. Cows are sacred fertility symbols in India; the Haida and Tlingit American Indians see in the moon a figure of a girl with a bucket, drawn there by mutual attraction.[24] Never mistake the finger pointing at the moon for the moon itself, a favorite Zen aphorism, applies here, for the poem gives us a sense of the beauty of the real-world object (the extensional moon), not the pointing finger (rational logic and language). In Zen "mirror knowledge" occurs when self and environment are one.[25] The warmth of the cows' breath, their unspilled milk, and the child's pure astonishment at the moon fuse in an ecstasy of amazement. In the concluding poems of *Wodwo* Hughes fully realizes his "new divinity," the objective of the volume's "single adventure."

The Renewing Sacred Spirit: *Crow*

Hughes originally conceived *Crow* (1970–72) as an epic folktale to affirm even more optimistically than *Wodwo* the human potential to integrate self and environment and thus transcend aggressive conduct and the utilitarian rape of the environment. Again the psychological and ecological remedy concerns the destruction of the defensive ego's fears and attachments to the purely physical. For Hughes the indestructible Crow was the embodiment of nature's "genetic potential" in the sperm, a "renewing sacred spirit" capable of creating a "new self" and fashioning a "renewed world." Hughes believed that "the optimism and creative joy" of Trickster literature testified to nature's desire to "enlarge and intensify life," and "this particular view of the Trickster Tale was my guiding metaphor when I set out to make what I could of *Crow*" ("Reply").

But the deaths of his companion Assia Guttman Wevill and her daughter Shura in March 1969 brought the Crow poems to an abrupt halt. Hughes dedicated the volume to them, but has not completed his original design. The first Faber edition carried a dust-jacket note stating that the verse inside derives from "about the first two-thirds of what was to have been an epic folk-tale." Almost all of the surviving *Crow* poems, including about 40 not printed in either trade edition (Scigaj, 326–27n), recount episodes in the tale *before* Crow annihilates his ego in "Truth Kills Everybody." Hughes's intentions regarding the narrative frame of this epic folktale and Crow's development are important guides to interpretation that should qualify treatments of Crow as a satiric buffoon. They also explain Hughes's use of Trickster folklore and violence in the sequence.

When Hughes gave personal readings of *Crow* poems in the seventies, he introduced them by explaining the master plan of his folktale narrative—a plan that unfortunately has never been published with the trade editions. Crow is the indestructible bird that survives even if it must eat battlefield corpses. In Celtic mythology Crow is associated both with the healing powers of Bran and the destructive powers of the war goddess Morrigu; these associations suggest that its functions are limited to the unvarying physical round of birth, survival, and death. Hughes drew from this tradition, adding the optimism of Trickster folklore material and the belief that Crow does have the power to transcend this destructive round by destroying his defensive ego in "Truth Kills Everybody" and forging an inner spiritual bond with his creator, nature. Crow does explode his "ego-shell" in the poem, but he handles the experience poorly and survives as "a Crow of more fragments, more precariously glued together, more vulnerable" ("Reply"). The incomplete sequence terminates well before Crow unites with nature, his bride.

The unpublished master plan of the *Crow* epic folktale can be summarized from reliable sources.[26] It begins when God has a persistent nightmare where a Voice and a Hand grab him, whisk him through space, plow the earth with him, and toss him back to heaven. At the same time Man (recounted in the uncollected "Crow's Song About God"[27]) sits exhausted and equally abused at the gate of heaven, ready to ask God to take back life. God refuses Man's request and the nightmare Voice mocks him. God challenges the nightmare to do better, and it creates Crow. Not considering this puny bird much of a competitor, God shows him around his creation and tests him by means of various ordeals. Crow not only survives, but begins tinkering with God's creation. He develops a bit of a conscience and begins to rebel and experiment on his own, with his usual combination of unflappable indomitability, grotesque humor, and mischievousness.

Crow was to succeed at the end of his journey after an encounter with an ogress at a river bank. The ogress refuses to let Crow cross the river unless he carries her on his back. As Crow carries his burden across the river, the ogress asks him seven puzzling questions about love. He sinks deeper into the water with each wrong answer, and his burden lightens with each correct answer. Psychologically speaking, the ogress forces him to attend to the burden of his psyche's confused, fragmented attitudes toward love and nature. As in many folktales, the ogress would probably transform herself into Crow's lovely bride Nature once he healed his psyche and found all seven right answers. "The Lovepet" in the American edition was Crow's answer to the question "Was it an animal? Was it a bird? Was it an insect? Was it a fish?" To the query "Who paid most, him or her?" Crow answered with "Lovesong." The *Cave Birds* poem "Bride and groom lie hidden for three days" was originally to have been Crow's correct answer to the question "Who gives most, him or her?"

Hughes stated that the objective of Crow's quest was to forge a "spirit link with his creator." "It is an inner link" that Crow regularly fails to create because he encounters "his own creator, God's nameless hidden prisoner . . . repeatedly but always in some unrecognizable form." These failed encounters occur in part because Crow's "ego-shell" projects his preconceptions on "the thing he seeks to unite himself with," and in part because the God who introduces Crow to his world is "the man-created, broken-down, corrupt despot of a ramshackle religion" ("Reply").[28]

The fear-and-projection motif of *Wodwo* also explains much of the Crow narrative. Once again the defensive ego, split from its nonlogical resources, becomes acculturated in the Protestant ethic to emphasizing rational analysis and placing taboos on the instincts. The nonlogical resources become repressed, then demonized, and finally projected outward in surreal distortions. Instead of forging the "spirit confidence" with his creator that Hughes spoke of in the Nicholson review, Crow soon begins to fear nature—as did the central persona in parts 1 and 2 of *Wodwo*—and spends his time fighting his own delusions and distortions of nature throughout his adventures. The uncollected "Crow the Just"[29] reveals just how much Crow is unable to destroy his own defensive ego, and how much he fights his own fears, desires, and attachments to a purely physical world of blackness and decay much like that in the *Sidpa Bardo*:

> Crow jeered at—only his own death.
> Crow spat at—only his own death.
> He spread rumors—only about his own death.
> He robbed—only his own death.
> He knocked down and kicked—only his own death.
> He vowed revenge—only on his own death.
> He tricked—only his own death.
> He murdered—only his own death.
> He ate—only his own death.
>
> This is how he kept his conscience so pure
> He was black
>
> (Blacker
>
> Than the eyepupils
>
> of the gunbarrels.)

Crow's "Lineage" begins with "Scream," the cry of animal consciousness, which soon begets "Eye," which begets "Fear." The eye of rational consciousness severs Crow's innate spiritual bond with nature. Even as a child Crow flees from nature: in "Crow and Mama" he recapitulates Western civilization's flight from a spiritual unity with nature into the defensive armor of machines—from automobiles to airplanes to rockets. Soon his repressed nonrational psychic energies appear in aggressive projections in "The Black Beast." Though Crow hides in its (his own) bed and sits in its (his own) chair, he prefers obsessive analysis of the external space he severed from himself rather than the recognition that the Black Beast is his own self imprisoned in his appetites and defensive ego. The imagery of blackness that recurs throughout the sequence recalls the unenlightened psyche's fears and attachments to the purely physical in the *Sidpa Bardo*.

Yet Crow is persistent and indomitable, and at this point the optimism of Trickster literature enters. Whether he is called Maui among Polynesians; B'rer Rabbit among black American slaves; Bamapama among Australian Aborigines; Spider among Africans; Gilgamesh among ancient Mesopotamians; Hercules and Mercury among ancient Greeks; or Coyote, Raven, Mink, Hare, Nanabozho, and countless other names among North American Indians, Trickster has always symbolized the optimism of a rudimentary stage of civilization. Most ethnologists, mythologists, and psychologists who have surveyed Trickster literature agree with Paul Radin that Trickster tales originally embodied the primordial urge of humans to express and develop themselves in an early world that did not differentiate between the animal, human, and divine realms. Trickster's most distinguishing traits—a perplexing mix of cunning, amoral wandering, hunger, sexuality, and lack of self-consciousness—reveal him as a creation of the needs of humans in the infancy of civilizations. As these civilizations developed, more sophisticated raconteurs rearranged the episodes and altered the focus to satirize Trickster's foibles or to assimilate his favorable traits into a culture-hero pattern.[30] Like Wile E. Coyote of the Warner Brothers Roadrunner cartoons (Coyote is the Trickster hero of the California Yokut Indians), the sly indomitability and phallic hardihood of Trickster convey the promise of differentiation into a more complex, socialized being.

After viewing Leonard Baskin's crow engravings in 1963 and then writing a review in 1965 of two folklore volumes by John Greenway that contained Trickster material,[31] Hughes rekindled a long-standing interest in Trickster narratives and began writing Crow poems. Later he stated that his purpose was to embody the "genetic potential" and "optimism of the sperm, still struggling joyfully along after 150 million years . . . learning a little but not much, from every rebuff, in the evolutionary way turning everything to his advantage, or trying to, being nothing really but a total commitment to salvaging life against all the odds, perpetuating life, renewing the opportunities for all the energies of life, at any cost." Crow was to progress by ultimately breaking through his "ego-shell" and losing his selfhood by "los[ing] himself in that spirit-link with his creator" ("Reply"). In essence Hughes en-

visioned *Wodwo*'s "single adventure" once again, from the flip side—
inherited genetic potential instead of inherited genetic aggression. The Crow
sequence commenced with the belief that Crow could conquer his fears and
his ego-attachment to a black world of desire and decay and finally recognize nature's splendor.
But Crow's gains are small in the poems Hughes did complete from the
first two-thirds of the sequence. When Crow begins to recognize that his
appetitive body limits his growth, and receives the dim inkling that he himself is the author of his actions, the first sensation of freedom leaves him par-
alyzed with fear. In "Crow Sickened" he finds himself

> Unwinding the world like a ball of wool
> Found the last end tied round his own finger.
>
> Decided to get death, but whatever
> Walked into his ambush
> Was always his own body.

When Blake in *Jerusalem* (plate 77) asks the reader to wind the golden
string into a ball, he suggests that it will lead to the freedom-filled Heaven's
Gate of an awakened creative imagination. But at the end of "Crow Sickened" Crow maims himself after experiencing fear so great that "His eyes
sealed up with shock, refusing to see." Crow is unable to transcend his appetites and regularly short-circuits his potential to grow.
    Throughout his adventures Crow sees mainly with the eyes of Blake's
single vision—the eyes of a passive scientific objectivity that ingests facts
and separates perceiving subject from objective data. Hughes follows
Blake's critique of empiricism as he shows that such eyes impede Crow's
awakening to a sense of the human self as the active organizer of experience.
In "The Door" Hughes suggests that the "eye's pupil" is itself a door that
has the potential to see beyond "the world's earthen wall." Most of the time,
however, Crow sees the black world of decay on the *Sidpa Bardo* side of the
wall.
    When Crow sees with single vision things stand in factual isolation and
disorganization in "Crow Alights." In "Crow Hears Fate Knock at the
Door," Crow perceives with empirical eyes that view nature as an "infinite
engine" broken into mechanical parts—"assembly, repairs and mainte-
nance." These eyes encourage a knee-jerk utilitarian satisfying of appetites.
In "Crow Tyrannosaurus" he stabs a grub with a "trapsprung" head, and the
world weeps at the separation between perceiving subject and distanced ob-

ject, as is often the case in Blake. When Crow meets the serpent in "A Horrible Religious Error," he converts this powerful pre-Christian agent of transformation and growth into a utilitarian relationship. After he "peered" at
the snake, he "Beat the hell out of it, and ate it." The birds of "Crow and the
Birds" have freedom to soar, but Crow remains "spraddled head-down in
the beach-garbage, guzzling a dropped ice-cream."

The grotesque connotations of words like "spraddled" and "guzzling" release the reader's buried instinctual life and balance Crow's empirically neutral "seeing" and "looking" and "peering." Crow's language is appropriate
for one who acts from the gut, the appetites. Hughes consciously chose a
rough, gritty, "super-ugly language" (Faas 1, 208) that would counter the
felicities of the Queen's English and probe the animal music at the base of
human volition. Verbs such as "blasted," "charred," "chopped," "crammed,"
"grabbed," "scorched," "screeched," "slammed," "squashed," and "vomited"
expose Crow's penchant for blunt, knee-jerk gratification and his inability
to control his instinctual life.

Crow becomes acculturated to a violent world at his birth: as he
"smashed into the rubbish of the ground" in "A Kill," Crow uttered "a
bowel-emptying cry which was his roots tearing out / Of the bedrock
atom." Neither Crow nor the universe created by his God exercises moderation and self-control. Verbals such as "belching," "blasting," "bulging," "jab-
bering," "racking," "rending," "screaming," "smoking," and "swivelling"
expose the violence in contemporary society.

Because Crow habitually perceives with empirical eyes, he limits his
power of perception to the defensive fort of an ego that wants only facts and
logic, but paradoxically leaves the repressed appetites in control of volition.
Hughes in "Crow's Last Stand" suggests that Crow creates his own obstacle
by trusting his limited empirical vision. This misplaced trust leads him to
fight a losing battle in the manner of Custer at Little Big Horn. Buddha in
his Fire Sermon at Benares counselled his followers to withdraw from the
fires of the purely physical world because they ignite the appetites, but the
one "obstacle" impeding Crow is his "eye-pupil, in the tower of its scorched
fort"—imprisoned in his burning desires.

Yet Trickster's hardheaded optimism primes him for survival no matter
how many errors he makes. In the Winnebago sequence recounted in Paul
Radin's *The Trickster,* Trickster survives with pluck and cunning no matter
how often he buffoonishly punishes his unwatchful anus by stabbing it with
a red hot poker; no matter how ignorant he is of the proper arrangement of
penis and testicles; and no matter how unperceptive he is of nature when
other animals dupe him, when he tries to slake his hunger by capturing the

reflection of plums in the water, or when he joins the celebration of the flies by imprisoning his head in an elk's skull. Trickster does acquire a minimal consciousness of self in the process, but his late ascent to the status of culture hero and demiurge at the end of the sequence is definitely the recension of raconteurs creating from a more sophisticated cultural vantage point. As John Greenway noted, Indians listening to the Trickster narrative would experience cathartic laughter at the breaking of tribal taboos and the general stupidity of Trickster, while at every moment recognizing that such conduct in themselves would prove counterproductive to survival and draw severe tribal censure.[32]

Crow's pluckish indomitability is nowhere more evident than in "Crow's Fall," where he saves face by concocting an explanation no one can disprove. His quixotic attempt to defeat the sun leaves him charred black, but his real fall lies in his slick use of rationalization to cover his embarrassment. This endears him to readers, most of whom have done likewise at some inglorious past moment. Similarly Crow in "Crow's Theology" uses logical fallacies to prove that, though God countenances the existence of evil in the world, he loves Crow. Crow seems aware of the inferiority of language to real-life event and appears impervious—unlike humans—to being duped by words in "A Disaster" and "The Battle of Osfrontalis." Here he has the animal savvy to be the less deceived. But when his bravado gets the best of him in "Crow Goes Hunting" and he uses words in a shape-changing battle with nature, he learns just how superior nature is to language, leaving him suitably agape, "Speechless with admiration."

At times Crow has the Trickster-like resourcefulness of an Old Testament Jacob in his struggles with Laban, though Crow's interference with nature is more profound and never does win him a bride. In "Crow Improvises" and "Magical Dangers," nature seems to contain so much repressed voltage as to annihilate him cartoonishly each time he tries to transform it. Death-inflicting jolts from nature's demonized power circuit raise Crow to a dim sense of self-consciousness ("A hair's breath out of the world") after a surfeit of laughter in "Crow's Battle Fury." Here, as when Cuchulain entered his chariot in book 9 of *The Táin* with a rage so strong its energy illumined his head, Crow's anger propels him to distance himself from his pain, and with this determined detachment "he comes forward a step" in self-consciousness.

A number of *Crow* poems—especially "Criminal Ballad" and "In Laughter"—combine laughter with violence. This unusual combination may create misconceptions. Hughes carefully distinguished the laughter in Trickster literature as essential to the optimism and creative joy of cultures at

nascent stages, as opposed to the black comedy of cultures at dead-end
stages, when their metaphysical beliefs have disintegrated ("Reply"). One
could go further and say that the laughter of Trickster literature and *Crow* is
an intelligent response to dread; it concerns surviving irresolvable incongrui-
ties and the crushing ambivalence of the unsponsored human situation. The
guilt for the anonymity of death caused by machines settles over everyone,
but laughter helps survival instincts to combat despair. Crow is always intelligent enough to survive.

Crow's intelligence does have severe limits, however, and his attempts
to interfere with creation are often ineffectual, exposing the obtuseness of
his jury-rigged practical solutions, however well intended. Crow cannot
heal the metaphysical rent in the fabric of God's relation to humans
in "Crow Blacker than Ever"; he can only manipulate by switching parts in
an ad hoc fashion. When Crow attempts the ancient ritual of eating the
god in "Crow Communes," he becomes only a "Half-illumined" adept of
sacred mysteries. His limited grasp of creation combines with the
playfulness of Trickster in ways that make his imperviousness to the rid-
dles of philosophy and religion an asset to his thick-skinned survival
instincts.

The limitations of Crow's intelligence surface especially when one considers Hughes's use of the nonrealistic fantasy fabric of Trickster narratives. In
a 1975 public reading, Hughes stated that Crow's "universe is one in which
all history is happening simultaneously."[33] Crow has the freedom to sample
and learn from all of earth's past cultures. But "like a leopard," Hughes's
tag for the Dionysian id in the *Wodwo* stories "The Rain Horse" and "The
Suitor," Crow in "Crowego" gazes greedily into "a fat land" to fuel his libido
with stories of the warrior heroes Ulysses, Hercules, and Beowulf.

Therapeutic and Satiric Violence   While the tragicomic
humor of Crow's exploits may endear him to the reader, the poems suggest
that Hughes also hopes to effect a serious emotional and intellectual cathar-
sis through the violence that often attends Crow's mischief. "Conjuring in
Heaven" and "Crow's Song of Himself" present Crow as an indestructible
part of creation—as indestructible as matter itself—that no amount of violence can annihilate. He believes he is "stronger than death" in "Examination at the Womb Door," but here he chooses to enter the *Sidpa Bardo*
round of reincarnation and enchainment to the appetites that Buddhist adepts are specifically exhorted to avoid—a world where delusions and violence occur with regularity (*Book of the Dead*, 175–88).

Hughes hopes that the violence of *Crow* activates compensatory powers in the reader's psyche. One can temporarily free the neurotic by using the right fantasy to activate repressed energies in the psyche. When these repressed energies are acknowledged and welcomed into conscious life, the psyche heals itself and personality growth once again becomes possible. Hence the violence in *Crow*, a literary fantasy, can help the reader to fashion his or her own mandala of psychic wholeness and personality integration. Writing on this subject in 1970, the year the first trade edition of *Crow* was published, Hughes stated that it is "the basis of Freud's whole therapeutic technique that the right fantasy can free the neurotic, temporarily at least, from his neurosis. . . . Once the fantasy has made connection with the demon and given him a role, the person feels cured" ("Myth 1," 58). Hughes believes that humans today are "dreaming a perpetual massacre" because their world of "rational scepticism" demonizes their split-off id (Faas 1, 198–99); one purpose of the violence of *Crow* is to release this demonized energy in the reader and bring it to consciousness, thereby fostering personality integration.

A great deal of the violence in *Crow* derives from Hughes's critique of the utilitarian science and sexual taboos of the Protestant ethos. Nature crackles with supercharged energy in *Crow* because it is the construct of what Hughes on the Claddagh Records dust-jacket of *Crow* called "the man-created, broken-down, corrupt despot of a ramshackle religion. . . . [who] accompanies Crow through the world, in many guises, mis-teaching, deluding, tempting, opposing and at every point trying to discourage or destroy him." The God of *Crow* operates his universe by means of Newtonian machine logic, abstract concepts, and sexual taboos. This acculturates the inhabitants of his creation to overdevelop reason, split it off from the rest of the psyche, and repress all else until nature itself becomes demonized.

Crow is not responsible for the world he is born into. His gestation in "A Kill" acclimates him to violence: "Flogged lame with legs / Shot through the head with balled brains / Shot blind with eyes." It is no wonder everything goes black when he hears the faint cry " 'It's a boy!' " He soon tries to flee his mother by creating the surrogate security of machines in "Crow and Mama," and near the end of his adventures he remains in flight from the sea of creative potential in "Crow and the Sea," though by then he has a dim presentiment that he is "crucified" to this world.

Crow's acculturation to violence continues with "Crow's First Lesson." God instructs Crow by teaching him the abstract concept, not the real experience. As God reiterates the command " 'Say, love,' " Crow forcibly represses his instinctual life, symbolized in the poem by the downward zoom of predatory animals. By the poem's end man and woman struggle in obvious discord. In "A Childish Prank" and "Crow Communes" God snores: he is a deistic Nobodaddy who absconds after creating a clockwork universe. Crow's playfully ad hoc attempts at rectifying creation only underscore his inability to comprehend life at any level beyond the brute physical. While God snores, Crow in "A Childish Prank" decides to give Man and Woman interdependent sexual organs; this solution not only fails to resolve the problem of granting humans souls, but reduces their interactions to a cave man ethic.

God cannot resolve the problem of how to relate the world of flesh and sex to his lordly domain; he grimaces with disgust at the serpent's intermediary agency in "A Horrible Religious Error" and turns his back on creation in "Crow Blacker than Ever," leaving Crow to rig a purely physical solution that becomes gangrenous. Meanwhile Crow, a willing pupil absorbing the rules of this clockwork empirical world, flees from nature's cyclic changes with great regularity, "cheered by the sound of his foot and its echo / And by the watch on his wrist" in "Oedipus Crow."

"Apple Tragedy" revises the Fall from grace and expulsion from Eden by splitting the inner spiritual unity of nature into "a new game" of self-conscious manipulation in a way that suits the Protestant ethos of Crow's God. Through the invention of language a new awareness of self quickly deteriorates to an intoxicating self-aggrandizement. God instructs Adam, Eve, and the serpent in the utilitarian manipulation of the environment, creating cider from the apples of Eden. A bathetic melodrama ensues: functioning like Freud's superego, the serpent ponders the social implications of this new situation and later tries to explain it. Eve satisfies her id and then uses language to repress the serpent's explanation. Adam, his ego crushed, gets drunk and becomes suicidal. God may be "well pleased" at his creation, but the deep division brings chaotically fragmented psyches and much self-indulgence. By appealing to rational consciousness and considering nature in utilitarian ways, God promotes violence.

For Hughes, the abstract science and mathematics of Western civilization since the seventeenth century are the products of an overdeveloped, split-off rational component that distrusts and represses the instinctual. Crow observes the world wars that ensue in "Crow's Account of the Battle." The Freudian repetition-compulsion urge that Hughes used in "Scapegoats and Rabies" (*Wodwo*) returns as cartridges explode "as planned" from trigger fingers programmed according to "excitement and orders." An eerie innocence prevails as machine weaponry distances soldiers and keeps their eyes "unhurt"—unbranded because they never see the bloodied bodies at close hand:

> The bullets pursued their courses
> Through clods of stone, earth and skin,
> Through intestines, pocket-books, brains, hair, teeth
> According to Universal laws
> And mouths cried "Mamma"
> From sudden traps of calculus,
> Theorems wrenched men in two,
>
> . . . . .
>
> Reality was giving its lesson,
> Its mishmash of scripture and physics,
> With here, brains in hands, for example,
> And there, legs in a treetop.

The Protestant God of *Crow* is the originator of this "mishmash of scripture and physics"; the consequence is a neutral machine logic that permeates his creation. Humans acquiesce in anesthetized unconcern to the devaluation of pain and the numbing of human sympathy. Today violence occurs "too easily / With too like no consequences."

"Crow's Account of St. George" presents in miniature the entire *Bardo* fear-and-projection motif. St. George develops his powers of analysis to the point of obsession with numbers and the vacuum of space. Meanwhile the nonrational portions of his psyche, repressed to the point of demonization, rear up in ever more menacing projections—from sharklike demon to lizard-eyed bird-head to a huge hairball with pincers and fangs. As St. George lifts a chair in defense, "fear lifts him" into ever more psychotic delusions and violent responses. Only after he hacks everything in sight with a sword does he realize that he has killed his wife and children.

If Crow were reciting the account of St. George, as the poem title seems to indicate, and exposing the hidden violence beneath the well-established Christian myth, then he would ostensibly experience a therapeutic release of repressed violence, grow in consciousness of self, and step significantly closer to marriage with his bride. Yet still to come are episodes where Crow attacks the sun ("Crow's Fall"), the serpent ("A Horrible Religious Error"), the two thieves at the Crucifixion ("Crow's Song of Himself"), and stone itself ("Crow and Stone"). At times the poem titles suggest a level of comprehension and dramatic irony that author and reader may have attained, but not Crow. Poem titles where Crow himself appears to narrate reveal an unresolved problem in point of view.

The violence of *Crow* is not gratuitous, for in each case Crow acts violently in response to violent attacks from God (as in "Crow's Song of Himself"), or because he becomes acculturated to the repressed violence of the Protestant "mishmash of scripture and physics." Many *Crow* poems ("The Black Beast," "Crow's Fall," "Crow Sickened," and "Crow and Stone") follow *Bardo* logic to exhibit Crow maiming himself by attacking projections of his own fears. Late in the sequence Crow battles stone, the ontological first principle of existence in many cultures, and alchemical *lapis,* symbol of the integrated self (Jung 13:101). Crow still has not learned how to embrace nature, his bride.

How much does Crow progress? In "Crow Tyrannosaurus" he experiences a faint glimmer of social responsibility as he contemplates becoming a savior, but he decides to feed his appetites rather than "become the light." He often means well in his myopic attempts to rectify creation ("Crow Blacker than Ever"), and he occasionally experiences guilt at his misguided tinkering ("Crow's First Lesson"). He develops some dim presentiment that pain exists in others in "Crow on the Beach," and he accuses himself of causing some of this pain in "Crow's Nerve Fails." In "Crow Frowns" he fails to find an essence beyond himself that defines his existence. Yet poems placed very late in the sequence— "Crow Sickened," "Crow's Last Stand," and "Crow and Stone"—indicate that Crow's fears, egotism, and aggressive behavior continue. Crow may advance "a step" in "Crow's Battle Fury," but the advance in consciousness as a reflex of pain does not enhance his potential to become whole and win his bride. Like St. George, he now lives with "His shattered brains covered with a steel cowl."

Interpreting "Truth Kills Everybody" is critical for defining the extent of Crow's progress toward his bride. Hughes has discussed this poem on two separate occasions, both times emphasizing four points: (1) that to attain his bride, his inner "spirit-link with his creator," Crow must explode his "ego-shell"; (2) that he does annihilate his ego at the end of the poem; but (3) that his use of force is wrong and results in immediate regression to a more vulnerable, fragmented creature; and yet (4) that this explosion constitutes his greatest step forward in his quest.[34]

"Truth Kills Everybody," a variation on Menelaos's battle with the shapeshifting Proteus to gain secret knowledge in book 4 of the *Odyssey,* takes place on a psychological plane. Here Crow must battle with his own menacing projections to gain the secret knowledge that he is the creator of his own values. His embattled ego defends itself with ever more fearsome delusions, including "The aesophagus of a staring shark," "a naked powerline, 2000 volts," and "The ankle of a rising, fiery angel." Crow musters so much force to capture, hold, and vanquish these projections that he actually learns little from the ordeal. His last appearance in the sequence, in "King of Carrion," occurs in a world of temporal decay; he has not yet freed himself from the self-imposed prison of the *Sidpa Bardo*. Crow's struggle to explode the defense mechanisms of his inadequate ego is compounded by his acculturation to the violent universe of his God. In this environment the feminine can barely manage to survive: she appears in "Crow's Undersong" as a frightened, easily bruised creature that nevertheless is the impulse behind all the civilizing tendencies in humans. When Crow attempts to sing about his vision of his bride in "Crow Tries the Media," he desires to cleanse his thoughts and "sing to her soul simply." But the glut of consumer goods, materialism, and weaponry pollute his vision. Singing becomes impossible when "this tank had been parked on his voice," "Manhattan weighed on his eyelid," and "His tongue moved like a poisoned estuary."

Glimpse   Crow's defensive ego and his acculturation to the abstract science and religious taboos of his Protestant God conspire to keep him in the *Sidpa Bardo* world of satisfying his appetites. If he could wipe his vision clean of these things, he could attain the oneness with the plenitude of nature that the central persona of part 3 of *Wodwo* attained in "Skylarks," "Gnat-Psalm," and "Full Moon and Little Frieda." In the *Sidpa Bardo* the initiate is exhorted to wipe away all traces of the phenomenal world from the karmic mirror of memory to attain the Clear Light of liberation (*Book of the Dead*, 166–69). In "Crow's Vanity" Crow looks into the "evil mirror" but cannot cleanse his polluted vision. As in "Crow Tries the Media," the skyscrapers and hanging gardens, the materialistic bric-a-brac of civilizations, obscure his vision. Without this glut of objects he would fare no better, however, until he annihilated his defensive ego, for he looks into the mirror for the wrong reason—"For a glimpse of the usual grinning face."

The closest Crow comes to attaining his bride in the incomplete sequence is "Glimpse." For a brief moment, before his analytic, categorizing reason overtakes his gaze, Crow transcends his separateness and sings silently, like an Oriental Whitman, and with a visionary stare like the "staring angels" of "Pibroch" (*Wodwo*). The leaf's edge has momentarily guillotined his fragmented ego's faith in language, and a sense of unity with the allness of nature suddenly leaks through in the "god's head instantly substituted." To experience a "god's head" is to feel unified with all of creation, as if the perceiving self were its creator. This is what happened to the persona of *Wodwo* in section 2 of "Song of a Rat" when he forced "the rat's head down into godhead" and transcended the phenomenal world. Sustaining his own godhead gaze would lead Crow to "a new divinity" and union with his bride.

Crow is Hughes's most well-known work, probably because its originality of conception and faith in survival balance its deep pathos and awareness of the cosmic loneliness of the human condition. The optimism of Trickster is tempered in the flames of struggle and risk. The reader, who laughs from the more knowing perspective that the built-in dramatic irony generously allows, learns to cry a little too, for Crow is every human being cheerily stumbling through life, looking for direction from the roadmaps of a bogus, exhausted culture. But occasionally flying. Even in its incomplete state *Crow* is a majestic success of creative insight and imaginative reach. It so brilliantly defines the condition of the postwar West that it belongs in the select group of works worthy of Nobel Prize scrutiny. It would be the crowning achievement of an illustrious career should Hughes finish it.

Chapter Four

Dissolution and Rebirth: *Gaudete* and *Cave Birds*

Reconciliation to the Goddess: *Gaudete*

As with Dylan Thomas, the conviction that impelled Hughes's poetry in the late sixties and early seventies concerned nature's imperative to grow or be sundered as a dead branch from the evolutionary tree. As a writer learned in structuralist psychology (Jung), anthropology (Lévi-Strauss), and religion (Eliade), Hughes recognized that growth involved organizing the psyche into time-tested mythic patterns of death and rebirth. While writing the gritty, "super-ugly" language of the *Crow* poems in 1967–68, Hughes also completed an adaptation of *Seneca's Oedipus,* a text that required an ability to convey in concise phrases human passions that are deep, urgent, and as overwhelming as the tramplings of lathered horses. When Hughes developed his *Orghast* mythology in Iran in 1971, he created a new language that attempted to mime the animal music that originates deep in the human subconscious, where volition first evolved language. In all three texts rebirth necessitates reconnecting oneself with nonrational resources: intuition, emotion, feeling, and instinct.

This rebirth pattern continues in *Gaudete* (1977). A small, aged Irishman with a "rough-snagged shillelagh" of a voice takes the Reverend Nicholas Lumb, a celibate Anglican clergyman, to a strange cave at the beginning of the narrative. Lumb's speechlessness when asked to revive the aboriginal, wolf-skinned Welsh muse Cerridwen is no accident: he cannot speak because he has lost all connection with the nonrational portions of his psyche. Demonized, these energies—as in *Wodwo* and *Crow*—appear in nightmarish projections, in this case of a North England industrial town whose streets seem littered with corpses "piled in heaps," "strewn in tangles," and lumped into mass graves. Like the Parzival of the epigraph, Lumb cannot aid others outside himself because he is not at peace within himself. Parzival shrank from Anfortas's wound just as Lumb shrinks from Cerridwen: neither is capable of selfless love early in the quest, and this lack of sympathy reveals a psychological flaw, a need for rebirth.

To heal Lumb's psyche Hughes in the central narrative of *Gaudete* explores a Celtic rebirth pattern that contains motifs shared with the ancient death-and-rebirth ordeals of Hercules, Attis, Dionysus, and Osiris. Originally written as screenplay in 1964, but never used, Hughes revised *Gaudete* in 1971–72, translating dialogue and camera directions into a riveting, supercharged prose-poetry intended to promote rebirth in the reader by activating repressed energies. He bolstered the mythic machinery of his central narrative with the mana power of his language, creating what he described as a "headlong narrative . . . like a Kleist story that would go from beginning to end in some forceful way pushing the reader through some kind of tunnel while being written in the kind of verse that would stop you dead at every moment" (Faas 2, 214). The "Epilogue" poems, written in 1975, indicate that the resolution of *Gaudete* concerns integrating the liberated instinctual energies with the rational in the reader's psyche to create a mandala of wholeness as the healed Lumb gropes his way toward a reaffirmation of nature's powers.

The result of this healing process, the 45 simple, cryptic lyrics addressed to the goddess of nature in the "Epilogue," attests to the unaccommodated soul's capacity to achieve a personal acceptance of mortality, and to recognize the necessity for the revitalizing power of love directed beyond the self. In their portrayal of the tormented spirit with austere verbal economy, unsparing candor, emotional nuance, and psychological resonance, these poems contain some of the most elegant verse ever written in the English language. Unlike "Crow Tries the Media" and "Crow's Undersong," where he bemoaned modern science's lack of reverence for the feminine, Hughes in the *Gaudete* "Epilogue" conveys a deep reverence for the feminine from a positive viewpoint—a perspective missing in his poetry since *The Hawk in the Rain.*

In the "argument" prefacing *Gaudete,* Hughes explains that "elemental spirits" abduct the real Lumb and leave a loglike changeling who "proceeds to interpret the job of ministering the Gospel of love in his own log-like way." The changeling motif introduces the reader to the psychological pattern of *Gaudete.* A staple of Celtic folktales concerned with the *daoine sidhe,* or "fairy people," the changeling motif can convey a state of temporary demonic possession as well as permanent physical deformity, according to Evans-Wentz, and fairyland, the "other world" where the "elemental spirits" have taken the real Lumb, may be a convenient label for a temporary state of supernormal consciousness as well as an imagined place. Evans-Wentz believes that these motifs of temporary abduction or lapses into abnormal behavior followed by a return to normalcy often express the psychological residue of ancient Celtic rebirth beliefs.[1]

The distinction between the real Lumb and his changeling, loglike double should not cause confusion once one realizes that the real Lumb appears only in the "Prologue" and the three-page interlude after the central narrative. Throughout 150 pages of supercharged prose-poetry in the central narrative, the loglike double's sexual escapades comprise a dream that compensates for the one-sided rationalism of the real Lumb and heals his fragmented psyche. In the central narrative dreamlike distortions occur in the loglike Lumb's minimal self-awareness and his hopelessly exaggerated and compulsive phallic escapades; in the abnormal reactions to sexuality by Westlake, Estridge, and Dunworth; in the surreal stretching out and foreshortening of time; in the curiously sound-deadened lack of direct conversation and a corresponding heightening of visual details; in the sensuality of music that rises to a crescendo of tribal orgy in the Women's Institute meeting; and in the use of characters in the central narrative to represent fragmented portions of the real Lumb's psyche (Scigaj, 168ff.). The real Lumb's poems, the spiritual record of healing and revitalizing the psyche, comprise the "Epilogue."

Prologue Dissolution   The real Lumb is not his normal self; in the first pages of the "Prologue" his psyche splits into fragments and demonic projections of repressed energies pour out. The central events of the "Prologue," the oak-tree flogging and the bath in the white bull's blood, are both remnants of ancient rituals that announce the rebirth motif as central to understanding the main narrative. In *The White Goddess* Graves wrote that to claim oracular poetic knowledge the male aspirant must court the White Goddess of nature—one of whose incarnations is the wolf-skinned Welsh muse Cerridwen—in full knowledge of his own mortality. He must woo her sincerely and passionately, in full knowledge that though he may idealize her in her virginal aspect and love her in her erotic aspect, he will ultimately suffer death, a tribute exacted by her hag aspect. Yet the knowledge that all erotic enticements ultimately end in death can lead him to an acceptance of his mortality and to a transfiguring spiritual illumination (Graves, 388, 444–48).

Greeks, Norsemen, and Druids associated the oak tree—symbol of royalty, power, and oracular knowledge—with midsummer fertility orgies and sacrifices—the lover and hag aspects of the White Goddess. Greek myths especially related the oak with Hercules as "the green Zeus," wielder of the oak-club, leader of orgiastic fertility rites, and sacrificial victim whose flesh is eucharistically eaten (Graves, 132). Through choosing the oak tree and being flogged, Lumb initiates himself into Hercules' royal cycle of immersion in sensual renewal for the first half-year, followed by a sacrificial death in the second half. According to Graves, in one midsummer rite Hercules was bound to the lopped oak, flayed and otherwise mutilated, and then cut to pieces, with his blood sprinkled among all to promote vigor. Thus "Cerridwen abides [for] poetry began in the matriarchal age, and . . . no poet can hope to understand the nature of poetry unless he has had a vision of the Naked King crucified to the lopped oak" with frenzied dancers shouting death cries (Graves, 448).

Lumb's bath in the white bull's blood after having been shot in the head identifies him with sacrificial rites of Dionysus, Attis, and Osiris, all of whom were vegetation gods associated with the fertility of bulls. Frazer recounts one rite of the Phrygian Attis in which a bath in the blood of a sacrificial bull purified the initiate and granted him eternal life.[2] Hughes's modernized version, complete with a darkened slaughterhouse, winches, electrified clubs, and infernal laughter, announces surrealistically the main narrative's psychological pattern. In the main narrative bulls function as tags to remind one of the loglike Lumb's phallic powers and his cyclic lot as vegetation deity in a death and rebirth pattern. Hagen mates bulls through artificial insemination, Mrs. Holroyd sunbathes near her pastured bull, Holroyd saws the horns off a bull, Lumb jumps a fence "padded with bullock's hair" in the final chase scene, and curious bulls attend Lumb's death.

The Double in the Dream   The main narrative, comprising the events of the last day of the loglike double's ministry, can be understood as the attempt of the real Lumb's subconscious to heal him by reattaching him to the nonrational psychic resources symbolized in the escapades of his loglike double. In his study of the shadow or psychic double, Otto Rank concluded that the narcissistic ego creates a split-off psychic entity within the self as a defense mechanism to repress a fear of dissolution at death or at the moment of self-surrender in love. In literature the refusal to become involved with the cycle of love and death can appear as a fight with the split-off double that often ends in suicide.[3] Lumb, apparently celibate of his own volition, has been denying his potential to grow through losing himself in love. Involvement in the love cycle would also lead to a consciousness of the limitations of mortality, the tragic fruit of the cycle of earthly love. Lumb's rational ego suppresses this knowledge.

Jung interpreted the doppelgänger or double in dreams to be a manifestation of the archetype of the shadow, the darker instinctual energies in the

Self that include sexual urges as well as the driving survival strength of libidinal energy.[4] The compulsive eroticism of Lumb's double in the central narrative compensates for the extreme rationalism of the real Lumb's "normal" behavior. Readmitted to consciousness, the combination of rational ego and its unconscious libidinal resources produces a synthesis: the more mature Lumb who composes the "Epilogue" poems. The "Epilogue" lyrics indicate that Lumb has more than healed himself; he has learned to accept human mortality with a superfine clarity of vision and an emotional equilibrium wrung from arduous self-colloquy.

"Lumb" is an old West Yorkshire term for the ruined factory chimneys that still dot the valleys. The loglike double of the central narrative dream certainly possesses the phallic energy and power of a factory in his inexhaustible sexual labors. His association with the oak tree solidifies that power, for the Greeks and the Norse believed the oak attracted the thunderbolts of Zeus and Thor. Lumb's double's sexual power thunders and crackles throughout *Gaudete*. The idea that Lumb may be having an affair with his wife "ignites the whole tree" of Hagen's nerves with "an insane voltage" (33). The same thought "strikes Westlake like a thunderbolt" (76). The loglike Lumb wrestles with his own projected double in thunderous twilight (78, 81), and feels after his ritual mating, unmasking, and beating at the final Women's Institute meeting like an effigy hit by lightning: "His whole being is in fiery tatters. / He is whirling in blazing rags, like a blazing rag effigy" (149). The march of the cuckolded husbands from the Bridge Inn after they have decided to kill Lumb occurs in "the thunderish atmosphere of evening catastrophe" (144). Lumb sees the men approach the rectory at the same moment his psyche momentarily remembers, "with electric shock fright in his every hair," the blade in Felicity's back (151).

Rooted in Mud   The tree of the loglike Lumb's psyche is rooted in the earth's cycles and limitations. In the central narrative Hughes introduces Lumb against a background of willow trees, with a prominent "long sallow skull" that is "dark as oiled walnut" (25). After lovemaking with Pauline Hagen, his after-nearness makes her want to "press her face into the soil, into the moist mould, / And scream straight downward" (32). Like young dogs "Unable to squirm free from their torturing infinite dogginess," Lumb and Mrs. Davies copulate ecstatically on bags of Irish peat in her potting shed (93). Lumb's favorite reverie (49–51) is a vision of simple freedom into which he could escape and be one of millions of free humans, but he also feels a hot "power that beats up against him, beating at the soles of his feet." His consciousness is irrevocably connected to the urgent desires of his body and their rootedness in the earth's vegetative cycle:

> He knows the blood in his viens
> Is like heated petrol, as if it were stirring closer
> and closer to explosion,
> As if his whole body were a hot engine, growing hotter
> Connected to the world, which is out of control,
> And to the grass under his feet, the trees whose shadows
> reach for him.

Lumb tries to fix his attention on his reverie of freedom, but learns he is imprisoned in stony "mother-soil":

> Between the root in immovable earth
> And the coming and going leaf
> Stands the tree
> Of what he cannot alter.
> As his heart surges after his reverie, with lofty cries
> and lifting wingbeats
> Suddenly he comes against the old trees
> And feels the branches in his throat, and the leaves at
> his lips.
> He sees the grass
> And feels the wind pulse over his skin.
> He feels the hill he stands on, hunched, swelling,
> Piling through him, complete and permanent with stone,
> Filling his skull, squeezing his thoughts out from his
> eyes
> To fritter away across surfaces.

Lumb hopes to escape in the final chase scene by plugging "his energy appeal into the inexhaustible earth" (163) and by sinking his "nerves into the current" of a beech tree's "powerline" (156). But his erotic energy is borne only of the earth: it waxes and wanes like the sun's daily round, and spends itself toward a deathly end because driven by mortal flesh and mud.

The culture dominating this mud is sterile. It fails to offer Lumb any guidance, any pattern for self-development and self-control, because its values distance humans from communal contact. It worships technological devices that are efficient mechanisms for analysis and judgment, but not for human sympathy. Binoculars, cameras, telescopes, and gunsights with their hard circular lenses dominate and lead to cycles of repression and explosion. Lumb first appears in the central narrative on Hagen's land, seen through the "hardening lenses" of his binoculars, and eventually dies there of a single shot from Hagen's Mannlicher .318. The loglike Lumb is incapable of finding a way out of Hagen's ice-cold Viking efficiency: he "jigs like a puppet" in Hagen's gunsights (165) after having run in a circle on his land (161). Estridge's telescope distances him from his daughters and from passions he refuses to face; Dunworth's gun affirms his psychological impotence; Holroyd's saw wire relegates his gaze to a narrow pragmatism, and Garten's photograph produces mindless rage in the cuckolded males—a mechanical substitute for self-knowledge.

Trees signified earthly finitude as well as godly election in mythological lore, and the tree imagery in *Gaudete* certainly has its darker side, further defining the loglike Lumb's limits. The oak tree attracts the lightning bolts of Thor and Zeus and is also destroyed by them. In the tribal past humans were sacrificed to Thor and Odin under the oak.[5] When Lumb prays for a successful escape with Felicity, he leans upon an ash tree (52–53), which in Graves is the tree where the White Goddess exacts justice—death, the mortal lot of all lovers composed of flesh and mud (Graves, 57, 68, 198–99).

Lumb's Olympian sexual exploits, hopelessly exaggerated as they should be in the unreality of the central narrative dream, nevertheless revitalize the psyche of the real Lumb and perhaps that of the reader with the periodically necessary jolt of sexual energy. But unless lifted to consciousness to fertilize the imagination and liberate the spirit, the loglike Lumb's sexual energy merely spends itself in cycles of ignorance. In the chase scene, Hughes likens Lumb to a hurt stag (162), recollecting the Roman myth of the stag-god Cernunnos, a spirit who cannot help but become the prey in the hunt of a foredoomed temporal cycle (Sagar, 202–3).

The psyche of the "Prologue" Lumb is evidently so arid that he needs an overdose of the erotic to activate his repressed energies. The central narrative is replete with erotic imagery as claustral and cloying as the "bulging green landscape" that oppresses Westlake (71) and the oppression Jennifer feels at the "fulness of her breasts" (41). Erotic imagery of music and flowers fills every page. In his 1971 *Orghast* drama Hughes developed the kinship between music and the subconscious in humans, where chords and deep moods operate below the level of rational discrimination; he agreed with Lévi-Strauss's distinction in *The Raw and the Cooked* that musical themes operate subconsciously and make us aware of our "physiological rootedness" (Smith, 117–18). In *Gaudete* the connection of music with sensuality begins with Jennifer's frenetic piano sonata and ends in the frenzied tribal music of the final Women's Institute orgy (Scigaj, 177–79).

Flower imagery conveys a cloyingly sweet hothouse sensuality that approaches the funereal. Lumb is introduced amid rhododendrons (25), a flowering plant that Hughes elsewhere associates with the sterility of graveyards (*Elmet*, 87), and Maud flings Lumb's suitcase out of the automobile and into rhododendrons as she prevents his escape (97). From the "creamy masses of the hawthorn blossom" Westlake smells a "nauseous sweet aniseed scent, an over-richness" (71). Dense honeysuckle covers Felicity's cottage (117); outside his own home Westlake stalks Lumb among the "peeled-back gorges of his rose-blooms" after driving into "the lilac secretness of the drive's curve" (73–74); and "the nectars of the white lilac / And the purple and dark magenta lilac" help to incapacitate Dunworth and leave him "Like a moth pinned to a board" after he fails to shoot Lumb (88). Maud arranges "Wet lilac and apple" blossoms in Lumb's room, and later brings apple blossoms to the empty grave where "Gaudete" is chiseled on the black stone (62, 94). Apple blossom in particular is the flower of consummation with the White Goddess and rebirth in wisdom (Graves, 253–59). *Gaudete*, Latin for "rejoice," from a hymn in the 1592 *Piae Cantiones* (Sagar, 188), reinforces through Christian symbolism the psychological death and rebirth pattern that the cloyingly sweet flower imagery accents.

In a lesser poet these mythological accretions of tree, music, and flower imagery would appear as lifeless catalogues of arid learning, but the charged urgency of Hughes's amalgam of prose and poetry awakens readers to admissions of how undeniably rooted we all are to instinctual desires that demand periodic satisfaction. We have all participated in the sensual drowse of Lumb's "hooded heavy eyes" (87) and Mrs. Holroyd's sleepy, sensual contentment while sunbathing "like a plant" (59). Yet the men of the central narrative refuse to recognize their rootedness. They are preoccupied by their binoculars, telescopes, gunsights, and photographs, and suffer from the same repression of the instinctual and overemphasis upon the rational as does the real Lumb of the "Prologue." Ultimately, the repressed energy of the men, as in *Wodwo* and *Crow*, turns demonic and results in explosive rage at being cuckolded by the loglike Lumb.

The entire central narrative in one sense expresses the single moment when the real Lumb brings to consciousness the instinctual energy he has repressed. According to Jung, self-development occurs only when the conscious mind assimilates unconscious material that the psyche has wrestled with successfully (Jung 16:152). In alchemy Mercurius assists in such transformations: he represents both the lowest form of earthly matter and the imprisoned spirit to be liberated from matter (Jung 12:65, 281). Garten, a shrewd poacher who knows the physical landscape of the village better than anyone else and is first to comprehend the loglike Lumb's escapades through following his wet tire tracks (61), is the debased mercurial intermediary who forces a recognition that ultimately integrates the psyche of the real Lumb. As he develops his lurid photo at a chemist's (107), Garten follows the dual function of the alchemical Mercurius. He conveys souls to the underworld, for his circulation of the photo initiates the loglike Lumb's death. He is also a godly messenger who brings to the consciousness of the real Lumb, a half-aware spectator of his central narrative healing dream, irrefutable evidence of what he must have to restore his wholeness: a recognition of the periodic need to attend to his instinctual life.

The loglike Lumb lacks the self-awareness and imaginative capacity to raise himself above a compulsive indulgence in the physical. Hughes throughout his career has maintained that individuals need a highly developed imaginative life to recognize and organize their energies and to reconcile needs and desires with the outer world of possibilities and limits. For Hughes, "what affects a person's imagination affects their whole life" because "imagination . . . [is] the most essential piece of machinery we have if we are going to live the lives of human beings" ("Myth 1," 57). Hughes strongly believes that "outer world and inner world are interdependent at every moment," and that if our inner world remains undeveloped it becomes a tool of the appetites, then becomes demonized, and finally ends in "an inferno of depraved impulses and crazy explosions of embittered energy" incapable of cohering into an individual self ("Myth 2," 90–91). The Lumb of the central narrative is incapable of composing the "Epilogue" poems because he cannot extricate himself from his rootedness in the purely physical world of satisfying his instincts. He lacks sufficient introspection to control his physical desires. His fishing and cattleyard slurry daydreams, the two significant dream-within-a-dream sequences in the central narrative, define his limitations.

After the loglike Lumb flees Westlake's double-barreled twelve bore, he relaxes at the edge of a river to wash a facial wound. In the sun's blaze he daydreams of fishing in a boat with Felicity (77–83). He is angling to possess the state of felicity or bliss, but his dream tells him that he is really playing the part of a sex-obsessed brute, a hairy monkey, and suffocating Felicity. The loglike Lumb projects a true picture of himself in a second double, and the ensuing fight represents his own inability to organize his psyche. The image of the hands wrestling with each other (82) is a staple of Trickster literature that reveals an infant state of consciousness. Lumb is at war within himself, but lacks a well-developed imagination to bring his impulses into control and to muster sufficient self-awareness to grow. Though the loglike Lumb fends off the hairy second double and saves Felicity from abduction and drowning, the dream ends with his nearly drowning Felicity in his rain-sodden grasp.

Not long after this a sudden rush of guilt becomes a flash vision of hairy hands grabbing Lumb's steering wheel, causing him to stop his van at the side of a road. A dark wetness grips him, and suddenly he is being pushed through a cattleyard slurry with other animals (98–106). As the cattle bellow and men in oilskins jab at him in the rain, he sinks deep into mud and soon notices that all his parishioners are similarly encased in the mud of a crater. As he strains to extricate himself, he notices a woman with a "baboon beauty face" configured in a "crudely stitched patchwork" similarly struggling to free herself. As he helps her, she grips him hard and he suddenly sees himself somehow giving birth to her while her grip tightens. Men in oilskins finally pull him free, with Lumb and the baboon woman intertwined, screaming painfully. Just as suddenly Lumb appears back at his van on the side of the empty road.

This demonic parody of a rebirth motif indicates that Lumb is indeed too rooted in the mud of physical instinct to develop his imagination. He comprehends so little of his daydream's significance that four pages later in the text he stares at the gross stone carving of a woman splaying her vagina wide open (110). Lumb finds himself so attached to this crude artwork that he packs it "snugly among underclothes" into his getaway trunk—the only nonclothing object, except for his magical apparatus, that he believes worth keeping (135). Lumb has Trickster's lack of introspection combined with the trademark sexual obsessions of Trickster that Hughes purposely excised from his *Crow* poems.

Hughes identified the baboon allusion as the Egyptian Thoth in an interview, but cautioned against interpreting the rebirth motif of the cattleyard slurry daydream positively, for he also said that "in *Gaudete* the women are being put together in a mistaken, wrong and limited way"(Faas 2, 214). In the surreal context of the daydream the baboon woman is a demonic Thoth symbol, a parody of the Egyptian god of healing through knowledge and sacred speech.[6] Lumb's erotic designs limit his vision of the feminine to disfigured, distorted versions in the central narrative. The deformed rebirth repeats the rebirth motif in a minor key and foreshadows the successful rebirth of the revitalized Lumb in the "Epilogue."

The baboon woman also foreshadows the rebirth of a positive treatment of the feminine in Hughes's poetry from a biographical perspective, possibly signifying a reconciliation with the departed spirit of Sylvia Plath. A year before her death Plath in a BBC biographical essay spoke of retrieving a wooden carving of a baboon from the sea at age three as recompense for the sense of separation from nature she felt upon learning of the birth of a brother. As an adult Plath interpreted the discovery of the carving as an early sign of future poetic election and associated it with the ancient Thoth baboon of the Nile.[7] The stitchwork on the baboon woman's face possibly alludes to the demonic muses of the de Chirico painting from which Plath drew the title of her poem "The Disquieting Muses."

Reconciliation and Transcendence   Unlike his loglike double, the revitalized Lumb of the "Epilogue" is able to transform the demonic baboon woman of the central narrative into the transcendent Goddess, the creative muse, through the mana power of Hughes's poetry. The poems record the ardent self-colloquy, the agonized intellectual and emotional tussle through which Lumb is able to achieve this transformation. Lumb begins his self-colloquy in despondent withdrawal, with a keen sense of having had an inexcusably naive attitude toward women and having been the victim of automatic, knee-jerk responses to instinctual drives. The combination has already produced catastrophe. Initially he wonders what is the use of writing, for language, even the language of poetry, comes after the fact—often as a Kafkaesque rationalization for human inadequacies—whereas the physical impulse happens instantaneously, without reflection, and with unforgiving urgency.

The three-page interlude that opens the "Epilogue" reintroduces Lumb in an almost prelapsarian landscape on the west coast of Ireland, where remnants of Celtic rebirth myths still flower in oral tradition. Lumb whistles up an otter from the lough for three girls; this experience, told to a local priest, whistles up an ecstatic sense of participation in nature for all four. The interlude reminds one of the Thoth-like creative potential of language, the dazzle that refreshes perception and activates psychic energies, for the priest becomes carried away by the ability of language to render a sense of the miraculous within the everyday. Turning the page to the poetry, however, one soon recognizes that Lumb initially lacks any confidence in his abilities and in the power of language to refresh perceptions and renew energies.

The first two "Epilogue" poems[8] convey Lumb's sense that language articulates the "aftermath" of experience "sublimed into chat," but not the honest "cries," the "sacred shout" of joyous pain that Hughes spoke of in his introduction to Baskin's work. In poem #3 Lumb appears alienated from any involvement in the processes of nature; whenever "the blood jumps" he experiences only a soured despondency at instinctual demands as old as his birth and "the age of the earth." Poem #4 presents Lumb as stymied by the eternal dilemma of humans torn between conflicting, incompatible relationships with nature: the rational ego's utilitarian desire to appropriate nature for self-serving designs, making it "a useful-looking world, a thrilling weapon," and the demands of the instincts to conform to ancient physiological and psychological patterns of revitalization—to resuscitate Cerridwen in her cave.

Like the persona of the part 1 poems of *Wodwo*, Lumb at this point seems capable only of withdrawing his libido from any direct contact with nature. Ironic humor at his aimless lolling in the sun, like a vegetable, seems to be his most sanguine response (#4); otherwise he feels very uneasy at the imperfections and mortality that he shares with nature—the sun's dust or sapphire's flaw (#5). Like the force that drives nature's green fuse in Dylan Thomas's early poem, the fuse of the lark's energy "sizzles" in Lumb's ear, but he knows that, as in the *Wodwo* poem "Skylarks," this fuse is timed, the "prophecy" foreshadows the final "plummeting dead drop" of the skylarks, and those borne of the "swelling earth" do not "stay."

Many "Epilogue" poems that appear elliptical or puzzling introduce with care and concision basic mythological symbols as touchstones for the gradual resuscitation of Lumb's spirit. Poem #6 presents the mummified spirit of Lumb receiving an infusion of new life, a trickle of inspiriting energy, through Egyptian symbology. In Egyptian burials stone scarabs, symbols of the beetle god Khepera are buried with the deceased to foreshadow resurrection, for the beetle renews vitality. The complex symbol of the tree growing inward from the navel may refer to an infusion of vital blood, the awakening of the arterial tree, and hawks are associated with Horus, the self-renewing divine spirit.[9] Though at the level of consciousness Lumb may feel his despondency abating, he has not consented to the magnetic impulse of the Goddess, the anima spurring him to partake of temporal action. She beckons at the end of poem #6.

Poems #7 through #10 present Lumb's regret at having abused his emotional and instinctual inheritance. Because he is lacking in patience and unable to manage conflicting impulses, the apple of sexual experience (#7) arrives with the violence of electrocution (#9). Before he is able to control and direct these impulses his "legs, though, were already galloping to help / The woman who wore a split lopsided mask" (#10). Sadder but wiser now, he is no longer the unconscious dupe of a comedy.

Lumb's feelings for the Goddess oscillate widely in these early poems, as in his self-colloquy he tries to puzzle out his honest responses to the important question of why one should participate in a world where every action seems wrapped in "Error on error / Perfumed / With a ribbon of fury" (#8). Real tragedy has occurred in Lumb's life: "She fell into the earth / And I was devoured" (#11). Lumb feels all passion has been spent in regrettable episodes that occurred without sufficient reflection. The music of the Goddess's passions has devoured him, leaving him drained of emotion and purpose—an emptied, rejected carcass (#12). Why should he become involved again? Yet in the next poem (#13) Lumb has a vision of the Goddess rescuing his aging frame from the sea of dissolution. Under the warmth of sunbathing stars the Goddess wades shoreward holding him pietàlike in her arms. No matter how emptied and rejected he feels, he has the mature, honest intuition that only the Goddess can heal his pain and make life vibrant and worth living.

Nevertheless passion, the musical maneater of poem #12, contains within it the "deaf adder of appetite" that operates "Ignorant of death" in #14; its bite actually obstructs the natural human desire to serve the Goddess to such an extent that humans, our appetites (her servant the snake), and the Goddess appear to work at cross-purposes, promoting deathly error. In #15 Lumb still hesitates to partake of the cyclic round of love-death. From a safe intellectual distance Lumb can grasp in a single image the whole process of the oak king's imminent death as he unites with his bride, the White Goddess, in midsummer fertility rites. Lumb remains undecided, but nostalgic for a return to the temporal cycle.

Lumb resolves his conflicting responses toward the Goddess with clarity and simplicity in #6. Without prevarication he asserts that whoever partakes of temporal experience plucks the Goddess's erotic love-death apple and must be willing to nail his heart on the cross of pain. The accretions of world symbology in the poem foreshadow the possibility of transcendent illumination as the distillation of pain. The ass and lion images convey the intractable flesh and the destructive energy of the Goddess. Mary, pregnant with Christ on the donkey, ushers him into the temporal world of death; Set, the evil brother of Osiris whose animal symbol is the wild ass, conspires with Isis in the yearly death of Osiris. Lions convey the destructive energy of fertility goddesses such as the Egyptian Sekmet and the Hindu Devi. But from this dissolution one can derive transcendent union and illumination: Siva and Devi ride a white bull across the heavens in Hindu symbology, and the white bull was an animal of divination in Celtic, Greek, and Cretan cultures.[10] At this point Lumb has a clear intellectual apprehension of the process, but still lacks the personal commitment to act accordingly.

As he considers making that commitment, Lumb recognizes that he needs an internal renovation. To participate once again in the cyclic hunt of life, he must "rend to pieces" what is under his coat (#17). This is a significant decision, and the initial aftermath is fear of the Goddess's incomprehensibility—the veils that the interrogating reason cannot penetrate (#18). He remembers the tragic consequences of having pursued former incarnations of the Goddess (#19). These experiences only produced self-annihilating anguish at the irretrievable loss of endearing relationships, feelings of being "defunct"—dead to the world of the living.

Strangely enough, feeling dead to the world can be transformed into a useful survival strategy. What experience has apparently taught Lumb is not to rely upon attachments to this world, not to trust the weak ego's needs for safety and reassurance. This leads, as was the case in *Wodwo*, to an Oriental loss of the ego and excarnation of the fleshly body. In poem #20 Hughes recollects his *Wodwo* position of sundering automatic attachments and instinctual responses to the earth, to become coextensive with the sun's pure "light"—a supernormal state of consciousness shared by various occult and Oriental disciplines. Lumb's "absence" in poem #21 after having "Crossed into outer space" recollects the *Wodwo* poems "Stations" and "Song of a Rat," where an Oriental excarnation of the fleshy body occurs. What is left is an aspiration to view life from the perspective of the sun—a transcendent plane of creative consciousness. The sun often appears in the Upanishads to signify the transcendent *ātman* consciousness where internal and external worlds unite (the "mind" and "space" of stanza 2). The sun bark is the transcendent abode of Thoth, Osiris, and falcon-headed Horus. The resurrected Hercules lived in the sun as doorkeeper of the gods.[11]

Poems #22 through #25 present a surrealistic recoil from the austerity of Oriental consciousness, a recoil that parallels Hughes's post-*Crow* return to Western mythology. Poem #22 presents a return to Cerridwen's cave after a surrealistic night wind depicts another loss of faith in the power of language: the "stone tower" torn away like the trees perhaps refers to the vanquished Tower of Babel (Gen. 11). The next three poems present surreal analogues for the psychological process of self-annihilation, a stage in the religious training of Shaman and Sufi adepts. The result is a reaffirmation of the Goddess as the one compass for his life in poem #25. Neither the physical earth nor the philosophical and religious systems of human culture ("the creaking heavens") can anchor Lumb; only the Goddess's needle of pain and the ardor of his pursuit of her can orient him.

Consent and dedication to the Goddess's cycle of love and dissolution follow in #26. Lumb implores her to take him into her service: "Let me be one of your warriors." An intensely erotic expression of devotion to the Goddess occurs in #27: Lumb sees her as the animating principle beneath all religious fervor. The language is arresting in its simplicity and grace, and in its unique synthesis of religious and erotic love. Churches are "erections" that topple in time, while the river purifies the breasts and thighs of the immortal Goddess. Lumb is becoming an impassioned lover.

The next five poems (#28 through #32) contain the ardor and emotional fluctuations of a lover. Lumb, no longer the distanced celibate and rational analyst of the "Prologue," sympathizes with the pain endured by incarnations of the Goddess he has known (#28) and feels acutely a cold ache of separation when her energies seem to wane (#29). Periodically he fears his own mortality (#30). Poems #30 and #31 express Lumb's resignation to the cycles of pain and exaltation he must undergo to feel near enough to articulate the touch of the Goddess without false rhetoric. Truth is the distillation of pain, and must be earned by pain that is not calculated or self-conscious (#31). The pain must derive from the delight and torment of Dionysiac abandonment—Dionysus is the "singing drunkard" who tramples and drinks him (#32).

Lumb is now ready to express a total commitment to the Goddess, hanging on to neither intellectual (hair) nor emotional (flesh) crutches (#33). He will give unreservedly, reaching "both hands into the drop" with a selfless openness. Lumb is now the mature Parzival who is ready to heal with a complete, sympathetic gift of self to other. He successfully revives Cerridwen by anointing her on the forehead with the blood of his soul's pain in a poem (#34) so clear in its spareness and tenderness that it rings with a unique elegance, like fine crystal. Lumb has touched the Goddess deeply; his pain and devotion have "Stirred" her, brought her presence back into his life.

The next four poems (#35 through #38) present Lumb's sympathy for all incarnations of the Goddess in the foredoomed temporal cycle (#35 and #36), express the great difficulty of trying to convey in words the experience of being near her (#37), and articulate the recognition that each experience requires a complete openness and a constant revision of old habits to digest the encounters (#38).

Lumb now feels confident enough to test his reinvigorated creative powers. Like Blake's Los at his fiery furnace in book 1 of *Milton,* Lumb in poem #39 breathes upon the steel mold of his verse, nearly giving its creations life, and knowing that if the creations of his pen live it is because the Goddess kissed them (#42). Hughes himself is one incarnation of the "steel man," the "reassembled infantryman" from the *Wodwo* poem "Out." Lumb's vision advances to a perception of the tiger of Los's creative energy pervading the entire universe in poem #40. In poem #41 Lumb awakens with incomprehension to a new dispensation, a new creative covenant, with a "rainbow silking [his] body" and wings fitted for spiritual ascent. His new powers make him infinitely more sensitive to the comings and goings of the Goddess's creative energy (#43).

The spiritual climax of the entire sequence occurs in the penultimate poem (#44). The temporary and eternal fuse as Lumb perceives the oak dancing "On the centuries of its instant." Eliot wrote that the function of the artist is to "apprehend / The point of intersection of the timeless / With time" ("The Dry Salvages") in order to consent to and suffer for the pattern of the "eternal action" (*Murder in the Cathedral*). What Hughes sees through Lumb is not religious orthodoxy, but the structuralist's eternal pattern of suffering and psychological death to gain illumination that earlier cultures perceived in myths of the oak king—one of which Frazer used as the centerpiece of *The Golden Bough*.

Unlike poem #15, where he distanced himself from the oak's raptures because his anxiety over mortality kept him from participating, Lumb in poem #44 becomes enraptured by the oak's cosmic round of suffering, death, and resurrection in the realm of spirit. All four elements of created matter interweave throughout the poem, affirming the mortal labors of Frazer's oak king, who could reign supreme in the Wood at Nemi so long as he could vanquish all contenders and keep them from plucking the golden bough (the mistletoe) from the oak.[12] He is the "guard" of line 6, and the dancer of the same line is Śiva, whose cosmic dance comprehends at every moment all potential for creation and dissolution (Zimmer, 30, 131–35, 154, 167). The black lightning that thrusts upward toward illumination signifies the alchemical union of opposites, the moment of illumination (Jung 13:160–61, 317). At the end of the poem Lumb grasps what Yeats desired in *A Vision:* reality and justice held in a single thought.

The flaming darkness of the final poem is another occult image of transcendent unity in passionate ardor. Just as the skin renews its molecules periodically, so the final lines of the sequence signify that the psychological pattern outlined by the entire "Epilogue" is one that must be completed periodically to gain spiritual renewal.

Socrates and the Alchemical Shaman: *Cave Birds*

Cave Birds (1978) developed from a recondite sequence for scholars and bibliophiles into an intimate psychodrama of personality growth. Originally Hughes wrote nine poems to accompany nine of Baskin's weirdly anthropoid cave birds drawings after he first saw them in 1974. The combination of poems and drawings was to be published by Baskin at his Gehenna Press. But after the Ilkley Literature Festival commissioned Hughes to do a public reading, he saw an opportunity to create a blueprint for personality growth that might appeal to a wider audience and prove absorbing as a dramatic reading. He wrote 10 more poems to accompany 10 more Baskin drawings, and cemented the sequence with 13 more poems not connected to drawings (Sagar, 243–44). This final group conveys the inner psychological anguish more directly in words that stretch the power of language to articulate deep feelings and psychological states.

Cave Birds is Hughes's most Jungian and most structuralist volume; these adjectives define some of its haunting uniqueness as well as its central limitation. Often Hughes's capacity to find visual imagery to translate Baskin's drawings into words is remarkable. It is surpassed in *Cave Birds* only by Hughes's astonishing ability to translate into words his own acute, feeling-toned awareness of his subconscious resources. Often the poems contain a brilliant opulence of imagery and imaginative strength matched with the instantaneous cuts and acid burns of an engraver. Occasionally, however, the Jungian paradigm obtrudes too nakedly, when emotion flags. At these moments a structural stiffness shows in overly forceful condensations and yokings of image clusters that blur the meaning of individual lines.

Hughes deserves praise for trying—and in the main succeeding—to adumbrate the delicate psychic stages of a rebirth process from a purely interior perspective, without the immediately recognizable plot narrative used in *Gaudete*. The cave of the sequence is the cave of the individual subconscious, with its roots in Jungian archetypes. To find words for moods, affective states, and psychoemotional curves and progressions that almost by definition reside beneath the resources of language was no simple task.

In his first "Myth and Education" essay Hughes affirmed the structuralist tenet that literary form comprises a kit of "blueprints" for organizing the heaven and hell of the reader's psychic life. It can release and synthesize the energies of the id, ego, and superego in a way that liberates the personality and promotes self-development ("Myth 1," 66–67). This is possible because in ancient and tribal societies around the globe the psyches of humans have utilized death and rebirth paradigms as the way out of static conditions of dread and culs-de-sac of the will. In a tribal society the shaman during his ecstatic flight experienced a psychological death-and-rebirth ordeal in which the clan vicariously participated to obtain psychological cleansing and spiritual liberation. The shaman's death-and-rebirth ordeal introduces a psychological blueprint, validated by 40 centuries of use, for the purpose of

healing the sick person and his society. In *Cave Birds* the central persona ac-
quires a shamanic helper, the eagle hunter; this totemic animal carries the
persona aloft to be dismembered and reborn.

Similarly Jung believed that literature—including the occult tradition
and the oral myths and folktales of tribal cultures—testifies over the length
of recorded history to persistent psychological needs and desires for wholeness and self-development in humans. Jung believed that two of the most
important ancient ancestors of his individuation process are shamanism and
alchemy (Jung 11: 306). One blueprint for the individuation process is the
"shaman's experience of sickness, torture, death and regeneration," which
implies being "made whole through sacrifice" (Jung 11: 294). To be transformed the shaman's "body must be taken apart and dissolved into its con-
stituents, a process known in alchemy as the *divisio, separatio,* and *solutio,*
and in later treatises as *discrimination* and *self-knowledge*" (Jung 11: 272).
For Jung psychotherapy began with the early cathartic or cleansing experience of putting the patient in touch "with the hinterland of his mind" (Jung
16: 59)—with the cave of his psychic resources.

In 1964 Hughes reviewed Eliade's *Shamanism* and like Jung agreed that
the shaman's death, dismemberment, and resurrection resulted in the dis-
semination of a "healing power" and a profound "cathartic effect on the audience." The structural anthropologist in Hughes responded with the
assertion that this process "lies perceptibly behind many of the best fairy
tales, and behind myths such as those of Orpheus and Heracles, and behind
the epics of Gilgamesh and Odysseus. It is the outline, in fact, of the Heroic
Quest."[13]

The Crime   In *Cave Birds* the heroic quest begins with a prideful
cockerel who is accused of a crime, then sentenced and swallowed by a
raven. In the underworld he locates a shamanic helper whose eagle assistants
allow him a new chance by means of alchemic initiation and ordeals in the
world of the eagles. Pain and dismemberment finally lead to the expulsion
of a scapegoat (the former self) and rebirth through marriage to a woman
and reintegration with his best psychic resources. This is the gist of
Hughes's own introductory comments in his 1975 BBC broadcast of *Cave
Birds* poems.[14] In the sequence Hughes weaves shamanic and alchemic material together with a psychological progression that includes confrontations
with Jungian archetypes.

The nature of the central persona's crime is revealed in the first, fifth, and
eighth poems, "The scream," "She seemed so considerate," and "In these
fading moments I wanted to say." Callous indifference toward human suf-

fering is the problem in "The scream," with Hughes openly referring to his own literary calling. While catastrophes and lobotomies occurred, the poet's hawklike artistic abilities remained unmoved; the hawk sat apart and "perfected its craftsmanship." This indifference creates a psychic split followed by a withdrawal from normal relations with the outside world. In "She seemed so considerate" the Jungian anima arrives to tell the persona that his "world has died" and to clasp him in an embrace that simultaneously accuses him of a crime against the feminine: " 'Look up at the sun. I am the one creature / Who never harmed any living thing.' " These lines capture the pained supplication of the Baskin drawing perfectly, where the semicircular globe of feathers seems to be wrapped in an embrace while the downturned beak conveys a note of rueful complaint. The anima of "In these fading moments I wanted to say" accuses the persona of a writer's aloofness: "Right from the start, my life / Has been a cold business of mountains and their snow / Of rivers and their mud."

Hughes gave titles to many of Baskin's drawings, and none is more important than that for the drawing that accompanies the 10th poem, "The accused." Hughes first titled the drawing "A Tumbled Socratic Cock," and then changed it to "Socrates' Cock" (Sagar, 243). Both Graves (Graves, 11–12) and Nietzsche consider Socrates' love of dialectical reasoning to be a turning point in Western civilization. Nietzsche especially emphasized across six sections of *The Birth of Tragedy* that Socrates, the prototype of the "theoretical optimist" and father of the scientific mind, actually believed that through a logical analysis of causation humans could plumb the mysteries of nature, correct nature, and "spurred by an insatiable thirst for knowledge," convert the energy of the solar system to "the practical, egotistical ends of individuals and nations."[15] This recollects "Crow's Account of St. George."

Hence the central persona's crime is wider in implication than simple moral indifference or the self-isolation of the artist. As in his sixties work, Hughes suggests that the progress of Western civilization, the liberation of the intellect, is paralleled by a corresponding lack of concern for human suffering and nonrational needs. As in *Crow,* the crime is against the feminine in nature and in the self, a patriarchal attempt to divest the self of everything—emotion, intuition, sympathy, feeling—except the intellect. Hence in the third poem of *Cave Birds,* "After the first fright," the persona "argued" his way out of his situation only to leave his split double, his emotional self, in mourning. Cries for "Sanity" and "Civilization" betray a faith in aloof rational inquiry that beg the question: "When I said: 'Civilization,' / He began to chop off his fingers and mourn." Hughes in his

BBC introductory comments to this poem characterized the persona as
protesting "as an honorable Platonist"; Plato was the Greek philosopher
whose dialogues, according to Nietzsche, betrayed a fervent devotion to
Socratic dialectics.[16]
    Archetypes were for Jung the genetically inherited repository of human
experience with adversity. They are not deterministic, but are purely formal
categories for kinds of psychic energies. The meaning of dream confrontations with archetypes can be ascertained only by interpreting the events according to the individual experience of the dreamer (Jung PC: xliv; Jung
16: 142–43). If the dreamer is willing to wrestle with his own unconscious
energies, the archetypes change from darkly menacing figures to helping
agents of transformation. The first archetype the persona of *Cave Birds* encounters is the shadow, the powerful chthonic energies and inferior personality traits that the individual normally refuses to recognize (Jung 9b:34;
Jung 11: 76–79). In "The summoner" the shadow's appearance is "Spec-
tral, gigantified, / Protozoic, blood-eating." His "grip" ends the self-
satisfied, cocky stance of the persona in the opening poem.
    The anima, Jung's archetype for the feminine creative and artistic lure in
the male, also first appears as menacing, in the guise of a Vulturess with a
"prehensile goad of interrogation" and X-ray probe in "The interrogator."
The gruff, chilling imagery of this poem graphically conveys the anguished
self-examination of the persona. Yet after the interrogation the anima becomes less menacing and offers a warm embrace in the next poem, "She
seemed so considerate." The anima is "The plaintiff," the "life-divining"
power of love in the persona's heart that Western civilization criminally
represses.
    "The judge" is a satiric portrait of the conscious intellect, the faculty
prized by Socrates and overdeveloped in modern Western civilization, according to Nietzsche's prophetic analysis. Like Urizen in Blake, this judge
spins a web that maps space into cold quadrants. Hughes presents the intellect as an oafish clown, ponderously overweight because it fattens on everything that invades its territory. The intellect transforms nature's warm
embrace into a distant, scientific "solar silence," and squats on its throne of
unalterable fact.

The Shaman's Alchemical Underworld   The black chaos
of the unconscious fills the persona, dissolving all discrimination and offering fresh possibilities for growth from its fecund energies in "The execu-
tioner." Jung portrays the unconscious as paradoxically dark but divine,
deceptive and revelatory, a primal chaos of blackness from which all cre-

ation springs (Jung 16: 187–92). To achieve a new self-image and a new world-orientation, the persona must risk dissolution and dismemberment of the former self. His willingness to undergo this dissolution announces the beginning of the interior journey in the central portion of *Cave Birds,* where alchemic and shamanic imagery act as signposts for stages of a transformation process that actually happens at levels beneath language.

The persona in "The accused" willingly offers himself for sacrifice, as in an Aztec ritual where Solar Eagle Knights armed with obsidian daggers slew captive warriors on the "flame-horned mountain-stone" of sun-god temples.[17] Swallowed by a raven, the persona becomes a quester starting on an interior journey in the raven's network of veins, bones, and intestines in "First, the doubtful charts of skin." Like Kierkegaard's existential knight of faith, the quester in "The knight" begins his quest without any certitude whatsoever, and with no armor save his zeal. His perfect submission is his only hope for spiritual renewal. Hughes's language achieves a stunning evocation of the quester's desolate piety and humility in a crisp image: "He is himself his banner and its rags."

Though once again the persona-quester finds himself unable to respond sympathetically to human suffering, his meek submission merits the aid of a shamanic helper to help him on his individuation journey in "Something was happening." The eagle-hunter's song, a shamanic invocation of a psychological pattern believed globally in tribal cultures "Two, three, four thousand years" ago, is "off key" only because it appears backward in modern cultures seduced by Socratic rationalism and science. As he bows before his trap the eagle-hunter recognizes the psychological truth of the mutual death-and-rebirth game he plays with the eagle he hopes to capture. Huge talons opened, the eagle descends in the accompanying Baskin drawing. Fearful, sweating, the quester cries out, and his "cry is like a gasp from a corpse. / Everything comes back. And a wingspread / nails [him] with its claws" in the next poem, "The gatekeeper."

Alchemical imagery dominates in the next two poems, conflating the annihilation and dismemberment motifs of shamanic flight and alchemical transformation with traditional underworld motifs. In "A flayed crow in the hall of judgment" Hughes imbues the traditional postmortem underworld judgment scene with imagery of blackness and putrefaction, the dissolution of the personality in the *nigredo* and *putrefactio* stages in alchemy. As Isis soothed and reconnected the parts of the dismembered Osiris, the feminine figure in "The baptist" bathes the quester's body "In winding waters, a swathing of balm." Sea and salt imagery—the salt sweat of human imperfections and the impurities of the salt sea—become the *aqua permanens* of alchemy or the *aqua vitae* of Isis, both of which scour the old self and then nourish it into a new synthesis (Jung 14: 19–20). The new self becomes a "seed in its armour" that will ultimately burst into flower ("The owl flower") as the "gem" of a new self ("Walking bare").

Jung believed that alchemical texts are important because the alchemist, writing in a less self-conscious age, was actually projecting the contents of his own unconscious into his writings and repeatedly articulating a desire for personality growth and spiritual rebirth through pseudoscientific terminology—thinly veiled, secularized amalgams of medieval Christian symbolism (Jung 12: 244–45). The alchemist is conventionally believed to be one who tried to transform dross into gold; actually the alchemist tried to transform dross into the *lapis,* the philosopher's stone (Jung 12: 227–483), the transformed personality or new self—Hughes's "gem of myself." In this context Christ was a type of Mercurius, the world-creating deity or new self imprisoned in matter that the alchemist labored to liberate (Jung 12: 35, 293–312).

The quester convalesces after the excision of the old self-concept in "Only a little sleep, a little slumber," and slowly begins to recognize the eagle as an aspect of himself, his anima. But the anima is a nixielike lure, full of illusions, and occasionally offers the comfort of unrealistic retreats into childhood maternal bonds ("A green mother") or prelapsarian ecstasy ("As I came, I saw a wood") that the quester must reject. His inner voice tells him he must work at the goal of wholeness in an imperfect, postlapsarian world where a bell of "cracked iron" tolls to summon him "To eat flesh and to drink blood."

The anima is the speaker of "A riddle." She challenges the quester with paradoxes that help him bring to consciousness the repressed feminine portion of his psyche. Because his psyche is the father of his anima, reunion with the anima as bride will cause him to be reborn, mothering him into a new relation with nature. This is not an easy process, for the quester (the "you" and "your" of the poem) has hitherto been content to use only the analytic portion of his psyche, thus alienating his anima and gradually brutalizing her. Hughes's poem offers a wonderfully clear, softly stated contemporary analogue for intuitions of the anima within the psyche in early cultures, as in the paradox of Isis as mother, bride, and sister of Osiris.

Rebirth   The delicate process of personality reconstruction continues with "The scapegoat," where the quester jettisons with ridicule and hyperbole the strutting cockerel, the prideful self seen at the beginning of *Cave Birds.* Here the image accretions become cloying overstatement and tend to weaken the force of the poem with overkill. Next comes an early stage in the gradual strengthening of the anima as a major psychic force in "After there was nothing there was a woman." For Jung the alchemical marriage of *sponsus* and *sponsa,* the royal opposites of brother and sister or spirit and body, was the absolutely necessary precondition for the healing of ills and the attainment of the *lapis,* the integrated personality (Jung 14: 475, 501).[18] From a state of decomposition the anima as *sponsa* slowly regains its psychic force in the male. In "After there was nothing there was a woman" Hughes presents an early stage in the resurrection of the anima as if this psychic power had atrophied and regressed to some beginning point in the primal slime of evolutionary history. Undaunted and nurturing, yet fragile, it has just enough energy left to clothe itself with the natural world and begin the arduous process of working its way back through mineral and animal states.

The anima speaks directly to the quester in "The guide," reminding him that she is his compass needle and divining rod, the intuitional direction-finder that orients him through all enterprises. She propels him through the red and black winds of the phenomenal world toward the single point of illumination and realization, what yogins call *samādhi,* an aspect of *nirvāṇa,* the "non–wind." Here the world fills the self, creating an easeful unity and stasis, a mood of contemplative rapture where the universe is seen as delightfully coherent. The anima is at this point simply reminding the quester of exalted states of perception that are possible once personality integration has been achieved, and generating momentum and conviction to complete the quest.

The quester in the next poem, "His legs ran about," tries to reorient his relationship with women, but has trouble finding his bearings and acquiring a balanced view. Finally *sponsus* and *sponsa* merge into one, with the attainment of stillness and peace. The quester experiences great relief at having finally put to rest the old self as if into a new grave. He feels spent but refreshed, sensing the newness of the earth moving among the stars— "Rushing through the vast astonishment."

Hughes's introductory comment for "Walking bare" is short and to the point: "he seems to be journeying into the sun." Here the quester becomes the solar falcon flying into the sun, the symbol of unity and wholeness in the final stage of the alchemical process (Jung 12: 80–82, 221). He experiences a new buoyancy, and yet feels exactly his weight. Unlike in the previous poem, he is now accustomed to the pull of gravity. Soaring above valleys and mountains, he unites with the sun's energy, becoming "a spark in the breath / Of the corolla that sweeps me," with all mean selfhood extinguished. Having survived the pain of the dissolution, dismemberment, and reconstruction of his personality, he achieves the *lapis,* the "gem" of himself. One of the best poems in the sequence, and arguably Hughes's most memorable love poem, is the beautiful "Bride and groom lie hidden for three days." The bride and groom of the title refer to the *sponsa* and *sponsus,* and the three days symbolize the time of an underworld rebirth journey (Jung 5: 331, 210–11). The successful reunion of psychic opposites in the poem derives more directly from Hughes's creative response to the sharing depicted in the Baskin drawing. Hughes conveys the pair's astonished delight at their careful refurbishing of bodily parts through fresh images and graceful actions in simple, active verbs. Like the solar falcon of the previous poem, the pair "keep taking each other to the sun" with each free exchange of loving care. Cleaning machine parts, an unusual image cluster, surprisingly does communicate the mutual caring and sharing of marriage. The freedom and graceful mutuality of the giving and sharing constitute the first genuine moment of Lawrentian star-equilibrium in Hughes's poetry since the beautiful "September" in *The Hawk in the Rain.*

The owl in the Baskin drawing that accompanies "The owl flower" fans out his ovoid splendor of feathers. Hughes perceives this pose as a mandala of renewal and wholeness, and develops the poem around images describing the rebirth of Osiris. "The dead one stirs" with imagery of springtime renewal: sap, nectar, pollen, seed sprout, egg hatch, and flower bloom. The entire rebirth process is distilled into a filament in the quester's psyche sensitized to receive a message of cosmic rebirth. The final, unified self lifts new wings in "The risen." The quester has become a cross, a symbol of the unified tension of opposites. His newly integrated selfhood galvanizes his imagination so that it soars with an energy that burns without consuming itself—a flaming bush that carries a measure of its own divinity. Yet like the comings and goings of the goddess in the *Gaudete* "Epilogue," humans exert a very imperfect control over inspiration. We cannot harness it or tame it; it will not "land / On a man's wrist" at his bidding.

The two-line "Finale" of *Cave Birds* is not an afterthought, but an important recognition that all stages in the individuation process are impermanent. The power and self-assurance of "The risen" will not last, for the psyche is a fragile faculty and circumstances change daily. Baskin's owl's-head cameo drawing that closes the sequence is a reminder that the goblin at the end of the ritual is itself a product of the human mind. As Jung learned from the *Bardo Thödol* and elsewhere, the mind contains the source of its own terrifying projections as well as its own ecstasies.

Chapter Five

Language and Ecology: *Remains of Elmet, Moortown,* and *River*

Dismantling the Scaffolds: *Remains of Elmet*

Having taken his structuralist critique of contemporary Western culture to the limit in *Wodwo* and *Crow,* and his Jungian paradigm for psychological renewal to the limits of mythic surrealism in *Gaudete* and *Cave Birds,* Hughes in the late seventies began to disassemble his superstructure and pare down his style to concentrate on his immediate responses to nature. A second marriage and work at the Moortown farm doubtless influenced this transformation, as did Hughes's well-known desire to explore the hinterlands of the psyche that makes him impatient with any achieved style. The result in his more recent poetry is a new humility and compassion for the role of all living creatures in the drama of life and death, and a deep reverence for the wonders of natural events. Instead of distanced jeremiads against rational empiricism, Hughes offers exempla of how to get in touch with our ecological second skin in *Remains of Elmet* (1979), *Moortown* (1979), and *River* (1983).

The Decomposition Process Basic ecology within the energy transfer of trophic or feeding organisms dictates that to restore nutrients to the soil for further growth, decomposers such as bacteria and fungi must comprise the largest biomass in the food chain after producers or plant life.[1] The main storage place for the nutrients, the capacitor for the energy transfer, is of course the earth. In an early BBC broadcast (1961), Hughes characterized the earth as the strongest of the elements, and also the most passive and silent.[2] Arranged as a dialogue among the four elements, *Remains of Elmet* contains a central analogy between this ecological process of decomposition and the dismantling of Hughes's great sixties monomyth: his indictment of the empiricism and religious repression of post–Industrial Revolution Western culture. Rather than continue to ascend the rungs of his monomyth ladder, Hughes dismantles it to arrive at the rag-and-bone-shop of his heart's immediate responses to nature.

Hughes began writing the poems of *Remains of Elmet* after Fay Godwin sent him the black and white photographs of West Yorkshire that appeared in the Faber and Harper and Row trade editions. Many of the photographs reminded Hughes of his youthful haunts at Mytholmroyd, his birthplace, and nearby Heptonstall. The innocence that seemed lost through adult sophistication was recoverable in part through memory, that Proustian *recherche du temps perdu* that Hughes hints at in the dedicatory poem. In *Elmet* Hughes seemed to agree with Wordsworth's dictum that the child is father of the man, for central experiences in his youth did form his character. Conflict with the dying Industrial Revolution textile culture of the Calder Valley, childhood meditations while fishing, family experiences that included memories of the Great War, and conflicts with the very landscape of the region—the high moors and Scout Rock—divided his soul and either nurtured or impeded his spiritual growth. From these elements, discussed in part in chapter 1 of this study, Hughes developed his worldview.

Yet a curious double movement exists in *Remains of Elmet*, for while the photographs revive memories of the dying Industrial Revolution factory system of his youth, Hughes at the same time deconstructs his interest in it through the decomposition process, a central organizational motif. The culture of his youth did form his character, but it no longer manifests such a tenacious hold upon his thinking and the photographs remind him of nearly forgotten experiences that no longer motivate. While the factories are abandoned and the stone walls of the Enclosure Acts sag and fall, the creative energy awakened by Hughes's responses to that culture is enfolded back into the poet's psyche for further growth. The birds (air or spirit), rain (water), and the peculiar purplish light of the region (fire—the sun's transformational energy) comprise elements of an ecological system that assists in the process of decomposition, with Hughes identifying most with the passive receptivity of the earth.

Acceptance of the past is the main posture of *Elmet*, with the silent earth reclaiming a spent personal and cultural adventure: "Cenotaphs and the moor-silence! / Rhododendrons and rain! / It is all one. It is over" (87). "Time sweetens" (43) a process of decomposition that includes even the stone walls and the phallic factory chimneys, the most conspicuous remains of the Calder Valley:

> Brave dreams and their mortgaged walls are let rot
> in the rain.

> The dear flesh is finally too much.
> Heirloom bones are dumped into wet holes.
> And spirit does what it can to save itself alone.
>
> Nothing really cares. But soil deepens
> . . . .
> Before these chimneys can flower again
> They must fall into the only future, into earth.
> (14)

Liberation from Mechanistic Culture   The titles and content of individual *Elmet* poems are very difficult to remember, for most are variations on a few central themes repeated in almost every poem throughout the volume. One important theme concerns the liberation of the land after enslavement by the rigid machine culture of the Industrial Revolution. Within a 25-year period beginning in 1765, all the essential inventions needed to spawn the Manchester factory system, England's first, occurred: Arkwright invented his waterframe for spinning thread, Hargreaves his spinning jenny, and Cartwright his power loom. Watt was perfecting his steam engine throughout this period, adding by 1790 his final important modifications: a pressure gauge and a governor for automatic speed control. In the next decade Manchester doubled in size to 100,000 in a country of small villages.[3] These events set the stage for the nineteenth-century textile trade in the Calder Valley.

In *Elmet* Hughes evaluates the remnants of Industrial Revolution culture. The walls of the Enclosure Acts are "Endless memorials to the labour / Buried in them"; as they enchained the land both "wore to a bowed / Enslavement," with the lives of spent humans becoming a compost dropped "into the enclosures / Like manure," leaving a "harvest of long cemeteries" (33). Rock, like the land, allowed itself to be "conscripted" into "four-cornered" factory and church walls, enduring patiently the "drum-song of the looms" that mesmerized humans into replaceable machine cogs:

> And inside the mills mankind
> With bodies that came and went
> Stayed in position, fixed like the stones
> Trembling in the song of the looms.
> (37)

This aggressive obstinacy and rigidity Hughes attributes in part, as he did in *Wodwo*, to continental invaders, especially the ninth-century Vikings.

Hughes considers their legacy in "For Billy Holt," a poem about a famous resident of nearby Todmorden (1879–1977) who epitomized the Yorkshireman's love-hate relationship with the mills. As a youth Holt worked as a weaver; as an adult he served in World War II, sailed around the world, and toured Italy on a 10-year-old horse. He wrote novels and travelogues, painted, and broadcast BBC programs. Though he received a patent for an improved shuttle for automatic weaving, he also championed workers' rights tirelessly as a socialist between the wars.

When Hughes introduced "For Billy Holt" in a BBC radio reading, he repeated the part of his *Elmet* introductory note about West Yorkshire having long been a hideout for criminals and nonconformists. Billy Holt took a "special pride" in the area's "laconic perversity of character," and Hughes in the poem responded by identifying some of the "Elmet" inheritance that formed the "rudiments" of that character. In a fine interweaving of ecological and anthropological insights, Hughes stated in a BBC radio reading that he used the word "Elmet" as a "naturally evolved local organism, like a giant protozoa, which is made up of all the earlier deposits and histories, animated in a single glance." The "remains" are "distortions peculiar to the ingredients," caught in the lens of the poet's eye ("Elmet").

In the poem Hughes reminds Holt that the badlands environment that he frolics in is depraved. Norse invaders reduced the land to private property and wealth, a "far, veiled gaze of quietly / Homicidal appraisal," one of the most chilling phrases in all of Hughes's poetry. Holt's exuberence is insufficient to escape a Viking inheritance that remains genetically anchored in his facial features and the limitations of his North Country culture.

The Industrial Revolution brought "the bottomless wound of the railway station / That bled this valley to death." Taking the long anthropological view, Hughes asserts that mills and railroads brought a machine rigidity that permeated the entire culture, repressed instinctual life, and ultimately led to anonymity and death—the cenotaph beneath a sky like an "empty helmet / With a hole in it" (34). The silence of earth and forests can "Muffle much cordite"; the "leaf-loam silence" can quiet the throb of the mills and the earth can accept the detritus of machine culture, the "old siftings of sewing machines and shuttles"(13).

Taoist Receptivity   Hughes's interpretation of the consequences of post–Industrial Revolution science and technology is not new; we have seen it before in *Wodwo, Crow,* and *Gaudete.* What is new is his posture of humble acceptance, the recognition that this cultural idea has lost its compulsive force as a theme in his poetry. As Lumb in *Gaudete* was compared to an oak tree, so the central persona of *Elmet* is compared to a tree that has learned the folly of fulminating and the wisdom of acceptance. In "Tree" Hughes feels the rhythm of nature only when he ceases his declamatory rhetoric. The persona of "A Tree," pummelled by natural forces like Lear in the storm, learns to divest himself of all self-serving uses of language. His ecological second skin tells him to accept the cycles of nature, to learn how to shed the old and let it decompose in silence. So he resigns himself "To be dumb" and receptive, to let his psyche be buffeted and renewed without goal-oriented volition. His body "Lets what happens to it happen."

This earth-oriented silence and receptivity in *Elmet* derives in part from the laconic, taciturn attitude toward nature of Hughes's Yorkshire nurture, and in part from an interest in Taoism that first appears in his work in *Elmet* (see my comments on Taoism in chapter 1). Chuang Tzu, for instance, writes that when the Great Clod bellows, the wind cries wildly among all the objects of creation. One should rather plant Hui Tzu's tree, a tree too gnarled to be useful, in the field of the Broad-and-Boundless, and relax, doing nothing, wandering freely. Taoist *yu,* free and easy wandering, activates the intuition and reminds us to delight in natural processes without becoming attached or possessive. One should blend or merge with the vastness of nature, in a single flow.[4] In America, however, the Taoist maxim "go with the flow" is too often torn from its ecological roots and twisted into "follow the crowd" or "conform"—to the urgings of mass media, mass merchandizing, or situational ethics.

The Taoist tenet of merging or becoming one with the changes or flow of natural events contains an important ecological application. For the ecologists Frank Darling and Paul Sears, for instance, ecological responsibility begins when one recognizes that the individual "is not just an observer and irresponsible exploiter but an integral part" of the ecosystem.[5] Feeling integrated with our ecological second skin does not promote the utilitarian abuse of the environment that one becomes acculturated to when rational empiricism is the model for dealing with nature. Crow can only "peer" at nature because his analytic ego divorces him from it; hence nature becomes one giant laboratory to be manipulated for possession and profit.

Elmet contains other important Taoist principles. " 'Think often of the silent valley, for the god lives there' " (13), the only quoted passage in *Elmet,* is a Taoist proverb that emphasizes the receptivity, acceptance, and womblike mystery characteristic of the feminine yin principle of Taoism, Lao Tzu's Valley Spirit.[6] Water emphasizes the virtues of patience and receptivity, as it follows the given contours of the land. Water at rest symbolizes clarity and perfect harmony.[7] In *Elmet* the rock, cut into a "four-cornered" sameness (37) that reflects the Protestant "hard, foursquare scriptures" (56), is no match for "the guerilla patience / Of the soft hill-water" (37).

Birds, messengers of the spirit world of air in *Elmet*, are most like Taoist sages in their capacity for free and easy wandering. In "Curlews Lift" the emphasis upon the birds' ability to strip away all but their cry parallels Hughes's new imperative to pare down his language to essentials. Roaming the spiritual vastness without the need to possess or analyze, the curlews merge into the allness of being. As the man observes the curlews "Drinking the nameleess and naked / Through trembling bills," he appears to grasp Lao Tzu's characterization of ultimate Tao as The Nameless.[8]

In "Widdop" Hughes appears to assert that the world was created from nothing and that all created being returns to nothing by pointing to the flight of a gull gliding "Out of nothingness into nothingness." Nothingness in Zen and Taoism also conveys a grasp of the nondifferentiated allness of being and the merging of opposites into unity, what Chang Chung-yuan considers the goal of Taoism.[9] The flight of Hughes's gull is most reminiscent of Chuang Tzu's parable of the white colt, where the life of all differentiated being, including the lives of humans, is likened to the passing of a white colt glimpsed through a crack in the wall.[10] Birds in "Dead Farms, Dead Leaves" similarly appear to "Visit / And vanish." Preoccupation with selfhood ceases when one grasps the allness of being.

Light on the moors is entrancing, elevating, and gradually in *Elmet* comes to symbolize a grasp of the spiritual dimensions of the environment, illuminated by the poet's visionary presence of mind. Hughes in his BBC essay about Scout Rock identified the light on the moors as "at once both gloomily purplish and incredibly clear, unnaturally clear," helping to create an "exultant" mood ("The Rock"). Bound to the wheel of pain in a world of opposites, light scalds trees (63), is ground by the millstone of sky (66), and alternately glares and throws glooms about the moors (68). Light is the testament of the sun's energy at dawn, "Bubbling deep in the valley cauldron," (121); after rain, light appears in a "golden holocaust" of sunshine at the cloud's edge (68). In other poems light imagery carries heavier philosophical freight. Beams of light become points of entry into the visionary world beyond phenomenality in "Heptonstall Cemetery," as in the Fay Godwin photo on the facing page. In "Open to Huge Light," Hughes creates a mood of meditative trance where the light bears the mystic wind-shepherds "From emptiness to brighter emptiness / With music and with silence."

The Nurturing Caddis   When Hughes unites all the elements in his fugue—light, stones, water, and wind—he creates the most astonishing image in *Elmet,* a memorable stanza attesting to just how much we depend upon our environment as our ecological second skin. Here the four elements are the infinitely fragile and infinitely necessary "armour of bric-a-brac / To which your soul's caddis / Clings with all its courage" (16). Hughes's reference to the caddis or larval case of the caddis fly signifies a faith in the real world as the point of origin for moltings into mystic visions.

Many of the poems in *Elmet* are meditations upon the poet's own caddis-case nurture, his days as a Yorkshire youth. Hughes's memories of his childhood are mostly positive, though some of the poems contain moments of regret, sadness, a disturbing sense of menace, or even a sense of outrage. Within the ecological design of the volume, Hughes reveals in these poems a sense of nature imparting a special gift that the poet responds to with a sense of stewardship. Hughes not only accepts the gift, but does so with the conviction that his Yorkshire environs provided a very adequate, even unique training ground for his spiritual development.

From his bedroom window Hughes as a child could see a football field on a ridge above and often watched soccer games from this distance. "Football at Slack" pays tribute to the indomitable spirit of sportsmen who braved the rain until the sun acknowledged their persistence, while "Sunstruck" probes deeper into the human desire for freedom and exhilaration that surfaces in our workaday world only on weekends, with the specter of Monday labor lurking in the shadows.

Other poems present a child's first consciousness of ecological issues through allusions to Eliade's *illud tempus* moment of original Edenic purity believed by tribal cultures around the world to have existed before cultural and social divisions.[11] "The Long Tunnel Ceiling" records the child's first encounter with a trout, a fish believed by the young Hughes to have magical properties because of its heritage in unspoiled nature. Hughes called the trout "the authentic aboriginal in that polluted valley, the holiest creature out there in its free, unspoiled, sacred world" ("Elmet"). In "The Canal's Drowning Black" Hughes records how basic ecology teaches moral values when a childhood expedition to capture loach places him in league with his confining culture. He rests the jam jar crammed with these small fish, pilgrims from the Oligocene, "On a windowsill / Blackened with acid rain fall-out / From Manchester's rotten lung," and soon feels guilty enough to liberate the expired loach by flinging them "Back into their Paradise and mine."

Another Eliadian moment of paradisial unity with nature occurs in "Cock-Crows." Here the young Hughes and his older brother Gerald had climbed up a high ridge before dawn and listened to the cocks crowing in Thornber's chicken farm below at first light ("Elmet"). The entire poem is an epiphany of unspoiled nature rising at dawn to greet them, with the "fire-crests" and "sickle shouts" of the cocks glazed in the molten metals of the sun's rays. "Cock-Crows" has a sustained strength of vision that is unmistakably Hughes's donnée, a quality in his work we too often take for granted.

From this moment of Edenic beauty and purity Hughes presents the postlapsarian departure of his brother Gerald in "Two." After Gerald moved permanently to Australia following World War II, the brothers seldom saw each other. Though Hughes was too young to fight, World War II has always reminded him of this great sadness in his family life. From the paradisal "morning star" the pair descend to the hills to find the violence of war. Hughes communicates an irreparable rift in his family bonding by suggesting a corresponding psychic shock in his art—the shaman's loss of his talismans for Edenic contact with nature: "The feather fell from his head. / The drum stopped in his hand. / The song died in his mouth."

Hughes celebrates medieval Christianity in "Heptonstall Old Church" by responding imaginatively to Fay Godwin's photograph on the facing page (119). Erected in 1260, St. Thomas à Becket Church has been a ruin since a storm badly damaged its roof in 1847. Hughes sees the remaining walls as the carcass of a "great bird" that once landed with an uplifting, civilizing idea. But the energy of that civilizing idea spent itself and the remnants, a comotose Methodism, became in Hughes's childhood a force that further separated him from paradisal union with family and the natural world.

In "Mount Zion" Hughes recounts his "waking nightmare" of being inducted into religious conformity at the age of five ("Elmet"). The Heptonstall area, just a few miles from Hughes's Mytholmroyd birthplace, was one of the cradles of West Yorkshire Methodism in the eighteenth century. A church there boasts a foundation stone set when John Wesley himself preached in the area, and Heptonstall's octagonal chapel constructed in 1764 is said to be the oldest Wesleyan chapel in continuous use. Hughes's induction into Methodism is macabre, ghastly; like a calf led to the slaughterhouse Hughes in "Mount Zion" is marched in, scrutinized by "convicting holy eyes," imprisoned with elderly women "crumpling to puff-pastry, and cobwebbed with deaths." Hughes controls the energy of this indictment with sardonic satire: the poem ends with the "mesmerized commissariat" engaged in "Riving at the religious stonework" to crucify a heretical cricket that dared to buck the rigid, foursquare catechism. Luckily Hughes, like Michael in the *Wodwo* story "Sunday," managed to escape regular church attendance and has never subscribed to any orthodox religion. Nevertheless, the gloomy shadows of Scout Rock described by Hughes in his BBC radio essay derived in large part from a nexus of patriarchal menace that included foursquare scriptures, machine monotony and pollution, and wartime deprivation. All left their accents upon the ecology and environment of the area. In "Under the World's Wild Rims," Hughes intimates that walking to school amid predawn darkness, factory soot, and watchful skylights became a horrific experience, like chancing upon a guarded excavation of a cultural disaster.

The geological and ecological environment of West Yorkshire affects the psychological and spiritual climate of all its inhabitants. As he introduced "Wild Rock" in his BBC radio presentation of *Elmet* poems, Hughes even contended that the textile trade grew up as an indigenous response to the geological and climatic environment, with Bradford worsteds a natural reply to the cold, frequent rain, and the pneumonia and rheumatism endemic to the area ("Elmet"). The wild energy, roughness, and penury of the West Yorkshire environment certainly affected Emily Brontë's spirit, as reflected principally in the stormy passion of Heathcliff in *Wuthering Heights.* Hughes comments upon the fatal attraction of the moors and Pennine cliffs to the Brontë family in "Emily Bronte" and "Haworth Parsonage."

Having become reconciled to the effects of his childhood environment upon his character, Hughes's visionary eye opens the Yorkshire landscape to offer a benediction for departed relatives in the penultimate poem of *Elmet.* Wind and spray impel the mind to spiritual flight in "Heptonstall Cemetery," the location of the Hughes family burial ground. Here the spirits of Hughes's mother Edith, uncles Thomas and Walter, and first wife Sylvia Plath become feathers on the wings of a giant swan flying westward. The swan vision leads to a dream recounted in "The Angel," the final poem of *Elmet.*

"The Angel," like the earlier "Ballad from a Fairy Tale" in *Wodwo,* concerns a dream premonition of Sylvia Plath's death some two years before her actual suicide (Scigaj, 253–54). The *Elmet* poem, a much less ominous recension, ends wih the poet's Yorkshire roots allaying his grief. Angels are embodiments of poetic intuition and spiritual revelation in the work of both Hughes and Plath. The macabre angel, made of "smoking snow" and "cast in burning metal," delivers a purely visual message in the dreamscape of the poem. Part of the Angel's message concerns the enigmatic white square of satin worn where the halo ought to be. Ted and Olwyn Hughes in conversation identified this satin square as the cloth covering Plath's face when Hughes first viewed the body.

Remains of Elmet may appear a slight volume upon first reading, for the relaxed rhythms and condensed thematic interweavings might imply that Hughes was content simply to ruminate upon photographs of his past without much direction or sustained pressure. But the more one reads the volume the more its subtle austerity and delicate moods become visible, and the more one discovers that its landscapes are imaginatively arranged to suggest how the confluence of regional geology and environmental powers do color our moods mold our character. Original images and apt cadences in *Elmet* offer the reader a glimpse of West Yorkshire that is as revealing and insightful as anything James Herriot has written. Consider the rough, tumbling cloudscapes of the region as "The witch-brew boiling in the sky-vat" (19), the soft "wobbling water-call" of the curlews invading the moor silence (28), and the wind like an anesthetic in the trees sending "swift glooms of purple" and "swabbing the human shape from the freed stones" (103).

Also consider the trancelike mesmerizing stare of "Widdop" or "Bride-stones," where Hughes's intense concentration produces poems that are deeply moving, activating obscure psychic energies for absorbed communion with the land. Consider the abundance of refreshing images in cleanly articulated, uncluttered lines, as when "The light, opening younger, fresher wings / Holds this land up again like an offering / Heavy with the dream of a people" (20). Consider the delicious play of assonance throughout the volume, with Hughes moving deftly up and down the register to reveal the moody bleakness of West Yorkshire, as in "The glare light / Mixed its mad oils and threw glooms" (68). Most of all, consider the new mood of serene acceptance in Hughes, which extends to include a sympathy with the dead and with aged pensioners "Attuned to each other, like the strings of a harp" (89).

Hughes is most sympathetic throughout the volume to the vast labor of generations, the human dreams and the human suffering seen in the ruins of the culture. Words in *Elmet* mean little to Hughes without experience—the hand of Lear smelling of pain and mortality. We see this especially in "Churn-Milk Joan," where linguistic deformation over time turned the *jamb* of a simple dairy farmer's payment stone into a *Joan*. A trite story developed to explain the use of Joan, a story that was an indigenous folktale product consonant with the peculiar desolate character of the moors. But for Hughes the story merits censure because "Her legendary terror was not suffered." The tale is pure fantasy, the product of weak imagining not grounded in actual experience.

Remains of Elmet is a rich glacial deposit of 50 years of Hughes's deep experience. Freed of his sixties monomyth, Hughes continued to follow the immediate responses of his spirit to compose some of his most riveting poems in the opening farm elegies of *Moortown* and the delicate riverscapes of *River*.

Words and Responsibility: *Moortown*

Having developed a richly complex mythic and surrealistic interpretation of contemporary Western culture in his sixties volumes, Hughes could have continued to fashion ever more intricate, esoteric works, as Blake did in his late prophetic visions. Instead he pared his verse to a compelling meditative stringency in the taut, spare lines of the *Gaudete* "Epilogue" and *Remains of Elmet*. Deeper states of consciousness became accessible to his probing as he also strove to achieve a greater fidelity of words to actual human experience.

Hughes was forging his own unique response to the great postwar devaluation of language. Language has lost its vitality, has become corrupted and exhausted by advertising and mass culture. In his essay "The Retreat from the Word," George Steiner wrote that the inflated rhetoric of oratory and propaganda has similarly devalued language in the postwar world, while the triumphs of science in harnessing the natural world appear to indicate that "reality" in the West lies outside verbal language—in the forbidding and specialized languages of mathematical symbols, equations, and scientific formulae. Steiner asserted that poets should resist, as did the French symbolists, confinement to fact and objective analysis, and prove again that language contains a magical "Power of incantation." Poets should be magical enchanters who liberate subconscious energies and "pass from the real to the more real" in language that is both clear and precise.

Had Steiner written his prophetic essay in 1981 instead of 1961, he certainly would have added Hughes to this privileged list of magical enchanters and liberators. In *Moortown* (1979) language attains a depth commensurate with subjective and objective experience richly lived and powerfully felt. Hughes's considerable linguistic and observational powers work at full tilt, often restoring to language the "measure of clarity and stringency of meaning" that Steiner feels is an absolutely necessary bulwark against cultural chaos.[12]

Hughes's response to the contemporary devaluation of language is a central concern of his most recent work. True to his English sense of culture as something rooted in the character of a geographic region and the actual lived experience of its inhabitants, Hughes in both *Moortown* and *River* strove to communicate honest actual experience and deep states of consciousness in words that are neither flattened nor inflated. Three years before publishing *Elmet* and *Moortown* Hughes wrote that he prized a language created by an imagination that is "both accurate and strong," that could envision blueprints of our deepest psychic life while integrating inner-world forces with the unvarnished actual conditions for living in the outer world. Hughes endeavored to create a clean, direct poetic line that could grasp inner and outer worlds simultaneously and flexibly, and a spare, precise language that "keeps faith, as Goethe says, with the world of things and the world of spirits equally" ("Myth 2," 92).

The Fresh Simple Presence   After the powerful and very unified *Crow, Gaudete, Cave Birds* and *Remains of Elmet, Moortown* at first appears a lesser work, an amalgam of previously published limited edition poems and uncollected magazine poems, some of which first appeared in the sixties. It possesses neither the epic and psychological grandeur nor the unity of subject of its predecessors. The first, second, and fourth sections of *Moortown* originally appeared as Rainbow Press limited editions— *Moortown Elegies* (1978), *Prometheus on His Crag* (1973), and *Adam and the Sacred Nine* (1979), respectively—while the third section, "Earth-Numb," reprints poems from the Rainbow Press *Orts* (1978) and from uncollected verse publications from as far back as 1963.

Yet Hughes has a purpose in combining these works, even though some of the poems in the "Earth-Numb" section remain esoteric, with their themes not fully realized. Elsewhere I wrote of the Blakean serpent alchemy in *Moortown* as a unifying principle: from the limited Beulah world of nature the poems progress through the worlds of Generation and Ulro finally to achieve the Edenic creativity of Los, with these four stages corresponding to the above four sections (Scigaj, 257–86). Hughes's struggle to find an adequate language to convey the inner and outer worlds of experience accurately and responsibly comprises another and equally significant unifying principle that functions as a reliable guide for interpreting *Moortown*.

When Hughes regularly worked in the early seventies as a farmhand on his Devon farm Moortown, managed by his father-in-law Jack Orchard, he carried a pocket journal in which he jotted down the fresh details of farm life for later use. Hughes soon switched from prose to verse jottings because he learned he was able to relive the experience more deeply in rough verse. When he tried to rework a farming experience into a poem weeks later, he found he lost much of the original freshness: his concentration gave way to inner-world considerations such as conscience while his nimble stylistic versatility began to rob the experience of its uniqueness and "assault it with technical skills." He found that his technical mastery "destroyed the thing [he] most valued—the fresh, simple presence of the experience," so he decided to discipline himself to catch the event honestly, near the moment he experienced it, and leave it in its unique freshness.[13]

The result was *Moortown Elegies,* a series of farming poems that are fine examples of Steiner's "clarity and stringency of meaning." Fidelity to the actual experience, rendered honestly but vividly, with a minimum of stylistic distortion, was a high priority for Hughes in every poem. Hughes had already written farming poems in his children's volume *Season Songs* (1974). Here vibrant description alternated with a touching sympathy that often aggrandized simple events in the natural world by adding mythic adornments or personification, or by using the pathetic fallacy or sentiment to capture the imagination of the younger reader and convey a sense of wonder and delight at nature's vitality and variety. Spring became a "tremendous skater" leaning into the curve of a new year in "Spring Nature Notes" or a young girl weeping rain at her coming-out party in "Deceptions." Hughes reworked the John Barleycorn myth in "The Golden Boy," developed the quest motif in "Autumn Nature Notes," rehearsed the myth of the dying vegetation god of the waning year in the stag hunt of "The Stag," and personified elements of the natural world in nursery-rhyme dialogues such as "Leaves" and "There Came a Day." The poems carried the fresh clean scent of a spring shower. A light touch modulated the sentiment of poems such as "A March Calf," but one saw on every page the gleaming technical mastery of the poet enriching and arranging the context.

As Hughes "keeps faith . . . with the world of things" in the opening "Moortown" section, adornments such as personification or use of the pathetic fallacy are rare. The image of the earth as an invalid surviving winter's operation derives from one of two poems ("March Morning unlike Others") reprinted from *Season Songs*. Rendering in human logic the bull's dissatisfaction in "While She Chews Sideways" or the calf's contentment in "A Happy Calf" is a very slight extension of a great wealth of descriptive detail from a sequence of real-world actions sustained throughout the poem. Here the focus remains firmly fixed on the individual animal. The depiction of the cattle standing in a "new emptiness," and the uprooted farmland left with "a great blank in its memory" after the death of Jack Orchard is sober and unsentimental, earned by the entirety of the sequence.

In the opening section of *Moortown* Hughes restricted himself to recording farming events as they actually happened. By writing very near the actual event he achieved a startling accuracy of observation with a minimum of adornment. Fidelity to the actual event liberated his style and allowed him to concentrate upon the simultaneous fusion of outer and inner experience in the honest passing of the lived moment. Intense absorption in small details in the outer world individualized farm animals and revealed character in situations where most readers would lump animal behavior into rude stereotypes and abstract categories. The net effect is to cleanse and refresh the reader's perceptions, to enable the reader to live more deeply and intensely. At the same time the reader witnesses the farmhand's inner-world engagement as a steady, willing submission to the requirements of managing the farm.

"Rain," the very first poem of "Moortown," not only introduces Jack Orchard's tenacious struggle with the elements, but erects the boundary of the actual around the entirety of the section as the men erect fence posts. Hughes recollects the same event in "A Monument," near the end of the opening section, as if to emphasize by formal means the boundary of the actual enclosing "Moortown." Orchard is the master farmer who shows his observant disciple how to manage nature—by plunging his bruised, soiled hands into it. Hands are levers with which to maintain the farm's ecological balance, but more importantly hands-on experience is a much surer way of immersing oneself in nature than relying upon words. Rain and mud test the mettle of the laborers while the stoic endurance of the sniffing animals nearby counsels patience. In "Dehorning," the next poem, the language renders the experience faithfully and vividly because Hughes limits his writing to the simple actual occurrences. Men "Grimace like faces in the dentist's chair" as they weather the shock and commotion of cows in pain. A severed artery squirts "a needle jet / From the white-rasped and bloody skull crater" as the men remain totally absorbed in their exacting work.

The opening section instructs the reader about the limits of the actual as it engages him or her in firsthand experience. Ultimately, managing the actual works farmers to death, a fact indicated by the concluding elegies, but death is here presented as the fulfillment of a deep commitment to living. In "A Monument" Hughes remembers the master farmer stubbornly "using [his] life up" erecting wire fence "through impassable thicket, / A rusting limit" or "boundary deterrent." Crucified to the world, his head is "Skull-raked with thorns" while his hands, like "old iron tools" completing necessary projects, weathered to "creased, glossed, crocodile leather" striated with the scars of painful accidents, as when snapped barbed wire ripped a half-inch furrow through them (63). But his stoic endurance of pain and his commitment to managing nature earns the farmer the blessing of the White Goddess. After his death the Goddess transforms his " 'bloody great hands' " into "a final strangeness of elegance" in the concluding line of the opening section (64), an apotheosis signifying union with the feminine principle of creation.

Unlike traditional elegies such as Milton's "Lycidas" or even Lowell's "The Quaker Graveyard in Nantucket," the concluding elegies of "Moortown" restrict their focus to the actual. Hughes avoids all conventions that emphasize technical mastery over actual observation: here are no invocations to the muse, personifications of natural forces, processions of mourners, digressions on the church, or enlargements of context to include pathetic fallacy invectives against death or consoling hopes for immortality. The boundary of the poet's penetration is the actual event. Yet the restricted gaze produces poetry that steeps the reader in the lush redolence of the actual, with images plump and clean as freshly washed grapes. The poetic line is simple, effective, and satisfying because the images are neither crammed into the line nor insisted upon.

Simple natural images alternate the feel of enduring the rough weather and crises of farm management with the quiet peace and contentment of uneventful days. Cows plant themselves against the wind at the Moortown farm "like nails in a tin roof" about to blow off (11), and sheep weather a snowstorm in a shed surrounded by "clapping wings of corrugated iron" while the snow nearly succeeds in "erasing" the blind oaks (24). The anxious hurry of rapid hay bailing under threat of a storm yields to the elation of accomplishment crowned by the rain's falling "Softly and vertically silver," creating a sudden "tobacco reek" as the last load nears the barn (50). Hughes accents a contented calf's meditations on the young "pulse of his life" by observing a buttercup that "leans on his velvet hip" (41), while "Sundown polishes the hay" and "The warmed spices of earth / In the safe casket of stars" nurse a sick calf (46). When a lamb born without the will to live dies in a day, "The wind is oceanic in the elms" (55). But when a dumb calf learns to suck, the mother stills her refractory behavior as "the happy warm peace gathered them / Into its ancient statue" (48).

Instead of a selfish utilitarian appropriation of nature, the master farmer and his assistant fulfill in their husbandry the laudable ecological goal of stewardship, assisting nature with hands that function equally well in heavy labor and in the delicate midwifery of reaching into animal wombs to assist lambings. The stewards save a calf striken by scour and trapped in a disk harrow (44–46), teach a dumb calf how to suck (47–48), and save the mother of a strangled lamb trapped in the womb at birth (32–33). Often nature can manage without aid, or the weather limits midwifery to a dab of antiseptic and a run for cover in a hailstorm (37–38). Herding new lambs

into a shed to save them from almost certain death in a late winter snowstorm merits a moment of satisfied prediction, for in a day or so the lambs
"Will toss out into the snow, imperishable / Like trawlers, bobbing in
gangs"(25).

Animal husbandry educates one to the limits of the purely natural, for
Hughes becomes extremely aware of the animals' dependence upon instinct
and habit, and their total lack of understanding. Lost in their cud-
munching stolidity, they are indifferent to management by sympathetic
human hands, and comprehend little. Their hooves are "knee-deep in
porage of earth" (11). Lambs and their mothers are distrustful, anxious,
and entirely unappreciative of being brought to the cover of a shed during
snowstorms (17–18, 24). Lambs freed for pasture in the spring fear it; they
long to return to the shed stalls of their birth (35). The lambs bleat woe as
they try to identify their newly shorn mothers; lacking any real freedom or
initiative, they simply "fit themselves to what has happened" (56). Rams
and bulls cannot understand their balked sexuality (28–29, 52–53). Meditations upon the animal world have limits; in their shit-patched uncon-
sciousness animals do not coax the artistic imagination to flower or soar, for
they are not "the soul's timely masterpiece" (36).

Tearing consciousness away from absorption in the actual creates problems. Conscience, introspection, and memory can obstruct action and sty-
mie participation in natural events. The assistant farmer worries himself
with instances where his tardiness or physical limits result in unsuccessful
calvings (8–10) or lambings (30–33, 54–55). When he meditates upon
the necessary technological extensions of his hands, he finds himself caught
in "a trap of iron stupidity" on his tractor (20). Simple natural events can
create a wild whir of "Crazily far thoughts" but no penetration into the right
cause for the surprising presence of the blue-black birth sac half-dropped
from a cow's tail (26). The potentially transcendent events of "Roe Deer"
and "Coming Down through Somerset" only confirm that the limits of absorption in the actual are severe; the actual sustains a "dimension" that is
very ordinary (22–23) and restricted to the temporal flow (42–43).
Hughes sees the physical labor and its pain etched in the folds of the master
farmer's hands, but can a farmer ever extricate his mind from passive submission to the actual?

Words Are the Birds of Everything   This is precisely
Prometheus's problem in "Prometheus on His Crag," the second section of
Moortown. An offshoot of his 1971 *Orghast* meditations upon the roots of
Western and Near Eastern myths, the 21 short poems of "Prometheus" con-

tain Hughes's attempt to resolve the problems of the relationship of consciousness and its wordy products to the pain, infirmities, and restrictions of actual living. Humans aspire to godlike freedoms and immortality, but live inside mortal, decaying bodies adrift in a world of pain. Perhaps the "numbness" Hughes spoke of as the motive for creating this sequence (Sagar, 147) was the numbness of living life restricted to the animal level of unawareness. Does the stewardship of nature allow life to be lived at levels above the numbingly passive submission to circumstances? Does a richer mode of consciousness exist beneath the surface preoccupation with objective analysis that Western culture valorizes? The lean language strips the poems to a stark majesty and a craggy intensity that is at once hypnotic and beguiling.

G. S. Kirk, in his Lévi-Straussian analysis of the Prometheus myth as contained in Hesiod, the oldest extant source, concludes that humans in this Greek myth lived in Edenic unity with the gods until Prometheus's cunning caused Zeus to withdraw fire from mortals and expell them. Both Zeus's withdrawal of fire from humans (after Prometheus tries to trick him with inadequate ritual food offerings), and the arrival of pain and disease (as Zeus retaliates with the vulture and Pandora), relate to the attempts of early Greeks to mediate human aspirations for divine freedoms and our actual enchainment to a world of pain. Prometheus's final return of fire to humans and his willingness to endure his daily pain mediates the opposites.[14]

Hughes dovetails the final fire theft, the pain inflicted by the vulture, and the arrival of disease and infirmity from Pandora's box by having Prometheus place the stolen fire in the wombs of females (#13) and in the potentialities of consciousness (#7).[15] Prometheus's liberation depends upon understanding the significance of what he has done and learning to mediate the opposites of aspiration and pain by developing his imaginative life. How can his salvation lie in his submission to the world of pain he has created? To some extent Hughes is utilizing the well-worked romantic myth, summarized by Northrop Frye, Harold Bloom, and countless others, of how consciousness sunders the naive unity of the mind with nature, making us aware of our separateness. The task is to transform self-consciousness into redemptive vision in the mediatory realm of the imagination.

Words, because they name discrete objects and are the tool of the reasoning mind, may reinforce a consciousness of separation and fragmentation, especially when in the service of empirical analysis, the world of Blake's Urizen. In Hughes as in Blake, this only exacerbates the loss, creating the cold equations of matter and space. Awakening to this fallen condition, Prometheus feels both fright (#1) and the strength of an individuality that paradoxically comes from sundering the Edenic unity of self and nature (#2).

Prometheus's first shout—intersecting self-consciousness, voice, and language—sunders the Eden of "holy, happy notions"; in its place he develops a consciousness of the daily pain that attends existence—the vulture (#3). The shout represents the awakening of language as an instrument that can either reinforce through objective analysis a sense of separation from the world, or function as a probe toward an awareness of deeper states of being that can possibly reestablish moments of unity. For Hughes "words are the birds of everything" (#19), and Prometheus must learn to use them to become aware of deeper levels of being, not simply to scatter his thoughts into identifications of separate categories through ordinary analytic thinking—the "space-fright" of poem #19.

From Prometheus's first consciousness of language, his first "world's end shout" that awakened the vulture, the birds of words have become "what birds have ever since been, / Scratching, probing, peering for a lost world" (#3). The vulture is created by the sun's fiery energy, and as it daily splays Prometheus it creates the "headline letters" (#4) of words, the vehicle for recording either the fragmentary ordinary world, as in the endings of poems #7 and #11, or for articulating the struggle to reintegrate the self and the world of pain into the visionary unity hinted at in poem #17.

To regain his freedom Prometheus must return authority to within himself. He had recently divested himself of authority by investing it in man and God, beings in the space outside the self (#9), and this has pinned him to the rock of space, leaving freedom possible only in his "soul's sleepwalking" (#15) after enduring the daily pain of having his liver torn out. As with Sogis in *Orghast*, Prometheus must transform the pain of existence into spiritual illumination. To be human is to exist between the godly and the animal, as Sogis exists between Pramanath and Agoluz in Hughes's *Orghast* mythology (Smith, 96–97). The lizard, an animal of divination for Castaneda's Yaqui shaman Don Juan,[16] gives Prometheus an intuition of how lucky he is to be human: to be between the extremes makes possible both the expression in words of the conflict between aspiration and pain, and the possible mediation of the conflict in the realm of the imagination.

Once Prometheus receives the lizard's hint in poem #18, he is ready for his crucial moment of understanding: the recognition that the daily pain of existence, the vulture, is a "Helper" toward extending his awareness of deeper levels of being that can reunite self and world (#20). Words, though they can only articulate circling images of these altered states of consciousness (#20), are nevertheless crucial for probing the self's unacknowledged legislator within and reempowering the self to overcome obstacles.

With volcanic force Prometheus's new understanding frees him of bondage to the fragmentary actual world in the final poem. Twenty-one bulletins of "Puddled, blotched newsprint" have recorded a genuine struggle, articulated in words, toward becoming aware of deeper levels of being where self and world do not stand isolated, separate, chained in objective analysis. In the concluding lines Prometheus "balances" self and world in a floating state of unison on "peacock film," a bird whose rainbow feathers Jung identified with the reintegrated self in alchemy and Gnosticism (Jung 9a: 375).

Words Magical and Unmagical   The confrontation between the poetry of incantation and poetry occasioned by the recording of events where limited consciousness constricts vision occurs especially in "Earth-Numb," the third section of *Moortown*. Hughes introduced his BBC reading of "Earth-Numb" poems by stating that he consciously strove to develop the boundary theme: "The boundary . . . runs between awareness, and unawareness, between the life of the one and the mere circumstances of the other, and the baffled sort of collision between them."[17]

From his introductory comments in both the BBC "Earth-Numb" reading and a different, taped recording of *Moortown* poems, it is clear that what Hughes means by "awareness" and "the life of the one" concerns the ability of words to produce magical, incantatory effects that liberate repressed energies while strengthening and deepening our sense of self, our grasp of deeper powers and levels of awareness. For Hughes, poetry is "a biological healing process" that is "energizing": it creates a "final mood of release and elation," an "upbeat" psychological state that promotes well-being and success. Hughes compares poetry by analogy to the magical chants that tribal hunters recited before the hunt to hypnotize themselves into a "state of alertness and concentration of perfect confidence" that would promote success.[18]

The poem "Earth-Numb" receives pride of place because Hughes believed its incantatory language actually ended a period of poor success at catching salmon. The poem begins with a stillness that is electric with tension. Hughes's concentrated "searching / Like the slow sun," is about to galvanize nature into an explosive response. The language packs great power into simple, concise description. Dawn is "a smoldering fume," with birds "simmering" and sycamore buds "unsticking." All await the sun's concentrated energy, which the poet mimes with his hypnotically steady, incremental imagery. The images of a flower opening and a surgeon conducting open-heart surgery create just the right mood of delicacy and hold-your-breath tension.

Suddenly the reader is jolted by the force of Hughes's language into an essential contact with the real event, as the fish grabs the hook with a bang and "the river stiffens alive" while a "piling voltage hums, jamming me stiff." Hughes vividly recreates the process of catching the fish with "terrifying / Gleam-surges" and "Cartwheels," as if he "were the current." The energy released in the descriptive language unites poet, fish, and reader in the moment of struggle. The mood finally relaxes as the trapped fish gags his last and his eyes absorb their final glimpse of reality.

Many poems in "Earth-Numb" reside on the other side of the boundary, where tourists, tramps, secretaries, and retirees are treated satirically for their inability to develop strong individual selves. They have negated their potential for becoming free, authentic beings and have become prisoners of cravings for food and drink (131) or the thrill of possessions (93, 102–3). Others wrap themselves in egotism (97–98), rigid religious orthodoxy (94–96), sexual conquest (101), or are left with the dregs of a life that has never cohered into a self-reliant strength of personality (99–100). Some poems remain obscure, their themes insufficiently realized (160–63), or their symbolism puzzling and inaccessible until one finds the proper referential key (111, 159, 164).

Heideggerian Language   Other poems appear to be Heideggerian extensions of Blake's critique of scientific space-time—Heideggerian because intimately concerned with the nature of language and being. For Martin Heidegger the uniform measuring of time and space into numerical units creates a "desert" of self-enclosed units, uniformly equal and indifferent, which become aggressive technological tools for the dominance of the earth.[19] Macbeth's four nightmares in "Four Tales Told by an Idiot" end in a fear of the scientific space he has divorced from himself—the Urizenic vacuum of Crow's "Black Beast." Technological conquest becomes a frantic digging at a black hole in space.

For Heidegger, it is the customary nature of language to bring the fourfold elements of the earth together in their nearness to the speaking subject through the "saying" of language. Though language itself has no *thinghood*, no essential being, it is at the essential core of humans' experience of the world. Words bring the elements together to constitute a simultaneous grasp of self and environment in the moment of their encounter, where past and present coalesce as one moves toward the future. Only through language can humans express their relatedness to the elements of the earth; the essence of language is relatedness, a bringing together, the expression of a potential coherence of self and the elements to constitute "world."[20]

In the last of the "Seven Dungeon Songs" the persona struggles to make the elements of the earth fuse into an essential wholeness of world that would "speak" (Heidegger would use the word "say" or "make appear") the self's sense of relatedness in the felt moment of experience. The opening songs suggest how difficult a struggle this is, for our Western understanding of experience is otherwise. In the first song the Western babe mortally wounds the cosmic wolf "in the jaw"; here the first consciousness of language (the babe's laugh and cry) is concurrent with a sense of injury and, in the second song, the desire to dominate the wolf's "offspring," the "space-earth" of the poem's first line. The elements that should cohere into a Blakean or Heideggerian "world" lie in their separateness, in "bits and pieces," while the creative principle mourns the division in the third song and the "Tree of light" weeps in the fourth. A Macbeth-like neurotic frenzy occurs in the fifth song, with the persona desiring to "rush to and fro" to attach broken parts.

The last two of the "Seven Dungeon Songs" suggest the possibility of wholeness should the persona recognize the self as the originator of one's experience of the world. The sixth song suggests that all beyond the individual is silent until called to "world" by the self's saying, for no oracle, witnesses, rocks, birds, dust, or light cohere of themselves. They await the human call to world in the act of speech, suggested in the final song's faith that cliff, water, and all the elements could fuse with a reconstituted body to articulate the truth of actual experience. The seventh song especially conveys Heidegger's sense of the "pure simplicity" that a mature poet can experience in his awareness of language's power to speak an originative event in a poem, a simultaneous constitution of self and the elements to produce "world."[21] The "Earth-Numb" poems "A Citrine Glimpse," "Life Is Trying to Be Life," and "Song of Longsight" are all concerned with failures to constitute the "world" of the moment; an alienation of all outside the self produces the deathly inertia of scientific measurement in the coldness of space.

"Acteon," possibly the most spellbinding individual poem in *Moortown*, presents the consequences of acculturation to a divorced, mechanistic space. Acteon's perception will never be a synergetic grasp of the other through the speech of a unified self, as it might be were Hughes to write an eighth dungeon song. The face or nodal point of coherence of the other (the finished puzzle) cannot be grasped when the self is speaking "hooverdust." Instead of uniting into a grasp of world, the puzzle pieces zigzag out of control when language speaks the speech of technological gadgetry. The elements, lacking relatedness, become devouring hounds, minions of dominance, while the technocrat speaker remains distant, unmoved, anesthetized. The children of "Deaf School," because they lack the ability to hear speech and to experience hearing their own speech, are likewise left to perform mechanistic gestures in space that will always remain separate and never cohere to a Heideggerian "world."

The predatory fish in section 1 of "Photostomias" (originally "Chiasmadon") is depicted as a mathematical calculus, a "final solution" intent only upon his prey. The second section, however, locates a corresponding fiery agent of transformation within the unconscious of humans, a "Buddha-faced" tiger that fuses self and the elements into a coherent world where "Earth is gulping the same / Opium as the heart." The third and last section indicates that this transformative agent can empower language to evoke something akin to Heidegger's nearness, that relatedness where self and earthly elements cohere in the moment of their saying. The tiger in "Tiger-psalm" is a "Beast in Blossom" because, one with its environment, it pounces upon its prey with an economical, instantaneous directness. The tiger for Hughes represents an analogous human power —the seizure accomplished in the act of perception itself. More exactly, it is the Oriental act of perception that annihilates discrete objects by transforming them into a unitive vision of allness. Conceived as a dialogue between the Buddha (the tiger) and Socrates (machine-gun dialectical logic),[22] "Tiger-psalm" contains a tiger that "Kills like the fall of a cliff, one-sinewed with the earth, / Himalayas under eyelid, Ganges under fur."

Many of the 25 sections of "Orts" (the word means "table leavings") are leavings from "Lumb's Remains," an early version of the *Gaudete* "Epilogue." Both sequences share the theme of grappling with the problems of consciousness, the erotic and aggressive components of the id, the world of pain and the inevitability of death in the quest to envision the White Goddess. In "Orts" the struggle to attain a clear vision of a feminine principle is still in process, and the only vision of the Goddess that the persona is capable of realizing is the dim Persephone-like figure who walks the lawn in the last section. Yet even more so than the *Gaudete* "Epilogue," the poems of "Orts" concern attaining the power to use language accurately and faithfully to record the struggle. The eyes are always open to achieve "being" as an astonished vision of a welcoming host or Yeatsian "swan launching / Into misty sunrise" (#1), but brain and emotions are seldom alert enough and sufficiently in concord to seize the moment fully and articulate it exactly.

Words in "Orts" scatter from humans like seeds from a tree, but are these seeds living—do they articulate the real originative event—or are they senile (#2)? Are words granite gravestones reminding the writer of what is missing (#3)? Do words function as they do for many poets: as glib illusions that cause the clear "simple light" to flee as it did when the first words of aboriginal humans fragmented experience into abstractions (#6)? Do "the airiest words" codify into rigid orthodoxy (#9)? Are words shadowy masks that obscure an ulterior purpose (#11)?

The instincts arrive with man-eating music, a *"Grosse Fuge"* (#7) or a powerful express train (#19), but the human capacity to turn erotic charge into spiritual vision is too often lacking. Our perceptions are narrowed and our transformative powers atrophied by a culture that prizes rational consciousness—the symbolic food fed to empty coats in insipid, unvarying highway restaurants (#5). Though children have the bravura to believe that the words they utter will be tools for the seizure of reality, an "occupying army" of vocables, their weakly articulated visions will wear them out, will function as decomposers, not as revitalizing inspiration. Their words are infected larvae that will devolve into bacteria (#23).

Adam's Words: The Birds of Everything   Some of the most dazzling poetry Hughes has written appears in "Adam and the Sacred Nine," the concluding section of *Moortown*. It testifies to the power of human speech to transform the self and to ascend beyond the mundane. Here Hughes adapts the shaman's ecstatic flight to enlist supernatural aid for the purpose of creating one's "world" anew and healing self and community.

Hughes introduced selections from *Adam and the Sacred Nine* in a BBC radio reading by stating that God, who has lost patience with Adam's torpor, sends down "nine divine birds to become his guardian exemplary spirit" after all the creatures of the world have failed to convince Adam to "pull himself together and get moving."[23] The phrase "guardian exemplary spirit" specifically refers to the shaman's practice of enlisting helping spirits at the outset of his spiritual journey. Adam will revive himself through a shamanic flight that is coextensive with a revitalization of the power of language within himself.

In *Shamanism* Eliade wrote that very often American Indian or Eskimo shamans mimic the calls of birds to enlist them as guides to the world of the dead, and as vehicles to impel the upward ascent to vision. The shaman's use of such animals signifies a desire to abolish profane historical time and return to the reempowering prelapsarian moment of unity with all creatures. The birds grant the shaman the power to travel freely through earth, underworld, and sky in order to ensure the success of the flight (Eliade, 96–109).

As with Sogis in *Orghast* and Prometheus in *Moortown*, Adam will revive himself by recognizing that within his inner world he has the capacity to transform, with the aid of language and the imagination, his "fallen" state into one of spiritual ecstasy and visionary fulfillment. Language and the imagination will enable him to mediate the contradictions of his situation and revive his prophetic "voice" when the Phoenix arrives (#11). Prior to this the magic of the sparkling, highly evocative language of the other birds enables Adam to integrate his faculties and reunite with the four elements to utter a Heideggerian world.

The fresh, vivid images combine with a clean poetic line that contains a wonderful combination of vitality and compression. Individualizing traits of bird species quickly and effortlessly develop symbolic dimensions, suggesting scarcely definable psychic powers in humans. The Falcon's powerful, direct flight suggests a kindred power within humans for grasping situations completely and instantaneously (think of the Mozart reference in the *Lupercal* poem "Thrushes"); the Skylark's long, liquid warble in flight becomes a continual labor of joyous energy to adorn the sun with its crest; the daylong flight of the Swift "Shears" its way with "Whipcrack" movements of its long, slender wings, expanding beyond its bodily limits to satisfy spiritual burnings; the restless Wren's loud, rasping succession of notes becomes "A blur of throbbings" where "His song sings him"; the earless Barn Owl's nonrotating eyes become a stare "fixed in the heart of heaven" while its screams lead to a chiasmic eating of heaven and earth by each other as if participating in an Indian Yab Yum ritual.

Then the Dove comes with its rainbow breast, suggesting peace, promise, and a great capacity to absorb pain. Possibly the first bird to be domesticated by humans, the dove sacrifices herself to the mutable world. The pain of Jack Orchard, Prometheus, the persona of "Orts"—the pain of the entire volume—becomes transfigured into vision as the Crow whispers survival and the Phoenix "voice" of prophetic utterance follows. In each poem the bird's perceptive powers and song (speech) combine to unite self and environment, reviving the fallen Adam by awakening his imaginative life, the mediating realm where words can flower into visions that know no boundaries. The sequence and the volume end with Adam's thoroughly refreshed vision and his first words. Words convey Adam's fresh grasp of his world as if he were "the first host, greeting it, gladdened."

The Ceaseless Gift: *River*

Though much of his seventies work criticized Western science and religion, Hughes also offered guides to heal and transform the inner self through developing one's imaginative life in the *Gaudete* "Epilogue," the Jungian alchemy of *Cave Birds,* and the "Prometheus on His Crag" and "Adam and the Sacred Nine" sequences of *Moortown. River* extends Hughes's meditations upon how to perceive the outer world, a project initiated with the Taoist vistas of *Remains of Elmet* and continued in the farming poems of *Moortown.*

As *Crow* is Hughes's *Iliad,* an account of a destructive battle with the environment caused by scientific objectivity and alienated instinct, so *River* (1983) is his *Odyssey,* an absolutely stunning poetic voyage that teaches us how to refresh our senses and, more importantly, save our planet. In *River* Hughes offers his readers a complete guide to a life-enhancing mode of perceiving that is consonant with the current thinking of ecologists, historians, ethicians, and theologians about how to live holistically and ensure the survival of our fragile planet. *River* will one day be recognized as one of the central literary masterpieces of the world; it should be required reading for all humans on our planet to help them attain responsible adulthood.

Ecological Animism   The historian Lynn White, Jr., in an essay often quoted by ecologists, argued that Christianity paved the way for the ecological ravages of modern science by condemning the animism of tribal cultures as an idolatrous belief in a spirit world inhabiting nature. Once Christianity drained the spirit out of nature, humans could exploit it without regard to the needs of animals and plants or the preservation of minerals. In the West the Medieval Church supported the biblically approved domination of humans over nature (Gen. 1:28) by sanctioning a spirit of inquiry into nature's operations and by considering Saint Francis—the sole environmentalist of the Medieval church—a near-heretic.[24]

White's bold assertions do have some validity, though they oversimplify. Civilizations based on other religious traditions certainly contributed to erosion, deforestation, and other forms of natural resource depletion. And the context surrounding Genesis 1:28 can lead to another interpretation: that humans are stewards entrusted with the care and preservation of all entities in nature's hierarchy. Human freedom and the weak will's tendency toward pride are the real culprits, and these are present at all times and in every civilization and religious denomination.[25]

Nevertheless, major ethicians such as Eugene C. Hargrove, K. S.

Shrader-Frechette, Holmes Rolston III, Paul W. Taylor, and others speak in accord with Christian theologians and cultural historians such as John B. Cobb, Jr., Thomas Berry, and Ian Barbour in advocating a new vision of Christian stewardship that would be ecologically sound and promote equality among nations. Some feminist theologians venture further, breaking with Catholicism (Mary Daly), Protestantism (Carol P. Christ), and Judaism (Judith Plaskow) by calling for a new, nonpatriarchal religion with an ecologically grounded creation story. Apparently what is needed is a vision that combines the sense of the sacred in nature found in the animism of tribal cultures with the humility of Saint Francis.

Most would at least agree with the position of the intellectual historian Roderick Nash, who wrote in his *The Rights of Nature* that nature, like humans, has rights. Bedrock would be the ecologist Aldo Leopold's position, first stated in his 1949 essay "The Land Ethic," that what is ethical is what preserves "the integrity, stability, and beauty of the biotic community."[26] Hence endangered species have the right to survive, rocks have the right not to be polluted with oil spills, and the ozone layer has the right not to be depleted. The perspective articulated by the Catholic cultural historian Thomas Berry in *The Dream of the Earth* summarizes the new ecological awareness: "What we need . . . is the sensitivity required to understand and respond to the psychic energies deep in the very structure of reality itself . . . [in a spirit of] cooperative understanding . . . [akin to] the ultimate wisdom of tribal peoples and the fundamental teaching of the great civilizations."[27]

Hughes's essays and poetry place him in the vanguard of this burgeoning ecological awareness. White's observations are almost indistinguishable from many 1970 essay statements made by Hughes concerning the failure of Christianity, and Berry's remarks are very similar to many statements Hughes has made in essays concerning what nature and tribal cultures can teach humans about survival. The gorgeous poetry of *River* is a distillation of Hughes's grasp of ecology. Far from being merely a group of lovely poems and photographs about fishing (unfortunately, the American Harper and Row edition does not include the vibrant Peter Keen color photographs of the Faber edition), *River* is an ecological primer about learning to perceive the animistic energies that the fisherman persona experiences in nature. Often the poems are rendered with a wonderful Heideggerian simplicity and nearness of language. The sacredness of nature appears on every page in the recurrent light and water imagery, and the persona achieves a sense of delighted participation in nature after first exercising a humble reverence for its processes.

In the second half of *River* Hughes confronts the original mythopoeic moment identified and discussed by Joseph Campbell: a consciousness of death as the loss of the inhabiting spirit, which prompts meditations about where that spirit came from and where it returns to.[28] Just as early hunters postulated Animal Masters, spiritual beings who provided the tribe's main sustenance, Hughes seems to posit in his exaltation of solar light and the water cycle a Spiritual Master who sustains a cyclic round consonant with the speculations of Taoists, Greeks, and many ancient and tribal cultures.

After the ecstasies of late summer leaping and midwinter mating, the salmon, who typify the survival struggles of all animate beings in *River,* await death patiently, ready to drop a body that is "simply the armature of energy" (73). Their spiritual essence will then return to a supratemporal Source, for throughout *River* a Spiritual Master illuminates and invigorates all with its animistic energy. Water is chrism for survival and light is revelation of the Source. In the title poem of *River* "water will go on / Issuing from heaven / In dumbness uttering spirit brightness," and in "Salmon Eggs," the concluding poem of the volume, the river's "piled flow" reveals a "ponderous light of everlasting."

Leopold once wrote that "The most important characteristic of an organism is that capacity for internal self-renewal known as health."[29] This health is dependent upon the dynamic interaction of healthy organisms in the ecosystem. Through the mana power of his language, Hughes in *River* attempts to convey a sense of intimacy and holistic interaction with the environment that promotes psychological renewal and a reverence for nature. This can lead to such intelligent conservation practices as fish hatcheries—the restocking of the salmon supply described so reverently in "The Morning before Christmas." Primarily, however, the poems in *River* indicate that Hughes is most often concerned with evoking a sense of astonishment and aesthetic delight in the powers and vitality of nature— something akin to the animism of tribal cultures—in order to promote self-renewal in humans and a reverence for nature.

"Animism," a term coined by Sir Edward Burnett Tylor in his 1871 study *Primitive Culture,* has come to be understood as a polytheistic system in which animals and the elements of nature are believed to be endowed with vitalistic spirits. Shamans on their ecstatic journeys could tap the energies of these spirits, and the psychological and spiritual health of individual and community depended upon enlisting the aid of these energies and avoiding offenses such as transgressing sacred groves, using resources wastefully, or offending through improperly executed rituals, food offerings, etc. Though many anthropologists still consider animism as a childish view of nature, ecologists have for decades been pointing out the environmental soundness of this so-called primitive system, for it promotes resource conservation and reverence for the natural world.

It would be wrong to ascribe to Hughes a deliberate intent to reintroduce the animism of tribal cultures, but his reading is steeped in cultural anthropology, and his belief in nature's vitality has only deepened since *The Hawk in the Rain*. *River* celebrates nature's powers to refresh one's perceptions and promote psychological renewal. The river, the central symbol in the volume, is the "Primitive, radical / Engine of earth's renewal" that "Tries and tries to wash and revive / A bedraggle of dirty bones" (17). Because the hydrological cycle of the river will "return stainless / For the delivery of this world," it is "a god, and inviolable. / Immortal. And will wash itself of all deaths" (51).

Brilliant sequences of imagery occur in *River* to convey a vitalistic energy that leaves one with a sense of astonishment and awe at the power and beauty of nature. The mana power of Hughes's language generates energies kindred to those felt within the animistic beliefs of tribal cultures. Most often the river's sustenance is linked to an overspill of the sun's energy, as if the river's true source were the sun's tipped bucket of molten metal or an electric current sparked from the sun's generator (7). Salmon leap in it (66) and live in its "surge-ride of energy" (73). When the folktale Trickster Mink leaves his Northern Night and enters the river, he becomes animated, "A-boil with lightnings / He can't get rid of" (21). Even a small salmon nibbling the fisherman's hook has an electric shock "flash of arm for leverage" to wrench the pole away (32). An ewe entering the river is "lowering herself / To the power-coils / Of the river's bulge, to replenish her udder." Here the river "Embellishes afresh and afresh / Each detail" as Hughes's language bathes the reader in a vitalistic energy that seems omnipresent and emotionally cleansing (18).

At other times Hughes conveys the animistic energy of the river through moments of sexual or religious ecstasy. During the low water of August, the river teases with the slow allurements of an idle woman, offering sensual delights where "Thrills spasm and dissolve" (60). Hughes captures the animated energy of even the lowly stump pool in spring, when it boils up with oxygen as if to burst its bonds and remove the hill-wood's bridal veil (27). When the river is perfectly calm, rivergazing can suddenly pitch a fisherman or birdwatcher into moments of ecstasy akin to the "epileptic's strobe," Muezzin's "Bismillah," or dervish's frenzy (71).

Most often Hughes portrays the spiritual component of the river's animistic energy through light imagery. Light imagery coalesces with river water regularly to imbue riverscapes with a numinous aura, a sense of the sacredness of the hydrological cycle. Cock minnows gathering in a pool at Easter work together solemnly in the "lit water," an image Hughes expands at the poem's conclusion to convey brightness from the Source blessing their labor "In the wheel of light— / Ghostly rinsings / A struggle of spirits" (23). On the island of Skye an encounter with a salmon leaves the fisherman with a sense of being momentarily absorbed into the spirit world after miles of hiking toward the river's source while staring at the pool tail's "superabundance of spirit" (31). Under water, the mystical sea-trout "Hang in a near emptiness of light" (40); the West Dart River "spills from the Milky Way, pronged with light" (39); and the river's "Unending" sustenance, a wine distilled from the harvest it helped to fertilize, is squeezed from hills packed "Tight with golden light" (45). An abundance of visual and auditory similes and metaphors revive in the reader a sense of participation in an ecosystem that fulfills much more than one's craving for facts and analysis.

A 1980 fishing trip to southeastern Alaska produced the epiphanic "That Morning," where Hughes and his son Nicholas stand waist-deep in a river so filled with golden salmon that they experience a momentary transfiguration during which the body drops its "doubting thought." The poem's title echoes Eliade's *illud tempus* moment of paradisal unity with nature that so frequently appeared at the core of tribal myth making. In a "dazzle of blessing" the freed body becomes a vehicle for the spirit, a "spirit-beacon / Lit by the power of the salmon." When two golden bears wade in to prong salmon beside the fishermen, as if no separation existed between the orders of humans and animals, light and water imagery once again coalesce: the poem ends with all "alive in the river of light / Among the creatures of light, creatures of light."

As in tribal animism, animals in *River* possess an energy, a power of concentration, and a singleness of purpose that at times makes them superior to humans. The sea-trout concentrate in yogic trance, oblivious to the ordinary (40–41), while the eel, alive in a body ill-suited for grasping the outer world, appears so patient and self-absorbed as to be otherworldly (69). The mink lives in such a frenetic expenditure of energy that he can make love "Eight hours at a go" (21), while the damselflies of "Last Act" rehearse the whole span of copulation and death within minutes, for the female's fierce embrace often kills the male and the oviposition of eggs near the water line soon after leaves her vulnerable to predators.

Kingfisher and cormorant have the ability to dive and grasp their prey with an instantaneous crackle of energy. The kingfisher dives with a sudden "blue flare," like a taut electric wire suddenly snapped. He exits with a diamond-cutter's precision, leaving a "rainbow splinter" of blurred energy. In his swift and precise movements he appears superior to humans, closer to god: "Through him, God, whizzing in the sun, / Glimpses the angler" (47). In "A Cormorant" the bird, unlike the preoccupied fisherman, achieves his purpose by concentrating so single-mindedly that he becomes one with his prey, like an aborigine still absorbed in his prehunt trance. A second, more incisive look at the cormorant in "A Rival" reveals a ruthlessness beneath the single-mindedness. Technological and predatory imagery characterize the cormorant as one whose self-interest and dictatorial iron will leads to ecological disaster.

Everything Is Connected   Unlike the cormorant, the river sustains an ecosystem that interrelates humans with animals, vegetation, the land and its minerals. "River Barrow" is one of many poems in which Hughes suggests that the best way for humans to refresh their perceptions and experience psychological renewal is to achieve a consciousness of this relatedness. Here language conveys a Heideggerian presence; Hughes refreshes our capacity for experiencing the nearness and relatedness of the environment by interweaving past and present while the river pulses with its "living vein" toward the future. Humans integrate peacefully with animals, insects, vegetation, and river water while appreciating a dynamic yet balanced ecosystem:

> We sprawl
> Rods out, giant grasshopper antennae, listening
> For the bream-shoal to engage us.
> The current
> Hauls its foam-line feed-lane
> Along under the far bank—a furrow
> Driving through heavy wealth,
> Dragging a syrupy strength, a down-roping
> Of the living honey.
> It's an ancient thirst
> Savouring all this, at the day's end,
> Soaking it all up, through every membrane
> As if the whole body were a craving mouth,
> As if a hunted ghost were drinking—sud-flecks
> Grass-bits and omens
> Fixed in the glass.
> Trees inverted
> Even in this sliding place are perfect.

All evil suspended. Flies
Teem over my hands, twanging their codes
In and out of my ear's beam. Future, past,
Reading each other in the water mirror
Barely tremble the thick nerve.
                                              Heavy belly
Of river, solid mystery
With a living vein.

Experiencing the ecological relatedness of nature can cleanse the self of the surface clutter of schedules and objectives that complicate one's life. Appreciating the beauty of nature at first-hand can relieve one of the stress of ordinary analytic thinking and egocentric decision making. "Go Fishing" is a triumph of sound ecological thinking that also synthesizes the advice of Patanjali's *Yoga Sutras* and most Zen and Taoist masters. The lambent mood and wonderfully tactile imagery point the reader toward desiring to bathe once again in the elements of nature and know them at first hand, in their honest, precognitive *suchness,* without labeling and distancing. This simplicity conveys the real relation of self to experience that Heidegger considers the fundamental purpose of language. To "Lose words" in the sense of losing the commonplace tags for objects, to "Let brain mist into moist earth" in the sense of divesting oneself of analytic thinking, and to be "Dismembered" by the "sun-melt" of river and the elements, is to experience anew the tactile relational presence of nature, the *whatness* that words refer to. Only at this moment can one "Try to speak and nearly succeed"—a further stage of progress than the subjunctive mode at the end of "Seven Dungeon Songs" in *Moortown.*

The Humble Fisherman   The fisherman persona whose adventures the reader follows throughout *River* is a hunter, a sport fisherman on a quest for the salmon. But his interest does not end with the challenge and finesse of catching a few salmon to eat. He has a deep curiosity about this marine survivor from the Paleolithic; he wants to locate its spawning grounds in the stump and source pools of rivers, learn its ways, and discover what the salmon have to teach him—what wisdom from prehistory they can impart (31, 55). He is responsive to the ecology of each area because he possesses a certain humility about the intervention of humans in nature, and respects the interrelatedness of things. He knows that, when humans disturb the meditations of sea-trout, the fish will "scram" (41) and he knows that he is an interloper (54–55) whose species has polluted the river with "bicycle wheels, car-tyres, bottles / And sunk sheets of corrugated iron" (74).

The fisherman's gentle, self-deprecating irony in many early *River* poems indicates that he is aware of the limitations of his ordinary rational mind and is willing to learn from nature. As he peers down at the salmon in the March river water, he experiences the sadness of separation: he views salmon "Trapped" in a "sand-storm boil of silt" while his consciousness, equally trapped in the element of air, is "a guttering lamp" (19). A cormorant can spear its prey with no aid save his naked eyes, wings, and claws, but the fisherman flounders in seven-pound waders, a heavy jacket, a sagging bagful of lures, a hat that embarrasses him, and a six-foot-long net that snags on every twig and fence-barb (25–26). For only a nibble from a small salmon he must walk for miles through suck-holes and clatterbrooks while repeatedly glancing at his watch so he will not miss the boat home (30–33). Always the self-deprecating irony is soft and ingratiating, for the fisherman (and the reader) soon become sensitized to how quickly toil can lead to astonished revelation in the unforgettable contact with a salmon.

Animal and Spiritual Master   "After Moonless Midnight" is a pivotal poem in *River*, for here the fisherman persona loses his ironic distance and becomes trapped in the river-fetch. From here on he begins to commune more directly with the river and to empathize much more deeply with the survival struggle of the salmon. The fish, with their "magical skins," initiate him into a mythopoeic drama of mortality and transcendence. The hunter becomes the hunted when the river whispers " 'We've got him.' " As the fisherman begins to understand the larger dimensions of the hunt ritual, a spiritual realm opens, revealing the origins of the idea of the sacred.

The salmon are magical creatures for the Indians of the Northwest Coast of North America, and it is no wonder that many of their great festivals coincide with the salmon runs. The salmon are their main source of food, and the salmon as provider reaffirm a religious dimension and inculcate an ecologically sound reverence for life. The salmon for these Indians are the gift of Salmon Woman or Bright-Cloud Woman, who ensures a plentiful supply of the fish as long as Trickster reveres her.[30] This is a type of myth that Joseph Campbell calls the Animal Master, a way Paleolithic hunting tribes resolved the problems of guilt arising from the necessary eating of an animal they otherwise admired. They postulated a spiritual realm that received the departing spirit of the animal who has lost a mortal body of little importance. Belief in a spiritual abode for humans appears to have first occurred at the same time among hunting tribes, for the earliest anthropological evidence of belief in an afterlife occurs with the cave paintings of the hunt and the deposit of tools, weapons, and treasures in the burials of hunting tribes. The cave was the cathedral of the spirit, a supratemporal dimension that tribal hunters actually believed to exist. Burial gifts were deposited in the belief that the spirit of the departed still lives in a transcendent realm.[31]

Though Hughes does not directly allude to Animal Master myths in *River,* his reverential language supplies the spiritual equivalent of the cave cathedrals of Paleolithic hunters, and we know from his *Crow* poems that he developed a very masterful and intimate knowledge of the Northwest Coast Indian Trickster myths. "The Morning Before Christmas," an early poem in *River,* conveys a sympathy with the survival struggle of the salmon, but without application to the spiritual needs of humans. Gradually the fisherman hunter does become aware of how the salmon's struggle reveals the mysteries of life and death and typifies the survival struggle of all beings. This awareness promotes a deeper, more sympathetic bond between hunter and hunted.

Hughes supplies some necessary factual information about the life cycle of the salmon in two *River* poems and a note. "The Morning before Christmas" mentions that the salmon's chances are "five thousand to one against survival." Though only Pacific salmon always die after mating, the survival chances of Atlantic salmon are also very poor. A note to a photograph on page 126 of the Faber edition states that very few survive the spawning run. At the river's mouth commercial nets and natural predators such as seals, sea lions, and otters await the salmon runs. Sport fishermen, winter cold, low river water, summer pollution, and the harvesting of sand-eel also reduce the Atlantic salmon population.

In "October Salmon" one learns that the Atlantic salmon return to spawn and probably die at an average of six pounds weight and four years of life. This prompts a cri de coeur in stanza 9, a very direct expression of grief over the shortness of life. Since Hughes has been an avid fisherman since age three and completed *River* past the age of 50, a biographical dimension appears obvious. To mediate and resolve the contradictions of mortality for humans as well as the salmon, Hughes adapts the Animal Master myth. The concluding salmon poems of *River* open a cathedral for the spirit and reveal the presence of the eternal in the temporal.

More than half of the poems following "After Moonless Midnight" are concerned with mortality and death. The meditative and often ironic "I" gradually disappears as the fisherman becomes absorbed in the drama of the salmon. Implicitly the salmon's deathward journey relates to the fisherman's own, and he slowly reconciles himself to his intuition that this journey is in harmony with the natural order of the ecosystem. As fall arrives the sense of the deathly in the river's flow becomes more intense and so does the fisherman's identification with the salmon. The poignant irony of the salmon's end—to die so soon after mating—is mediated by the hope for the continuance of the inhabiting spirit in a transcendent realm, the abode of a Spiritual Master.

Immersing oneself in first-hand experience does have its dark side, as does the river. The river in "Last Night" smells of sickbeds and slimes at night, leaving the fisherman feeling as if he "stood in a grave" when he stands "In the dying river." "In the Dark Violin of the Valley" conveys a similar feeling of temporality and death as the fisherman senses the gradual, unrelenting erosion of the river "Cutting the bed-rock deeper" with its dark violin music at night. These poems develop earlier reflections on the mortality of all who depend upon the river. The river may be an immortal god, but the "river's cargo" in "Four March Watercolours" is "A solution / Of all dead ends—an all-out evacuation / To the sea." A leaping trout must return immediately to water, a "peculiar engine" that "works it to death" in "Ophelia."

As August ends, the salmon and sea-trout move up the river to mate and spawn in hollowed-out riverbed grottos. In low water "An August Salmon" is a bridegroom "rapt" in visions and patient in his wedding cell. He has "the clock of love and death in his body" and like a monk kneels and "bows / Into the ceaseless gift / That unwinds the spool of his strength." Moved by the salmon's martyrlike resignation to the natural order, the fisherman becomes aware of a cosmic dimension, an instance of White Goddess drama with her male consort, as he observes the salmon awaiting "execution and death / In the skirts of his bride." When the river begins to cool toward winter, the fisherman senses in "August Evening" a sacred drama in the "religious purpose" of the sea-trout processions: "Robed in the stilled flow of their Creator / They inhale unending. I share it a little." The sense of mutuality in a sacred drama becomes more acute.

Hughes revised "The Gulkana," another poem written about his 1980 Alaskan fishing trip, for the American Harper and Row edition, adding about 42 lines. Thirty of these added lines occur at the point where the fisherman lands a huge Chinook salmon and gazes into its eye. The added lines speak of a resignation to the cycle of love and death as ordained by nature. This is expressed through an imagined ritual on a tribal "platform of water" where the river tears the flesh from the fish in a "dance-orgy of being reborn." Also added are lines suggesting a premonition of the fisherman's own death as he writes the poem "Word by word" on the return flight. Here he admits that the "burden of the river" caused "a secret bleeding of mourning / In my cave of body" as he inspected the huge salmon's eye. Once again Campbell's original mythopoeic moment occurs: knowledge of eventual death directly precedes the hope for the continued existence of an essential spiritual core.[32]

The final three salmon poems in *River* contain an apotheosis of the plight of the salmon with emphasis upon the sacredness of a drama preordained by nature and in accord with her ecological cycle. The intense identification of fisherman with his prey is reinforced with sacramental and light imagery to arrive at a mystical participation in the salmon's death, as in Animal Master rituals. Consent to the cycle as ecologically providential transforms death into resplendent rebirth, with a majestic assertion at the conclusion of "Salmon Eggs," the last poem, that *"only birth matters."*

A patient, humble acceptance of his role adds dignity to the salmon of "September Salmon." Oblivious to weir and insects, he wears his scars of age. Buoyant in sacramental imagery, he appears "sacred with lichens" for an autumn benediction. In the final stanza he "adds his daub" as he leaps into the September sun. "October Salmon" is a more rhetorical testimonial to the salmon's toil and a sympathetic outcry against death. Having served nature loyally, the salmon returns home, his skin leprous with sores for badges. A steady veteran, he finds the pool of his birth an appropriate home for his death. He expects no favors; indeed the river's "flow will not let up for a minute."

As the fisherman cries out against the salmon's subjugation in "October Salmon," a bonding occurs: through an intense sharing in the salmon's suffering, the fisherman becomes the salmon, the salmon is the fisherman. The eternal aspect of the life and death cycle dawns upon the fisherman, and the full message of death breaks in upon him: "And that is how it is, / That is what is going on there." The body is just the "armature of energy," a vehicle to be dropped to free the spirit for a return to "that covenant of Polar Light." Yet here the fisherman communes so intensely with the physical agony of the salmon and the indignity of its plight that he fails to take any consolation in the heavenward return of the spirit.

Only by losing his ego in "Salmon Eggs," the concluding poem of *River,* is the fisherman prepared for the final spiritual revelation. When "my eyes forget me" (the "me" of egocentric selfhood), the fisherman becomes one with the "piled flow" and the "ponderous light of everlasting." He consents to the holiness of the process, the "Perpetual mass / Of the waters," for he recognizes the eternal within the temporal, the presence of a Spiritual Master who has ordained this process. All issues from "the swollen vent / Of the nameless," the Tao or supratemporal first principle. The poem is superbly crafted, with short stanzas that mark deepening stages of insight. Subtly evocative rhythms buffet a language that whispers softly a sense of spiritual beatitude, as if spoken in Chartres. The fisherman disappears into the river's great silence, swathed like a Zen adept in the allness of nature.

"Where there is no vision, the people perish," states Proverbs 29:18. All of *River*, but especially "Salmon Eggs," offers a wonderfully positive and life-enhancing alternative to Crow's myopic vision. Hughes has constructed a cathedral of ecological vision to show his readers how to enliven their imaginations and save our planet.

Chapter Six
The Direct Grasp: *Flowers and Insects* and *Wolfwatching*

The Simplicity of Fable: *Flowers and Insects*

Since becoming poet laureate, Hughes has had to adjust to increased requests from his public and more limited writing time. Recently he stated that he receives approximately six requests for appearances and readings every day. Accepted requests for just an hour's appearance—often at the other end of the United Kingdom—may reduce the month's available writing time by two or three days each.[1]

Nevertheless, when Hughes does find time to write, he is often capable of reaching a level of penetration, incisiveness, and synthesis that resolves complex problems into the simplicity of a minidrama or microtragedy. His more recent verse records the mind's groping toward a final resolution in deceptively simple language, with a voice that is increasingly more supple and flexible, yet also able to convey complex emotions with an audacious alternation between a powerful directness and equally powerful, consciousness-raising tensions created by oblique juxtapositions of worlds of reference. Single objects or simple situations become the locus for a cosmic drama or a revelation of mysteries at the heart of existence. As Hughes wrote in a 1980 introduction, poems that appear to contain simple description may be the lucid result of a complex struggle that "has the simplicity of an inclusion of everything in a clear solution." This happens when "the experience of having gone through the complexity has changed the observer, and brought him to a direct grasp of the inner sources of the subject, which are always simple."[2]

Though at first reading they may seem extraordinarily direct and simple, the 17 poems in the 1986 *Flowers and Insects* are not children's poems precisely because of Hughes's ability to reveal essential human dramas and mysteries in his meditations upon the beautiful Baskin drawings they accompany. Like mandalas, Baskin's luxuriantly colorful drawings often coax Hughes's psychic resources into an exalted state similar to a yogin's ecstatic meditations, where complex problems are resolved into clear solutions that appear on the page directly and simply. Metaphors and images are not ornamental and the tone is not sentimental, as in much of the children's verse; all is essential to the "spiritualized morality" where a "strong imaginative grasp" records "visionary parables" in individual poems.[3]

The meditative poetry of *River* has undergone a transmutation into the concentrated simplicity of fable in *Flowers and Insects*. Just as fables are simple tales that actually distill centuries of wisdom, so too Hughes's recent poems are visionary distillations of a lifetime of meditation on the human condition. The poems of *Flowers and Insects* are Hughes's own unique compositions, yet as meditations on human foibles their ancestors include Jotham's bramble and Aesop's vain jackdaw and idle grasshopper. Often the tone of these poems is ethereal and the point of view cosmic, with a combination of serene control and deep pity somewhat like that of Chaucer's Troilus at the end of his tale as he peers down upon human pain and folly from his eighth-sphere remove. At other times the mood conveys a majestic solitude where the poet's consciousness seems to levitate in a palpable spiritual quiet, like Michelangelo, the "Long-Legged Fly" whose "*mind moves upon silence*" in the late Yeats poem.

The opening flower and landscape poems of *Flowers and Insects* are meditations on mortality that express some anxiety concerning the mutable world, but not the surrealistic fright of the opening poems of *Wodwo*. A stronger grasp of essentials leads Hughes to ponder more directly and with greater control the similarities of human and plant life. Both are imprisoned in decaying forms. Human brain and blood cells are as unaware and blindly groping as brambles (12). If the numbness wears off and a dim level of awareness enters, humans become susceptible to delusions of rebirth into a protective heaven, like narcissus bulbs wintering in the earth (9). Yet the elements grind the earth and the landscape crumbles, with no relief. Humans are as frail and as momentary as the violet at Lough Aughrisburg (10–11).

The riddle of mortality that surrounds the early flower poems like a nimbus or halo comes to the foreground in "Daffodils." Since he moved to Court Green, Hughes had become accustomed to picking and selling the thousands of daffodils that bloomed every spring near the garden (*Letters Home,* 453). For Hughes the blooms originally conveyed the lushness of spring rebirth in the prime of one's life, but now as he ages he suddenly notices that, as in Christmas tree rituals, cutting the flowers actually reveals the impermanence of life, the fleeting, substanceless passing of days that have "Hardly more body than a hallucination!" Very erotic description in which cutting daffodils is linked by images to the act of deflowering maidens contrasts with the eerie description of the odorless stalks that whisper the numbness of the grave in the night's dreams that follow. One dream's attempt to transform the blooms into resurrection trumpets occurs, only to be rejected as the mind's delusion. The persona awakens to comfortless shivers and draughts as the poem concludes.

Living as bulbs of the earth, the loglike Lumb and the townsfolk of *Gaudete* are prevented from attaining any final knowledge of mortality and the meaning of life by the distractions of summer and the drunken dream of sexuality. Similarly, in *Flowers and Insects* the surprise at the conclusion of a brilliant extended metaphor reveals summer as a trapper "In the Likeness of a Grass-hopper." Summer is herself the trap, a "wicker contraption" containing a spring tensed and baited with Aesop's grasshopper to attract with his violin the song of the "wild earth." Efficient and uncaring, she leaves to set more traps.

Sexuality is a drug that also prevents humans from achieving a lucid grasp of their condition. The "Two Tortoiseshell Butterflies" are "drunk with earth-sweat" and "conscripted" into courtship, filled with titillations and tremblings, intoxicated and absorbed in an infinitely delicate ritual. But they have no freedom; they do "what's required / Of the splitting bud." The erotic hawthorn flower and apple blossom addle both the starlings and the poet trying to concentrate on writing a letter (32), the "everted" blooms of the iris overpower a bee entranced by its "loosely dangling helplessness" (36), and the floppy breasts of the foxglove make one's drugged head swim (44). The poppy's huge petals, like "carnival paper skirts," seem like the urgent abandon of a mafia queen whose core bleeds inwardly, hidden from view by her flamboyant carelessness. After only a few days, the petals drop all at once, revealing a withered, early old age, a self-created coffin, a body whose drugged core burned its fuel too quickly (53).

Hughes finds no easy solution to the riddle of mortality, but he does face the problem honestly rather than avert his gaze. Again and again the poems reveal that the best humans can do is raise their level of awareness to the point of delighted trance, of mystic participation in the allness of being, in the freedom achieved through a moment-to-moment interfusion of self, world, and activity. This is the mystic trance of the *Elmet* wind-shepherds, the sea-trout of *River,* and the nostalgia for a Yeatsian unity of being in "Thrushes," where one longs to be "Blent in the prayer." In *Flowers and Insects* the "Tern," as with other Hughes animals, achieves instinctively an instantaneous fusion of self and world in the moment of its activity. Its body and brain fuse into a well-honed harpoon that prongs the sand-eel. The tern's actions speak "a precarious word" and its "meaning has no margin," no limits, no separation of self and action, no division into parts.

Hughes's prescription against anxiety concerning mortality in *Flowers*

and Insects is to achieve states of mystic exaltation that transcend the deep
divisions and fears created by a conscious mind apprehending an objective
world. Probably the most famous parable that articulates this transcendent
condition is the butterfly dream of the Taoist mystic Chuang Tzu: "Once
Chuang Chou dreamt he was a butterfly, a butterfly flitting and fluttering
around, happy with himself and doing as he pleased. He didn't know he
was Chuang Chou. Suddenly he woke up and there he was, solid and unmistakable Chuang Chou. But he didn't know if he was Chuang Chou who
had dreamt he was a butterfly, or a butterfly dreaming he was Chuang
Chou. Between Chuang Chou and a butterfly there must be *some* distinction!" The humor and the point of the parable is that there should not be
any distinction: become the free butterfly through an act of self-
transcendence. Interfuse self and environment; recognize no distinctions.[4] In
Flowers and Insects advice from a mystical adept occurs in "Cyclamens in a
Bowl" and in "Saint's Island."

Rapt in meditation, "quietly gazing" at the flowers, the persona of "Cyclamens in a Bowl" sees serpent stem open to "butterfly face." The peculiar
posture of the flower, at once plunging like a horse but with "five petals
elated— / A still of tensile flight!" coaxes persona and reader into a visionary leap where flower parts and bodily organs merge in the stanza following
the two-line parenthesis. When the spirit moves, the bulky body follows.
The poem ends with the cyclamen leaves, the "solid" and worn "physiques
of substance," opening palms to air that is "simple and good"—not cold
and mutable, as in the opening poems.

In "Saint's Island" the molting mayfly at first appears ludicrous. It develops in the mud for a year only to do an obligatory mating dance for a few
hours before dying. Because the mayfly is so incongruous in our world, with
jaws and digestive tract useless during its few hours of unfeeding flight, the
fisherman asks "What is it doing on earth, anyway?" But once the fisherman
empathizes with its frenzied flight, with its complete unity in the moment,
unselfconsciously using up every ounce of energy like the gnats of the
Wodwo poem "Gnat-Psalm," he recognizes blood cells that are awake and
alive—the reverse of "Brambles." The mayfly's weak vision becomes "A rose
window in blood-cells, / A Holy Grail of neurons." Its last molting is really
a dropping of the physical body to put on spirit. Like a Dervish, the mayfly
is "Drunk with God." Astonished at the mayfly's capacity to live the fleeting moment ecstatically, the fisherman reverses his initial position and wonders "What are we doing on earth?" The ideal would be to forget these
divisive questions and bring awareness to that pitch of penetration where for
a period of time the fisherman becomes mayfly like Chuang Tzu became

butterfly. This state of consciousness would be far preferable to the persona's anxious worry in "Eclipse," where, magnifying glass in hand, he wonders when the male spider will be crushed in the grasp of the female—another White Goddess ritual death for her consort.

Psychic Ecology: *Wolfwatching*

The poems of *Wolfwatching* (1989), Hughes's latest volume, are not for the faint of heart. The 21 poems are nearly equally divided between poems about animals and *Elmet*-type poems of growing up in West Yorkshire. Each poem in the latter group presents an unvarnished, unblinkered stare, powerful in its directness or image juxtapositions, at all that does not go gentle into that good night; they range from a cri de coeur at the thwarted dreams and disconnected meanderings of the elderly to attacks on the stifling impositions of a monolithic culture that has stunted the spiritual growth of the youthful and the aged. Yet the direct stare releases a wealth of often contradictory feelings that readers will recognize as being close to the richness of life as it is actually lived. Many poems offer portraits of parents and close relatives, disarmingly candid portraits that are more humane than those in Lowell's *Life Studies* because Hughes is less interested in exposing individual weaknesses of character than he is in revealing how incredibly ubiquitous are the effects of a diseased, impoverished, warped cultural heritage upon the spiritual potential of all its inhabitants.

The family portraits of *Wolfwatching* are poignant in their candor, with a deceptively simple language and narrative flow that at times generates emotions so complex, painful, elemental, and overpowering that the reader may momentarily avert his or her gaze. These almost embarrassing glimpses of the naked and tortured spirits of the elderly reveal the hopelessness of lives ending with a bleak finality that is as sour and fungoid as the leaf mold beneath their feet. What the decayed leaves contain, as in the poems of *Elmet,* is the residue of the science, religion, and machine technology of the Industrial Revolution, and the carnage and detritus of the Great War. As usual in Hughes's poetry, the warped culture is related to the violent catastrophe as cause to effect.

Wolfwatching contains portraits of a father who survived Gallipoli in a coma of silence punctuated by grotesque public laughter and intermittant private weeping. The son matures in a cracked cultural crucible where he inhales "visionary defeat" (7) while his father convalesces from the psychic wounds of Gallipoli. His mother's wisdom is a perpetual *Missa Solemnis* of mournful folklore that mixes the most minute elements of the environment with the cloth trade and the war. Rolling a pine needle is like threading a sewing machine; an ant's egg looks like Billy Holt's shuttle (39).

A psychic ecology operates throughout *Wolfwatching.* Just as humans in their proximity to one another affect each other's actions and beliefs as they watch, converse, and cooperate, so too the content, the energy, and the quality of their interactions can either exhaust or renew the spirit. Liberation and periodic renewal must occur if humans expect to cohere in a dynamically interconnected ecosystem, but what are the opportunities for liberation and renewal in the West Yorkshire culture of Hughes's youth? Hughes admits that to survive he used up "a lot of spirit" as the psychic ecology of the family subtly placed him in the position of being his father's "supplementary convalescent" (13). The mother's folklore works its inexorable way into her son with exponential effect, so that he feels like her "step-up transformer" (39) as he becomes enchained to the gruesome West Yorkshire heritage of looms, bibles, and clog-irons.

At one level *Wolfwatching* updates Balzac's intuition from *La Peau de chagrin* (The wild ass's skin) that humans are endowed with a certain mass of psychic energy at birth, and one can exhaust this magical skin quickly or slowly according to the drives of will and power, or transform it into renewable intellect and spirit. Though he may not have read Balzac, Hughes's intuitions about the finite endowment and spiritual potential of psychic energy certainly indicate some shared beliefs. Hughes's major modification concerns the force of received cultural myths in the growth or exhaustion of spiritual potential. If the cultural myths do not liberate, ennoble, and renew, than everyone is conscripted into a futile dependency where each preys on the spiritual reserves of the other. Throughout *Wolfwatching* the culture is the main villain, scalding and bleaching the spirit until, scarred and numb, it fails to connect at all with the environment in old age.

The elderly in this culture have not attained a vision that can grasp the environment with the inbuilt gyroscopic wisdom of age; at best their vision captures shards and pieces in a very loose net, or reposes in inertial numbness, failing to grip the external world with any vestige of the viselike lock of Hughes's early animal poems. In perhaps the most painful of all the poems in the volume, Hughes in the two-part "Walt" records how a sniper's bullet from the war temporarily maimed his uncle's body but left his spirit in a state of perpetual paralysis. Though he became a very successful garment factory owner, that bullet "brought him and his wife down together, / With all his children one after the other" (44). At 84 he still fails to "grasp what's happened," for "His frown / Won't connect." All he can do is drown his alienated soul in wine, steroids, and tranquilizers and utter a periodic, heart-rending monosyllable: " 'Aye.' "

The end of the second part of the poem is particularly affecting. Unable to "just die," Walt in his pain stares toward the Atlantic from a mountaintop fence rail. Every whiff of the sea "Is another swell of overwhelming. / Meaningless." Almost able to place his finger on the cultural wound, he breathes another " 'Aye' " and his stare suddenly meets Hughes's watchful gaze head-on. The moment is too searingly electric with poignancy and too nakedly painful even for the very caring and sympathetic embrace of the poet's eye. The poem ends with Hughes crying "Walt! Walt!" silently in his heart and burying the emotion of the momentary encounter in an averted gaze, a flustered downward glance. All is deposited "Hugger-mugger any-how / Inside my shirt." A poet whose main interest is reputed by some to be violence could never experience the compassion needed to write this poem, nor communicate the pain with such a depth of pity.

Of the other *Elmet*-style poems in *Wolfwatching,* "Climbing into Heptonstall" best reveals the cultural dilemma. Here a guide leading tourists through the Hebden area of West Yorkshire remarks tonelessly that " 'You will notice / How the walls are black.' " This remark provokes a "madman" in the group to shout a lengthy sardonic eulogy for the textile culture of the valley, demanding that the sooty walls be scrubbed, that the penury and cold comfort of the candle and psalms be exorcised, that the region be swept clean of its empty factories and its anesthetic "penny-hunger" herb that seems to embody its depravations. After the madman leaves with a "tuneless wail," the guide, heedless, returns to his empty sermon for tourists: " 'Before us—stands yesterday!' "

This is an earthier, crustier Hughes railing at human folly like the wild old men in late Yeats, and feeling the Eliotic delights reserved for age: the lacerating laughter at what no longer amuses and the powerless rage at human folly, as in the doppelgänger passage of "Little Gidding." *Wolfwatching* functions as the flip side of the *Elmet* coin or the second part of a dyptich, a reversal of the optimism that a decade earlier confidently deposited the remains of Industrial Revolution culture in West Yorkshire into an ecological compost heap for future renewal. In *Wolfwatching* the poisoned culture infects each succeeding generation; both walls and psyches may be too stained to be scrubbed clean.

The non-*Elmet* poems of *Wolfwatching,* mostly about animals and environmental concerns, also promote the psychic ecology theme. Recently Hughes supplied helpful comments on three key poems.[5] Hughes explained that "Macaw" developed a fantasy of Iago's punishment: "to be re-

born as Malvolio in the form of a caged parrot." At the end of *Othello* Iago is
remanded to the Lord Governor for imprisonment and torture, but the
exact nature of the torture is never specified. In the poem Hughes half-
comically suggests, after meditating on a real parrot, that jammed down the
bird's gullet is a plastic reed, a "Torture instrument of brittle plastic" that
emits grotesque screeches. Its coat of bright blue feathers is a mockery, and
its nervous kneading on its perch yet another part of a diabolic punishment
for Iago's heinous crime. In *Othello*, to "speak parrot" is to babble
(2.3.281); the macaw's garbled voice seems a fitting punishment for one
whose false counsel caused irreparable human tragedy.

Hughes's rebirth motif in "Macaw," where the Macaw is a reborn
Malvolio, has a more widespread application to *Wolfwatching*, for
Pythagoras's belief in the transmigration of souls underlies Hughes's comments about "Macaw" and knits together the animal poems and the *Elmet*-
like poems in the psychic ecology of the volume. Imprisoned as a lunatic in
Twelfth Night, Malvolio undergoes a comic examination of his sanity by the
Clown disguised as Sir Topas the hermit. When Malvolio professes not to
believe in Pythagoras's doctrine of the transmigration of souls after death
into beasts or birds, he is pronounced still insane and left in prison (4.2. 54–
63). Pythagoras's doctrine, one of the animistic beliefs of tribal cultures, applies to most of the bird and beast poems of *Wolfwatching*, especially "A
Sparrow Hawk," "Little Whale Song," "The Black Rhino," and "A Dove,"
the optimistic concluding poem to the volume. Unlike the elderly victims of
West Yorkshire culture, these birds and beasts are intimately connected to
their environment. Their grasp and grip grant them control and a liberating, renewing freedom unless they unwittingly become entrapped in the
diseased cultural myths of humankind.

The bird's eyes in "A Sparrow Hawk," the opening poem of *Wolfwatching*, are "wired direct" to the sun's core. In the first two stanzas Hughes
suggests that the sparrow hawk's tenacious grasp of the earth at one level
personifies a power within humans, a capacity for penetrating vision whet-
ted by "The sun's cooled carbon wing" that makes its swift and intuitive
connection with the sun's energy long before one's first lumbering
thought clarifies. Poets who have learned how to develop and train this
power usually call it the creative spirit or the visionary imagination. In his
letter Hughes stated that in "A Sparrow Hawk" he attempted in part to
suggest "Yeats' poetic self as Cuchulain reincarnated in a bird—a sort of
Celtic Horus."

The dominant motif of vision in "A Sparrow Hawk" and Hughes's allusions to Cuchulain and to the Egyptian Horus combine to specify the poetic

imagination as the liberating ideal. From this plateau the reader descends to the enfeebling West Yorkshire culture in the ensuing poems. Horus, the solar falcon in Egyptian mythology, is the chief of the spirits in the Egyptian Book of the Dead and certain Pyramid Texts. Its right eye is associated with the rising and setting sun and the healing power of Thoth.[6] According to Joseph Campbell, Horus embodies the resurrected creative power of his father Osiris, and this creative power contains the *ka* or eternal vital force that lives in all gods and all earthly beings (Campbell 1962, 87). The recurrent eye imagery of "A Sparrow Hawk" suggests that a liberating creative power for spiritual renewal is always available to promote a psychic ecology among humans, but the twisted myths of certain human cultures in the history of the species have often stifled rather than promoted the development of this power. With his vision bruised to a state of paralysis by his culture, Walt— like a contemporary everyman in Beckett's plays—can perceive only meaningless vistas when he gazes toward the Atlantic.

Other animal poems in *Wolfwatching* indict a diseased Western culture as the cause of ecological and environmental tragedy. The "global brains" of whales in "Little Whale Song" possess an "all-dimension / Grasp" of the world, and their song is a diving and rising rhythmic merge into oneness with "the world's lit substance." A cosmic dance renews at each moment the felt presence of the world as a beautiful fusion of self and other—a more leisurely version, on a colossal scale, of the mayfly's ecstatic frenzy in *Flowers and Insects*. Yet these cetaceans are a royal family acting out a tragic drama, rising for a dive that is "The most terrible fall." Commercial whaling has exterminated the gray whales, and other species are endangered and nearly extinct despite international controls.

The problem is that, though most animals are so perfectly attuned to their environment that they move with its motions and restrict predatory behavior to personal necessity, humans can distance themselves from the environment and use their powers of abstraction in ruthlessly utilitarian ways. When these ways become encoded into a culture's beliefs, they foster a diseased mode of perception that perpetuates utilitarian abuse on a global scale. As more and more of the globe becomes assimilated into the dreams of an infected Western culture, the diversity and autonomy of nature vanishes. When the rhino of "The Black Rhino" cries "You are the crime" to the pensive scholar in the vision that comprises section 2 of the poem, the animal does more than echo Oedipus's personal realization in Hughes's *Seneca's Oedipus,* for the rest of "The Black Rhino" suggests that the criminal "you" of human culture acts like a step-up transformer, magnifying the slaughter far beyond the scope of a one-city contagion. The rhino "is in-

fected / With the delusions of man"; it has "blundered somehow into /
man's phantasmagoria, and cannot get out."

As the technological power of the machines devised by the Industrial
Revolution grows, cultural delusions have become more powerful than the
checks nature can devise through environmental hazards, distances, and the
vagaries of weather. The *Wolfwatching* endnote about the slaughter of the
black rhino details some of the background information of the slaughter, to
which one can readily add other important details. Diseased Oriental and
Near Eastern myths combine with Western technology and supply-and-
demand marketing to facilitate the tragedy. Though the rhino's horn is
composed of keratin, the same substance that comprises fingernails, it is
prized by Oriental cultures for having magical medicinal and aphrodisiac
properties because the rhino's prodigious strength is believed to be contained in its horn.

Worse is the poem's own statistic in section 3: most of the 50,000 North
Yemenite youths who each year reach maturity want rhino-horn hilts for
their daggers, as macho proof of virility, and those rich with oil profits can
pay the price. But the wounded rhino bleeds to death after its horn is reck-
lessly severed, and as of 1989 fewer than 4000 rhinos remained on this
earth. One rhino horn can earn a poacher enough money to feed his family
for months, and in the international market in 1989 the horn is more dear
per pound than cocaine, selling at three times the price of gold.

Even more disastrous, however, was the Thatcher government's handling
of the 1984–85 coal workers strike, for it seemed to doom an entire social
class of humans to extinction. "On the Reservations" obliquely compares
the demise of the English coal workers with the late nineteenth-century demise of the Indians in the American Southwest. Blue-collar workers in England have never achieved dignity or the confidence of equality within their
culture; in the poem Hughes argues that the Iron Lady's rigid handling of
the yearlong strike is another expression of a diseased culture's inhumanity.
The workers returned grimly to the mines in March 1985, having achieved
nothing but empty wallets and stomachs from their opposition to the
Thatcher government's decision to streamline operations by cutting capacity and closing enough inefficient mines to place 10 percent of Britain's
nearly 200,000 miners on the dole. Slaves of the empire, the dejected workers in the poem appear as relegated to extinction as the whale or rhino. They
have become "a surplus people" purged from the culture like the American
Indians or Stalin's enemies.

The blackened faces and sooty garb of the coal miners in the poem appear to be their mark of Cain, emblematic of having been tossed into pits by

a culture whose "bible of coal" spawns throwaway humans in a cultural laboratory, the coal belt between the Mersey and Humber rivers. They gain only the blue scars of coal dust permanently embedded in their pores as they fuel British industry. In section 1 Hughes combines artifacts of the mining industry with those of an uncaring consumer culture. Adapting the defacing techniques of postmodern painters to poetry, Hughes juxtaposes this agglomeration of artifacts, a hideous melange, as a grotesque bulge in the Christmas stocking of the quietly dignified Sitting Bull. In the second section a woman widowed by a mining disaster cannot eradicate her waking nightmare vision of mines having become mass graves, formicaries of consumer indifference and the callousness of a government in some ways as ruthless as Stalin's Russia.

The Ghost Dancer of section 3 breathes the miners' last hope—to "Start afresh, this time unconquerable." A shamanic dancer lost like a dervish in the ecstasy of his dance and his resplendent garb, he prophesies a "lightning stroke" deliverance that "Puffs the stump of Empire up in smoke." Yet the epigraph identifies the dance as a weeping entreaty for life. The historical context of the dancer's actions, never intruding into the muscular energy and vivid description of the lines, changes hope to despair, for the Indian cults of Ghost Dancers in the 1880s and 1890s who prophesied the imminent end of white dominance were a last gasp of transmogrified despair. Like Nora's tarantella in *A Doll's House,* the Ghost Dance that concludes "On the Reservations" signifies that the cultural environment suffocates the human spirit.

The same sort of complexity underscores the title poem of the volume. It is initially pleasant to see Hughes again composing poems about wolves, as he did in the early poetry and "Seven Dungeon Songs" in *Moortown,* and pleasant to see a poet in his ripe age focusing upon the lineaments of age in the animal. The mood is relaxed, almost laconic, mirroring the aged wolf's shuffling of "useless weight," his "Jumble of leftover scraps and bits of energy / And bitten-off impulses and dismantled intuitions." But when the poet's gaze shifts to a young wolf also trapped in a zoo cage, and focuses upon that young animal's slowly growing neurosis as his self-assured boredom, his muscular power, energy, and razor-sharp senses slowly fester with disuse, one's pleasant mood evaporates. What the young wolf fails to recognize in the withered spirit of his elders is that the future bodes disaster, a cheating repetition of the same spiritual torpor. The closing lines present a vista of despair, as barren as a landscape in de Chirico or Tanguy, where the young wolf suffers like the hanged god in Frazer, with a pair of eyes "Like

doorframes in a desert / Between nothing and nothing." This culture exhausts without renewing, incarcerating both body and spirit in futility.

Amid all this bleakness Hughes remains heroically engaged in the
human enterprise, suggesting in his final poem a spiritual potential that,
with an overlay of Pythagorean optimism, remains available for all who can
attain it. In the concluding poem of *Wolfwatching* the "snickering" wings of
"A Dove" mount its dream of love and peace into space. Then it cavorts with
a companion, expending a throwaway energy captured in the plosive
"plungings" and "explosions" of the poem. Like the "Acrobats" of *Lupercal*
in their effort and grace, the doves knit together the psychic energy of animals (the porpoises) and humans (the temple-dancers) in the psychic ecology of *Wolfwatching*. Their road of excess resolves struggle and despair into
the palace of renewed spiritual potential. The words of the poem supply
both the direction and the spark of spiritual renewal. Even in this bleak volume Hughes affirms that the world of art—especially the reader's contact
with the poems—provides the environment for a consciousness-raising
vault beyond a diseased culture.

Where Where?

To ask the question "Where is Hughes's poetry headed?" is to fall into
the *Moortown* tractor's "trap of iron stupidity." Hughes has been remarkably
consistent in his vision, and will continue to use events from his daily life as
opportunities to deepen his grasp of the human condition and articulate its
joys and limits. He knows as did Yeats that consciousness is "fastened to a
dying animal / It knows not what it is," but he offers neither a comfortable
nor a desolate heaven for the swan of the human soul to leap into. His verse
is maturing into the ripeness of age, and his counsel, spoken directly into the
teeth of decay and death, is to become absorbed in life like the gnat, mayfly,
or dove—with whatever intensity and vision one can muster. There exists a
very rich ecology of ideas in Hughes; instead of predicting where his verse is
heading, being receptive to whatever his meditative reach raises up out of
the lough can prove more satisfying.

Hughes's work has throughout affirmed that the world of art—the
words on the page—can renew the spirit and liberate the individual from
ignorant adherence to malformed cultural myths. His poetry also provides
eloquent testimony that there are moments of connectedness and even ecstasy that punctuate our days, moments when life does make sense, and
moments when it is joyous to be human. Having read through the entirety
of his poetry many times, one of my very favorite lines by Hughes is one of

the simplest: that lizard breath that Prometheus hears, his own intuition telling him " 'Lucky, you are so lucky to be human!' " (*Moortown*, 84). That line is woven into the binding of every volume Hughes has written.

As a coda, I would like to direct attention to some of Hughes's accomplishments that did not fit the interweaving of life and literary influences in chapter 1 of this text, but are listed in the chronology. I mention them because they tell something of the character and commitment to real education through literature and living that makes Ted Hughes's career one of remarkable coherence and distinction. As an educator of children, he has published more than a dozen children's works, broadcast dozens of self-scripted talks for children, reviewed children's books, and for 25 years has been a judge of a national children's poetry competition.

As an educator of adults, Hughes has widened our knowledge of poetry by helping to translate and publish the work of many Eastern European poets. For years he was the coeditor with Daniel Weissbort of *Modern Poetry in Translation*. By selling his Lumb Bank home to the Arvon Foundation and providing regular assistance to the foundation, Hughes has helped to offer affordable creative writing courses taught by established writers in a unique country setting where tutors live with the students and work individually with them. Martin Booth, in a recent survey of contemporary British poetry, called the Arvon experience "at the core of what British poetry ought to be doing these days."[7] Hughes was also a leading organizer of the first Arts Council International Poetry Festival, now held every summer in London.

Although through the years Hughes has allowed fair copies of his poems to be auctioned to raise money to save trees and salmon, or composed poems to help raise funds to save rhinos, or donated the proceeds from first newspaper printings to environmental organizations, he is an activist primarily in desiring a better psychic and cultural environment for humans. Normally his poetry preserves the human spirit, raises the worth of the shares we nearly forgot we owned in our stock of uniqueness and selfhood, and enhances our potential for living rich, satisfying lives on planet Earth.

Notes and References

Chapter One: Introduction

1. Austin Layard, *Discoveries among the Ruins of Ninevah and Babylon* (New York: Harper & Brothers, 1859), 271–72.

2. "The Hanged Man and the Dragonfly," in Alan Fern and Judith O'Sullivan, *The Complete Prints of Leonard Baskin* (New York: Little, Brown, 1984), 20.

3. "Modern Poetry," *BBC Talks for Sixth Forms,* prod. Tom Butcher, recorded 24 May 1963, 3.

4. On the function of the libido in Jung and its relation to the therapeutic healing process, see also Wolfgang Hochheimer, *The Psychotherapy of Carl Jung,* trans. Hildegard Nagel (New York: G. P. Putnam's Sons, 1969), 34, 62–67.

5. See also "Secret Ecstasies," review of *Shamanism,* by Mircea Eliade, *Listener,* 29 October 1964, 677–78.

6. Review of *Primitive Song,* by C. M. Bowra, *Listener,* 3 May 1962, 781.

7. Paul Shepard, "Introduction: Ecology and Man—a Viewpoint," in *The Subversive Science,* ed. Paul Shepard and Daniel McKinley (Boston: Houghton Mifflin, 1969), 1–10.

8. H. D. F. Kitto, *Greek Tragedy* (Garden City, N.Y.: Doubleday, 1954), 139–42.

9. Shepard, "Introduction: Ecology," 1; John Jones, *On Aristotle and Greek Tragedy* (New York: Oxford University Press, 1968), 83–87.

10. Quotations from the poems of Ted Hughes used throughout this text derive from the American Harper & Row, Viking, Knopf, or Farrar, Straus & Giroux editions listed in the Selected Bibliography. Page numbers in parentheses are added whenever poem titles are omitted.

11. In a letter to the author, dated 28 July 1989, Hughes slightly revised the account quoted from a 1967 W. S. Merwin letter in Paul Carroll, *The Poem in Its Skin* (Chicago: Big Table Publishing, 1968), 149–50.

12. Letter to Aurelia Schober Plath, dated 22 August 1960. The letter resides in box 7, folder 2, of the Sylvia Plath Manuscripts 2 Collection, Lilly Library, Indiana University.

13. The following digest of the marriage of Hughes and Plath, and of her suicide, derives principally from Anne Stevenson, *Bitter Fame: A Life of Sylvia Plath* (Boston: Houghton Mifflin, 1989), and from Linda Wagner-Martin, *Sylvia Plath: A Biography* (New York: Simon and Schuster, 1987). My summation also derives from half a decade of teaching Plath in university courses, numerous readings of Plath's *Journals* and *Letters Home,* and familiarity with a great deal of secondary

criticism on Plath, mostly feminist in orientation. I have also reviewed the entirety of Plath's correspondence, including passages deleted from *Letters Home,* at the Lilly Research Library, Indiana University. See Plath, *The Journals of Sylvia Plath,* ed. Ted Hughes and Frances McCullough (1982; reprint, New York: Dial Press, 1982); *Letters Home,* ed. Aurelia Schober Plath (New York: Harper & Row, 1975).

14. See J. M. Newton, "Mr. Hughes's Poetry," *Delta* 25 (Winter 1961): 6–12; Sydney Bolt, "Ted Hughes: Laureate of Leucotomy," *Delta* 42 (February 1968): 4–11; Ian Hamilton, "Ted Hughes: *Crow,*" in his *A Poetry Chronicle* (London: Faber & Faber, 1973), 165–70; Calvin Bedient, "On Ted Hughes," *Critical Quarterly* 14 (Summer 1972): 103–21; and David Holbrook, "Ted Hughes's *Crow* and the Longing for Non-Being," in *The Black Rainbow,* ed. Peter Abbs (London: Heinemann, 1975), 32–54.

15. See, for instance, the account of an event that Dido Merwin reports Hughes said was a turning point in their marriage (Stevenson, *Bitter Fame,* 206, 334). One morning in early February 1961 Moira Doolan interviewed Hughes about doing a children's series for BBC radio. Plath had mistakenly surmised that the Irish lilt in Doolan's telephone voice suggested a young woman who would become a rival for Hughes's affections. When he returned late for lunch because the interview went well, he saw his drafts of about half a year's work—poems, a play, notebooks, and even a favorite edition of Shakespeare—torn to shreds. Plath never mentioned incidents such as this in *Letters Home.* As Linda Wagner-Martin observed (*Sylvia Plath,* 174), "Sylvia seemed to use her letters home to explain away her impolite behavior. It was as if her letters allowed her to fictionalize the real events of her life—Aurelia [her mother] was far away and so she would never know the truth of Sylvia's stories."

Plath believed in *manipulating* events in the service of more important poetic truths (see Plath's introductory statement to her reading of three *Ariel* poems in *The Poet Speaks* [Argo Records, PLP 1085]), but this belief often left family and friends to suffer from her venomous satire. She satirized close friends in *The Bell Jar,* presented unkind portraits of her mother in "Medusa" and of Dido Merwin in "Face Lift," turned her mother's own childhood ballet experiences against her in "The Disquieting Muses," and turned the gentle horse Ariel into the breakaway Sam of her Cambridge years (see "Whiteness I Remember") for the title poem of *Ariel.* Similarly, Plath in "Daddy" transformed her father, a lifelong pacifist, into a Nazi, and her husband, idealized for years in *Letters Home,* into "A man in black with a Meinkampf look/And a love of the rack and the screw." Pangs of conscience after the 14 January 1963 publication of *The Bell Jar* may have influenced her final bout with depression.

In a 12 October 1962 letter to Aurelia, Plath told her mother that she was writing "as if domesticity had choked me." It was a hugely manipulative "as if." Readers of *Ariel* are left to infer that Hughes was an unfeeling patriarch and Plath a diaper-ridden domestic drudge. The situation in rural Devon in 1961–62 was hardly a sexist purgatory. Soon after moving in, Hughes and Plath equipped the home with a Bendex washer, and Nancy Axworthy, the cleaning women who regularly worked for the former owners of Court Green, did ironing, floor scrubbing, and light cleaning two mornings each week. And Hughes cared for the children every morning while Plath wrote.

16. "Tricksters and Tarbabies," review of *Literature among the Primitives* and *The Primitive Reader,* by John Greenway, *New York Review of Books,* 9 December 1965, 33–35.

17. Northrop Frye, *Fearful Symmetry* (Princeton: Princeton University Press, 1969), 32.

18. For the best summary of basic Jungian tenets, see Jolande Jacobi, *The Way of Individuation,* trans. R. F. C. Hull (New York: Harcourt, Brace & World, 1967), 42–48, 60–81.

19. Carl Jung, "On the Psychology of the Trickster Figure," in Paul Radin, *The Trickster* (New York: Greenwood Press, 1969), 206–11.

20. "The Environmental Revolution," review of *The Environmental Revolution,* by Max Nicholson, *Your Environment* 1, no. 3 (1970): 81–83.

21. "The Gentle Art," *BBC Home Service,* recorded 24 February 1961, 3.

22. Patanjali, *The Authentic Yoga,* trans. and ed. P. Y. Deshpande (London: Rider, 1978), 19, 118; Mircea Eliade, *Yoga,* 2d ed. trans. Willard R. Trask (Princeton: Princeton University Press, 1969), 47.

23. Mai-Mai Sze, *The Tao of Painting,* 2d ed. (Princeton: Princeton University Press, 1963), 3; Arthur Waley, trans. and ed., *The Way and Its Power* (New York: Grove Press, 1958), 52, 110–12.

24. See Freud, "Revision of the Theory of Dreams," in *New Introductory Lectures on Psychoanalysis,* trans. and ed. James Strachey (New York: Norton, 1965), 7–27; for Jung, see Jung 16: 139–61.

25. See the chapter on Lévi-Strauss in G. S. Kirk, *Myth: Its Function and Meaning in Ancient and Other Cultures* (Berkeley and Los Angeles: University of California Press, 1970), 42–83.

26. For excellent introductions to the work of Derrida, see Gayatri Chakravorty Spivak, "Translator's Preface" to Jacques Derrida, *Of Grammatology,* trans. Spivak (Baltimore: Johns Hopkins University Press), ix–lxxxvii; and Jonathan Culler, "Jacques Derrida," in *Structuralism and Since,* ed. John Sturrock (New York: Oxford University Press, 1979), 154–80.

27. Thomas West, *Ted Hughes* (New York: Methuen, 1985), 51–52.

Chapter Two: The Hawk in the Rain and Lupercal

1. In a 26 February 1976 letter to the author, Professor David Trump of the Cambridge University Department of Archaeology and Anthropology stated that no one has kept departmental reading lists for the 1954 tripos. Trump, however, had himself read for this tripos in 1953, and remembered some of the works and authors on the list: Evans Pritchard's *Nuer* and *Witchcraft among the Azande,*

Firth's *We the Tikopia* and *Elements of Social Organization,* Malinowski's *Coral Gardens of the Pacific* and *Sorcerers of Dobu,* van Gennep's *Rites de Passage,* and books by Mayer Fortes, Margaret Mead, Ruth Benedict, R. F. Fortune, and Durkheim. Trump misremembered one reference: R. F. Fortune wrote *Sorcerers of Dobu.*

2. Hughes, "Creatures," *BBC Home Service,* prod. Owen Leeming, recorded 5 May 1960, 1.

3. See Jacobi, *Individuation,* 51–56.

4. As quoted in John Horder, "Desk Poet," *Manchester Guardian,* 23 March 1965, 9.

5. Mary Douglas, *Evans-Pritchard* (Sussex, England: Harvester Press, 1980), 1–38, 49–73.

6. Robert Cassidy, *Margaret Mead* (New York: Universe Books, 1982), 22–41.

7. Kirk, *Myth,* 42–83.

8. Claude Lévi-Strauss, *Totemism,* trans. Rodney Needham (Boston: Beacon Press, 1963), 77–90.

9. John Crowe Ransom, *The World's Body* (Baton Rouge: Louisiana State University Press, 1938), 112–42; *The New Criticism* (Norfolk, Conn.: New Directions, 1941), 279–336; "The Concrete Universal: Observations on the Understanding of Poetry," reprinted in Ransom, *Poems and Essays* (New York: Vintage, 1955), 159–85.

10. Cleanth Brooks, *The Well-Wrought Urn* (New York: Harcourt, Brace & World, 1947), 213–14.

11. "Ted Hughes Writes," *Poetry Book Society Bulletin,* no. 15 (1957):1.

12. Franz Kafka, letter to Oskar Pollak, dated 27 January 1904; reprinted in Kafka, *Letters to Friends, Family, and Editors,* trans. Richard Winston and Clara Winston (New York: Schocken Books, 1977), 17.

13. Agnes K. Michels, "The Topography and Interpretation of the Lupercalia," *Transactions of the American Philological Society* 84 (1953): 47–51.

14. Max Weber, *The Protestant Ethic and the Spirit of Capitalism,* trans. Talcott Parsons (1930; reprint, New York: Charles Scribners' Sons, 1958), 62–63, 108–17.

15. "Poetry and Performance: 4," *BBC Home Service,* recorded 2 August 1960, 8.

16. See also Peter Elfred Lewis, "The New Pedantry and 'Hawk Roosting,' " *Stand* 8, no. 1 (1966): 58–65.

17. Alfred Alvarez, "An Outstanding Young Poet," *Observer,* 27 March 1960; Stanley Kunitz, "The New Books," *Harper's Magazine,* September 1960; 103-4; E. Lucas Myers, "The Tranquilized Fifties," *Sewanee Review* 70, no. 2 (1962):218–20; Alun Jones, untitled review, *Critical Quarterly* 2, no. 2 (1960): 184–85; John Holmes, "A Poet Seeks the Limits of His World," *Christian Science Monitor,* 25 August 1980, 8.

Chapter Three: Wodwo and Crow

1. Freud, *Totem and Taboo,* trans. James Strachey (New York: W. W. Norton, 1950), 141–61; *Beyond the Pleasure Principle,* trans. C. J. M. Hubback (London: Hogarth Press, 1922), 19–25, 44, 54, 76.

2. "The Poetry of Keith Douglas," *Listener,* 21 June 1962, 1069–70; Introduction to *Selected Poems of Keith Douglas* (New York: Chilmark Press, 1964), 11–14; "The Crime of Fools Exposed," review of *The Collected Poems of Wilfred Owen,* ed. C. Day Lewis, *New York Times Book Review,* 12 April 1964, 4, 18; untitled review of *Men Who March Away,* ed. I. M. Parsons, *Listener,* 5 August 1965, 208.

3. "Superstitions," review of *Astrology,* by Aldus, and *Ghost and Divining Rod,* by T. C. Lethbridge, *New Statesman,* 2 October 1964, 500.

4. "Arnold Wesker: 'A Sort of Socialism,' " review of *The Wesker Trilogy, Nation,* 19 November 1960, 402.

5. Alan Moorehead, *Gallipoli* (New York: Harper & Brothers, 1956), 360–61.

6. Untitled review of *Men Who March Away,* 208.

7. "Vasco Popa," *Tri-Quarterly* 9 (Spring 1967):202.

8. See also Jacobi, *Individuation,* 30, 39, 88.

9. For Celtic rebirth doctrines, see W. Y. Evans-Wentz, *The Fairy-Faith in Celtic Countries* (1911; reprint, New York: University Books, 1966), 42, 182.

10. Ernest Wood, *Yoga* (Baltimore: Penguin, 1962), 60–61.

11. D. T. Suzuki, *An Introduction to Zen Buddhism* (New York: Grove Press, 1964), 50–51.

12. Sir James G. Frazer, *The Golden Bough,* abridged ed. (1922; reprint, New York: Macmillan, 1951), 628–29, 664.

13. "The Brother's Dream," *BBC Third Programme,* recorded 8 November 1965.

14. Eliade, *The Myth of the Eternal Return,* trans. Willard R. Trask (New York: Pantheon Books, 1954), 6, 9, 12–17.

15. "On Writing for Radio," *BBC New Comment,* recorded 16 January 1963, 3.

16. Frazer, *Golden Bough,* abridged ed., 709–17.

17. "Vasco Popa," 204-5.

18. Suzuki, *Essentials of Zen Buddhism,* ed. Bernard Phillips (New York: E. P. Dutton, 1962), 402–14.

19. Jung, "Trickster Figure," in Radin, *Trickster,* 202-9.

20. Franz Kafka, "Reflections on Sin, Pain, Hope, and the True Way," in *The Great Wall of China,* trans. Willa Muir and Edwin Muir (New York: Schocken, 1948), 298–99.

21. On science and religion, see Albert Einstein, "Religion and Science," reprinted in *Ideas and Opinions,* ed. Carl Seelig (New York: Dell, 1973), 46–58; on

164 TED HUGHES

music and science, see Ronald W. Clark, *Einstein* (New York: Avon Books, 1972), 140–41.

22. Suzuki, *The Essence of Zen Buddhism* (London: Buddhist Society, 1947), 13–14.

23. "Superstitions," 500.

24. Hartley Burr Alexander, *North American Mythology*, vol. 10 of *The Mythology of All Races*, Louis Herbert Gray, gen. ed. (Boston: Marshall Jones, 1916), 257.

25. Suzuki, Erich Fromm, and Richard De Martino, *Zen Buddhism and Psychoanalysis* (New York: Harper & Row, 1960), 56.

26. Sagar, 106, 235; and Terry Gifford and Neil Roberts, *Ted Hughes: A Critical Study* (London: Faber & Faber, 1981), 115–17, 257n.

27. Hughes, Ruth Fainlight, and Alan Sillitoe, *Poems: Ruth Fainlight, Ted Hughes, Alan Sillitoe* (London: Rainbow Press, 1971), 16–17.

28. See also the record-jacket blurb for the Claddagh Records recording of *Crow* (CCT 9–10, 1973).

29. Hughes et al., *Poems: Fainlight, Hughes, Sillitoe*, 18.

30. Radin, *Trickster*, 124–28, 145–46, 155–56, 164–69.

31. See chapter 1, note 16.

32. Greenway, *Literature among the Primitives*, 80.

33. As quoted in Gifford and Roberts, *Ted Hughes*, 116.

34. Letter to Terry Gifford and Neil Roberts, dated October 1979, reprinted in Gifford and Roberts, *Ted Hughes*, 256n. See also Hughes, "A Reply to My Critics."

Chapter Four: Gaudete and Gave Birds

1. Evans-Wentz, *The Fairy-Faith In Celtic Countries*, 18, 252, 358–96, 469, 490–91.

2. Frazer, *Golden Bough*, abridged ed., 351–52.

3. Otto Rank, *The Double*, trans. and ed. Harry Tucker, Jr. (Chapel Hill: University of North Carolina Press, 1971), 69–86.

4. Jung, "Trickster Figure," in Radin, *Trickster*, 202–9; Jung 9a: 284–85; Jung 9b:34; Jung 11: 76–79.

5. Frazer, *The Golden Bough: A Study in Magic and Religion* (London: Macmillan, 1911), 2:361–65.

6. E. A. Wallis Budge, *Osiris*, rev. ed. (New York: University Books, 1961), 1: 10, 65–66, 82.

7. Plath, "Ocean 1212-W," reprinted in *Johnny Panic and the Bible of Dreams* (New York: Harper & Row, 1980), 24. Aurelia reported to Anne Stevenson (*Bitter Fame*, 14) that Plath manipulated the events of "Ocean 1212-W": Sylvia's younger brother Warren crawled into the waves, and a family friend recovered the baboon carving. Plath narrates both events as her own actions.

8. The *Gaudete* "Epilogue" contains 45 short poems, separated by diamond-shaped dividers, but not numbered. In my discussion I number them for

convenient reference. The first Harper & Row and Faber & Faber editions, however, omitted a diamond divider after #20. Poem #20, "I said goodbye to earth," should end with the line "On a dark sill, and to bleed."

9. Budge, *Osiris*, 1: 277–78, 281; 2:40, 326 (scarab & Khepera); 1:46, 148; 2:37, 39, 315, 326 (Horus).

10. For Sekmet and Devi, see Campbell 1962, 5–6, 90–91; Zimmer, 48, 70, 138, 139; and Wendy Doniger O'Flaherty, trans. and ed., *Hindu Myths* (New York: Penguin, 1975), 247–49. For white bull, see Zimmer, 61, 137–38, 197–99; and Graves, 105–6, 134.

11. For sun and *ātman*, see Robert E. Hume, trans. and ed., *Thirteen Principal Upanishads*, 2d ed. (1931; reprint, New York: Oxford University Press, 1971), 27. For Hercules as doorkeeper of the gods, see Graves, 177.

12. Frazer, *Golden Bough*, abridged ed., 1–7.

13. "Secret Ecstasies," 677–78.

14. "Cave Birds," *BBC Radio 3*, prod. George Macbeth, recorded 26 May 1975.

15. Friedrich Nietzsche, *The Birth of Tragedy and The Genealogy of Morals*, trans. Francis Golffing (Garden City, N.Y.: Doubleday, 1956), 93–94.

16. Ibid., 86.

17. George C. Vaillant, *Aztecs of Mexico*, rev. Suzannah B. Vaillant (Garden City, N.Y.: Doubleday, 1962), 32, 42–44, 166.

18. See also Jacobi, *Individuation*, 59, 74–75.

Chapter Five: Remains of Elmet, Moortown, and River

1. R. J. Putman and S. D. Wratten, *Principles of Ecology* (Berkeley and Los Angeles: University of California Press, 1984), 84.

2. "Earth," *BBC Light Programme*, recorded 28 September 1961.

3. Donard Worster, *Nature's Economy: The Roots of Ecology* (1977; reprint, Garden City, N.Y.: Doubleday Anchor, 1979), 12–13.

4. Chuang Tzu, *The Complete Works of Chuang Tzu*, trans. Burton Watson (New York: Columbia University Press, 1968), 36, 47, 94, 168.

5. Paul Sears, "Ecology—a Subversive Subject," *Bioscience* 14, no. 7 (July 1964): 12.

6. Waley, *The Way and Its Power*, 149, 174, 178, 206, 217.

7. Chuang Tzu, *Complete Works*, 74.

8. In Waley, *The Way and Its Power*, 141.

9. Chang Chung-yuan, *Creativity and Taoism* (New York: Harper & Row, 1970), 5, 7, 36; Suzuki, *Essays in Zen Buddhism, First Series*, ed. Christmas Humphreys (1949; reprint, New York: Grove Press, 1961), 214–66.

10. Chuang Tzu, *Complete Works*, 240.

11. Mircea Eliade, *Myth and Reality*, trans. Willard R. Trask (New York: Harper & Row, 1963), 139–40; *Myths, Dreams, and Mysteries*, trans. Philip Mairet (New York: Harper & Brothers, 1960), 15.

12. George Steiner, *Language and Silence* (New York: Atheneum, 1970), 12–35.

13. "Moortown," *BBC Radio 3,* prod. Fraser Steel, recorded 6 February 1980, 1–2.

14. Kirk, *Myth,* 196–97, 226–30; *The Nature of Greek Myths* (Baltimore: Penguin, 1974), 136–43.

15. Discussion and poem numberings refer to the "Prometheus on His Crag" section of the 1979 Harper & Row *Moortown.* The original 1973 Rainbow Press *Prometheus on His Crag* contained encounters with Pandora (#5) and Io (#12), and a poem discussing Prometheus's understanding of his fire theft (#17). For the *Moortown* version Hughes deleted these three poems. The *Moortown* "Prometheus" poems numbered 5, 7, and 17 are new. See Scigaj, 269–72 for an analysis of these changes.

16. Carlos Castaneda, *The Teachings of Don Juan* (New York: Pocket Books, 1974), 109–19. This is the first of Castaneda's *Don Juan* books; Hughes reviewed the fourth, *Tales of Power,* very enthusiastically for the London *Observer,* 5 March 1972, 32.

17. "Earth-Numb," *BBC Radio 3,* prod. Fraser Steel, recorded 6 February 1980, 1.

18. In *Ted Hughes and R. S. Thomas Read and Discuss Selections of Their Own Poems. The Critical Forum* (Battle, Sussex, England: Norwich Tapes, 1978).

19. Martin Heidegger, "The Nature of Language," in his *On the Way to Language,* trans. Peter D. Hertz (New York: Harper & Row, 1971), 105.

20. Ibid., 57–108.

21. Ibid., 69, 92.

22. Sagar, "Fourfold Vision in Hughes," in *Achievement,* 307.

23. Hughes, "Earth-Numb," *BBC Radio 3,* 11.

24. Lynn White, Jr., "The Historical Roots of Our Ecologic Crisis," *Science* 155 (1967): 1203–7.

25. See Robert H. Ayers, "Christian Realism and Environmental Ethics," reprinted in *Religion and Environmental Crisis,* ed. Eugene C. Hargrove (Athens: University of Georgia Press, 1986), 154–71, for a solid response to White's argument.

26. Aldo Leopold, *A Sand County Almanac* (New York: Oxford University Press 1949), 224–25. See the discussion of Leopold's integrity concept in Roderick Nash, *The Rights of Nature* (Madison: University of Wisconsin Press, 1989), 63–74.

27. Thomas Berry, *The Dream of the Earth* (San Francisco: Sierra Club Books, 1988), 48–49.

28. Joseph Campbell, with Bill Moyers, *The Power of Myth,* ed. Betty Sue Flowers (New York: Doubleday, 1988), 71.

29. Leopold, *Sand County,* 194.

30. Franz Boas, *Tsimshian Mythology* (Washington, D.C.: U.S. Government Printing Office, 1916), 76–79, 668–70.

31. Campbell, *Power of Myth,* 69–89.

32. Except for single word alterations, Hughes lengthened the revised "The Gulkana" in three places for the American Harper and Row edition. At the beginning of the poem he suggests a mythic scenario with the addition of nine and a half lines. Only the lines from "Strange word" through "crumpled map" occurred in the original Faber version. The most major revision is an expansion of 30 new lines beginning with "And its accompaniment" through "Into that amethyst." The final major revision is the addition of three and one-half lines beginning with "The burden of the river moved in me" through "In my cave of body."

Chapter Six: Flowers and Insects and Wolfwatching

1. Letter to the author, dated 1 February 1989.

2. Introduction to *The Reef,* by Keith Sagar (Bradford, Yorkshire, England: Mallett & Co., 1980), 2–4.

3. Ibid.

4. Chuang Tzu, *Complete Works,* 49.

5. Letter to the author, dated 10 October 1989. Quotations from Hughes concerning the poems "Macaw" and "A Sparrow Hawk" in ensuing paragraphs derive from this letter, as does the main thrust of the interpretation of "On the Reservations."

6. Budge, *Osiris,* 1:65–68.

7. Martin Booth, *British Poetry 1964 to 1984* (London: Routledge & Kegan Paul, 1985), 25.

Selected Bibliography

This bibliography is limited to the major trade editions of Hughes's adult and children's work, and the most important articles, interviews, recordings, book reviews, and introductions Hughes has published to date. Selected secondary sources are limited to books.

For an elegant, comprehensive bibliography through 1980 of Hughes trade editions, Rainbow Press and other private press publications, broadcasts, broadsides, essays, recordings, and contributions to periodicals, as well as all secondary criticism (books, articles, and reviews) written about Hughes, see the Keith Sagar and Stephen Tabor bibliography. Sagar and Tabor have again contracted with Mansell to produce in 1996 an updated bibliography covering the years 1946 to 1995.

Though short biographical summaries and vignettes appear in many of the critical studies listed under secondary sources, no adequate biography of Hughes exists. Sections of some of Hughes's articles, interviews, book reviews, and introductions are collected in the two appendices of Faas, *Unaccommodated Universe*, 163–215.

PRIMARY WORKS

Trade Editions

The Hawk in the Rain. London: Faber & Faber, 1957; New York: Harper & Brothers, 1957.

Lupercal. London: Faber & Faber, 1960; New York: Harper & Brothers, 1960.

*Meet My Folks!** London: Faber & Faber, 1961; New York: Bobbs-Merrill, 1973.

*How the Whale Became.** London: Faber & Faber, 1963; New York: Atheneum, 1964.

*The Earth-Owl and Other Moon People.** London: Faber & Faber, 1963; New York: Viking, 1976, as part of *Moon-Whales*.

*Nessie the Mannerless Monster.** London: Faber & Faber, 1964; New York: Bobbs-Merrill, 1974, as *Nessie the Monster*.

Wodwo. London: Faber & Faber, 1967; New York: Harper & Row, 1967.

*Poetry in the Making.** London: Faber & Faber, 1967; New York: Doubleday, 1970, as *Poetry Is* (shorter edition).

*The Iron Man.** London: Faber & Faber, 1968; New York: Harper & Row, 1968, as *The Iron Giant*.

Seneca's Oedipus. London: Faber & Faber, 1969; New York: Doubleday, 1972.

*The Coming of Kings and Other Plays.** London: Faber & Faber, 1970; New York: Viking, 1974, as *The Tiger's Bones*.

*children's work

Crow. London: Faber & Faber, 1970; New York: Second Faber & Faber edition, augmented, 1972.

Selected Poems: 1957–1967. London: Faber & Faber, 1972; New York: Harper & Row, 1973.

Season Songs.* New York: Viking, 1975; London: Faber & Faber, 1976.

Moon–Whales and Other Moon Poems.* New York: Viking, 1976.

Gaudete. London: Faber & Faber, 1977; New York: Harper & Row, 1977.

Moon Bells and Other Poems.* London: Chatto & Windus, 1978.

Cave Birds. London: Faber & Faber, 1978; New York: Viking, 1979.

Remains of Elmet. London: Faber & Faber, 1979; New York: Harper & Row, 1979.

Moortown. London: Faber & Faber, 1979; New York: Harper & Row, 1980.

Selected Poems: 1957–1981. London: Faber & Faber, 1982; New York: Harper & Row, 1982.

River. London: Faber & Faber in association with James & James, 1983; New York: Harper & Row, 1984 (without photographs).

What Is the Truth?* London: Faber & Faber, 1984; New York: Harper & Row, 1984.

Fangs the Vampire Bat and The Kiss of Truth.* London: Faber & Faber, 1986.

Flowers and Insects. London: Faber & Faber, 1986: New York: Knopf, 1986.

Tales of the Early World.* London: Faber & Faber, 1988.

Wolfwatching. London: Faber & Faber, 1989; New York: Farrar, Straus & Giroux, 1991.

Articles

"Context." *London Magazine*, n.s., 1 (February 1962): 44–45.

"The Poetry of Keith Douglas." *Listener*, 21 June 1962, 1069–70.

"The Rock." *Listener*, 19 September 1963, 421–23. Reprinted in *Writers on Themselves*, edited by Herbert Read, 87–92. London: Cox & Wyman, 1964.

"Sylvia Plath." *Poetry Book Society Bulletin* 44 (February 1965):1.

"Notes on the Chronological Order of Sylvia Plath's Poems." *Tri-Quarterly* 7 (Fall 1966):81–88. Reprinted as "The Chronological Order of Sylvia Plath's Poems," in *The Art of Sylvia Plath*, edited by Charles Newman, 187–95. London: Faber & Faber, 1970; Bloomington: Indiana University Press, 1971.

"Vasco Popa." *Tri-Quarterly* 9 (Spring 1967):201–5.

"Myth and Education." *Children's Literature in Education* 1 (1970):55–70.

"Ted Hughes's *Crow.*" *Listener*, 30 July 1970, 149, 156.

"Sylvia Plath's *Crossing the Water:* Some Reflections." *Critical Quarterly* 13 (Summer 1971):165–72.

"Myth and Education." In *Writers, Critics,* and *Children,* edited by Geoff Fox et al., 77–94. New York: Agathon, 1976. [Completely different from the 1970 essay above.]

*children's work

"A Reply to My Critics." *Books and Issues* 3–4 (1981):4–6.

Recordings

The Poet Speaks. London: Argo Records, 1965. PLP 1085. Hughes reads nine
poems from *Wodwo.*

Crow. Dublin, Ireland: Claddagh Records, 1973. CCT 9–10. Hughes reads almost
the entirety of *Crow* on two records.

The Poetry and Voice of Ted Hughes. London and New York: Caedmon Records,
1977. TC 1535; cassette CDL 51535. Hughes reads 27 poems, principally
from *Hawk, Lupercal,* and the "Epilogue" of *Gaudete.*

*Ted Hughes and R. S. Thomas Read and Discuss Selections of Their Own Poems. The
Critical Forum.* Battle, Sussex, England: Norwich Tapes, 1978. Hughes reads
and discusses six poems from the "Moortown Elegies" section of *Moortown.*

Ted Hughes and Paul Muldoon. London: Faber & Faber Poetry Tape, 1983. ISBN
0-571-13090-9. Hughes reads eleven poems from volumes 1978–83, including "Bridge and groom lie hidden for three days," "February 17th," "Go ⟨
Fishing," and "October Salmon."

Book Reviews

Primitive Song, by C. M. Bowra. *Listener,* 3 May 1962, 781.

An Anthology of West African Folklore, by Alta Jablow. *Listener,* 18 October 1962,
629–30.

Vagrancy, by Philip O'Connor. *New Statesman,* 6 September 1963, 293–94.

Folktales of Japan, by Keigo Seki, and *Folktales of Israel,* by Dov Noy. *Listener,* 12
December 1963, 999.

Myth and Religion of the North, by E. O. G. Turville-Petre. *Listener,* 19 March
1964, 484–85.

The Collected Poems of Wilfred Owen, edited by C. Day Lewis. *New York Times Book
Review,* 12 April 1964, 4, 18.

Astrology, by Louis MacNeice, and *Ghost and Divining Rod,* by T. C. Lethbridge.
New Statesman, 2 October 1964, 500.

Shamanism, by Mircea Eliade, and *The Sufis,* by Idries Shah. *Listener,* 29 October
1964, 677–78.

Men Who March Away: Poems of the First World War, edited by I. M. Parsons. *Listener,* 5 August 1965, 208.

Literature among the Primitives and *The Primitive Reader,* by John Greenway. *New
York Review of Books,* 9 December 1965, 33–35.

The Selected Letters of Dylan Thomas, edited by Constantine Fitzgibbon. *New
Statesman,* 25 November 1966, 733.

The Environmental Revolution, by Max Nicholson. *Spectator,* 21 March 1970,
378–79. Expanded review appears in *Your Environment* 1 (Summer 1970):
81–83.

A Separate Reality, by Carlos Castaneda. *Observer,* 5 March 1972, 32.

Book Introductions

Introduction to *Selected Poems of Keith Douglas.* London: Faber & Faber; New York: Chilmark, 1964.

Introduction to *A Choice of Emily Dickinson's Verse.* London: Faber & Faber, 1968.

Introduction to *Selected Poems of Vasco Popa,* translated by Anne Pennington. Harmondsworth, England: Penguin, 1969. Later augmented for *Collected Poems: 1943–1976.* Manchester, England: Carcanet, 1977.

Introduction to *A Choice of Shakespeare's Verse.* London: Faber & Faber, 1971; New York: Doubleday, 1971, as *With Fairest Flowers While Summer Lasts.*

Introduction to *Selected Poems of Janos Pilinszky,* translated by Janos Csokits. Manchester, England: Carcanet, 1976.

Introduction to *Amen,* by Yehuda Amichai. London: Oxford University Press, 1977.

Introduction to *Johnny Panic and the Bible of Dreams,* by Sylvia Plath. New York: Harper & Row, 1980.

Introduction to *The Reef,* by Keith Sagar. Bradford, England: Yorkshire, 1980.

Introduction and notes to *Collected Poems,* by Sylvia Plath. London: Faber & Faber; New York: Harper & Row, 1981.

Foreword and notes to *The Journals of Sylvia Plath,* edited by Ted Hughes and Frances McCullough. New York: Dial, 1982. Reprint. New York: Ballantine, 1983.

Introduction to *The Complete Prints of Leonard Baskin,* by Alan Fern and Judith O'Sullivan. New York: New York Graphic Society in association with Little, Brown, 1984.

SECONDARY SOURCES

Interviews

"Ted Hughes Writes." *Poetry Book Society Bulletin* 15 (September 1957):1.

"Desk Poet." Interview by John Horder. *Guardian,* 23 March 1965, 9.

"Ted Hughes and *Crow.*" Interview by Ekbert Faas. *London Magazine,* N. S., 10 (January 1971):5–20. Reprinted in Faas, *Unaccommodated Universe,* 197–208.

"Orghast." Interview by Tom Stoppard, *Times Literary Supplement,* 1 October 1971, 1174.

"Playing with Words at Persepolis." Interview by Ossia Trilling. *Theatre Quarterly* 2 (January-March 1972):32–40.

Interview. In Smith, *Orghast at Persepolis,* chs. 2 and 3.

"Ted Hughes and *Gaudete*." Interview by Ekbert Faas. In Faas, *Unaccommodated Universe*, 208–15.

Books

Bold, Alan. *Thom Gunn and Ted Hughes.* Edinburgh: Oliver & Boyd, 1976. Bold primarily evaluates Hughes's comparisons between humans and animals in the early volumes through *Crow*, and finds a bleak pessimism toward human aspirations informing the poetry. 136 pages.

Faas, Ekbert. *Ted Hughes: The Unaccommodated Universe.* Santa Barbara, Calif.: Black Sparrow, 1980. After excellent opening chapters that place Hughes's poetics within a new multicultural and interdisciplinary tradition that included Oriental influences, Faas concentrates on the hero's descent to the underworld to save his desecrated bride in *Crow* and *Gaudete*. Faas's two interviews with Hughes, printed as Appendix 2, are absolutely essential. 230 pages.

Gifford, Terry, and **Neil Roberts.** *Ted Hughes: A Critical Study.* London: Faber & Faber, 1981. A very careful and informed study of language in Hughes that responds to charges of obsessive violence by patient evaluation of individual poems to determine the main characteristics of Hughes's style. Gifford and Roberts find Hughes to be a somewhat uneven but richly imaginative poet who normally controls and disciplines his considerable stylistic talents to serve a consistent and generous vision. 288 pages.

Hirschberg, Stuart. *Myth in the Poetry of Ted Hughes.* Dublin, Ireland: Wolfhound Press, 1981. A source study that begins by treating the early poems as animal totems and then concentrates upon mythic expiatory rituals involving the shaman, Trickster, and scapegoat consort of the White Goddess in Hughes's middle period: *Crow* through *Gaudete* and *Cave Birds.* 239 pages.

Robinson, Craig. *Ted Hughes as Shepherd of Being.* New York: St. Martin's, 1989. Robinson explores parallels between Hughes and Heidegger that redefine responsible adulthood. A person who is open to Being disdains clichés and narrow ratiocination. Words should humbly record fresh experiences that involve feeling, intuition, and the sense of our physiological rootedness. Lacks footnotes to specify material borrowed from previous scholarship. 220 pages.

Sagar, Keith. *The Art of Ted Hughes.* 2d ed. Cambridge: Cambridge University Press, 1978. An excellent study that devotes a chapter to each volume of Hughes's adult poetry, *Hawk* through *Cave Birds* and *Gaudete,* and synthesizes a great deal of Hughes's intellectual and stylistic influences into clear, concise prose. 280 pages.

———, ed. *The Achievement of Ted Hughes.* Manchester, England: Manchester University Press; Athens: University of Georgia Press, 1983. A first-rate collection of substantive scholarly essays that convey the range and complexity of Hughes's work and delineate many of the elements of his complex vision.

Topics range from Hughes's landscape, his mythic view, his dramas and children's poetry, to his relationship with England, Shakespeare, Blake, the Movement, and Eastern European poets, and contemporaries such as Redgrove, Heaney, and Plath. 377 pages.

Sagar, Keith, and Stephen Tabor, eds. *Ted Hughes: A Bibliography 1946– 1980.* London: Mansell; New York: H. W. Wilson, 1983. An elegant and exhaustive bibliography of Hughes's books, pamphlets, broadsides, essays, contributions to periodicals, translations, interviews, recordings, and broadcasts, as well as all secondary books, essays, and reviews through 1980. A must for the Hughes scholar. 260 pages.

Scigaj, Leonard M. *The Poetry of Ted Hughes: Form and Imagination.* Iowa City: University of Iowa Press, 1986. I discuss a three-stage development in Hughes's poetry: a fifties New Critical formalism, a sixties mythic surrealism, and, from the midseventies through *River,* a mystic landscape poetry. While reserving separate chapters for each major poetry volume, I attempted to synthesize major influences from depth psychology, myth, alchemy, Trickster folklore, Blake, and many Oriental disciplines. 369 pages.

Smith, A. C. H. *Orghast at Persepolis.* London: Eyre Methuen, 1972. A descriptive and interpretive summary of the summer 1971 Peter Brook *Orghast* production at Teheran, Iran, including two chapters of comments, notes, and drawings by Hughes that pertain to his invented language and unpublished script. 264 pages.

Uroff, Margaret. *Sylvia Plath and Ted Hughes.* Urbana: University of Illinois Press, 1979. By focusing primarily on landscape poems and poems of surreal self-exploration, Uroff studies what Plath and Hughes shared and learned from each other as each artist achieved a mature early poetry and then developed beyond it toward articulating the inner world. 235 pages.

Walder, Dennis. *Ted Hughes.* Milton Keynes, England, and Philadelphia: Open University Press, 1987. A very elementary exploratory discussion of the themes of surprise, personal roots, war, tradition, satire, and nature in Hughes, concentrating on four or so poems per theme. 108 pages.

————. *Ted Hughes and Sylvia Plath.* Milton Keynes, England: Open University Press, 1976. A short outline for a Hughes/Plath unit of a twentieth-century poetry course. The 30 pages devoted to Hughes contain thin and unrevealing comments.

West, Thomas. *Ted Hughes.* London and New York: Methuen, 1985. A tight focus on what West perceives as the "radical subjectivity" of an "inner drama" in Hughes produces insightful comments on the early poetry, but becomes reductive in spotty and uneven discussions of *Gaudete, Moortown,* and *Elmet.* Focusing upon an inner drama in Hughes without considering his well-known influences from the depth psychology of Jung and Freud substantially weakens the argument. 126 pages.

Index

The Author

Leonard M. Scigaj is associate professor of English at Virginia Polytechnic Institute and State University, where he has taught twentieth-century literature and writing courses since completing his Ph.D. at the University of Wisconsin-Madison in 1977. He has published articles on Ted Hughes in *The Achievement of Ted Hughes* and in journals such as *Twentieth-Century Literature* and *Perspectives on Twentieth-Century Literature,* an article on Sylvia Plath in *Centennial Review,* and articles on the science fiction writers Frank Herbert, Ray Bradbury, and George Lucas. His first critical study of Ted Hughes, *The Poetry of Ted Hughes: Form and Imagination,* was published by the University of Iowa Press in 1986. He is presently completing the *Critical Essays on Ted Hughes* volume for G. K. Hall.